The Company Citizen

Business doing good is doing good business; this book learns from the era where governments ruled the world, pre-globalisation, a world in which business looked after itself. Back then dealing with climate change, resource depletion, even poverty and hunger were not thought to be the responsibility of business.

The Company Citizen concludes that not only are these key issues for business today but that the world will not be able to manage these issues without active participation – even leadership – from businesses of all sizes. Aware of the shortcomings of both government and civil society the author argues that a strong business case exists for companies to address environmental sustainability, economic and social inclusion and the better management of resources – let alone a moral one. This book examines that case for the company citizen on global, national and community levels, working alongside others as citizens do. Never has the conscientious company citizen, as presaged by 19th-century Quaker philanthropists, been more needed; and never has that business case, for a long-term commitment to corporate behaviour for good, been more clear.

Drawing attention both to the businesses that are taking the lead and those who are holding us back, the author concludes that only by involving business can we tackle the great issues of the day, and survive: as communities, nation and planet.

Tom Levitt is a writer and consultant on 'using the tools of business to create public good' and a former Member of Parliament. He is a science graduate, former school teacher and a serial charity chair, with extensive experience of working in community and international development. In 2011, Tom was awarded an Honorary Doctorate by the University of Derby.

'The challenges of our modern world, and the need for an effective new social contract, are well documented. In this timely and interesting book, Tom Levitt brings practical knowledge, and credible policy solutions to the question of business, and makes a compelling case about the potential of business to help us all change the world, and our economy, for the better. What is more he articulates a clear duty for business to play its full role as corporate citizen – a hugely important and resonant message for our times.' – **Julia Unwin, Chair, Independent Inquiry into the Future of Civil Society**

'With £275b of fines from misconduct being paid by the banks so far since the financial crisis and trust in business generally having fallen sharply, Tom Levitt argues that it is high time that firms start thinking of themselves as "company citizens" with a duty to contribute to the well-being of the wider economy. This means assuming responsibility for the environment in which they operate, avoiding excessive pay for senior executives, treating their employees and customers with fairness and dignity and paying appropriate amounts of tax while not being scared to take a stance against injustice. The win is an improvement in business reputation and longer term business sustainability. It really is as simple as that. But as this book demonstrates it requires a new mindset for it to work.' – **Vicky Pryce, founder of GoodCorporation and former Joint Head of the UK Government Economic Service**

'In his latest book Tom Levitt weaves together a tapestry from a variety of sources and analysis of global trends to argue for company citizenship, a concept which reaches beyond both company social responsibility and corporate philanthropy. This concept offers an exciting potential to resolve some of the long standing criticisms of capitalism and provide a new paradigm for business to engage positively with society.' – **Professor Alex Murdock, London South Bank University**

The Company Citizen

Good for Business, Planet, Nation and Community

Tom Levitt

Routledge
Taylor & Francis Group
LONDON AND NEW YORK

First published 2018
by Routledge
2 Park Square, Milton Park, Abingdon, Oxon OX14 4RN

and by Routledge
711 Third Avenue, New York, NY 10017

Routledge is an imprint of the Taylor & Francis Group, an informa business

British Library Cataloguing-in-Publication Data
A catalogue record for this book is available from the British Library

Library of Congress Cataloging-in-Publication Data
Names: Levitt, Tom, author.
Title: The company citizen : good for business, planet, nation and community / Tom Levitt.
Description: Abingdon, Oxon ; New York, NY : Routledge, 2018. | Includes bibliographical references and index.
Identifiers: LCCN 2017028728 (print) | LCCN 2017041089 (ebook) | ISBN 9781315164038 (eBook) | ISBN 9781138058729 (hardback : alk. paper) | ISBN 9781138063037 (pbk. : alk. paper)
Subjects: LCSH: Social responsibility of business. | Citizenship. | Corporations—Moral and ethical aspects.
Classification: LCC HD60 (ebook) | LCC HD60 .L48 2018 (print) | DDC 658.4/08—dc23
LC record available at https://lccn.loc.gov/2017028728

ISBN: 9781138058729 (hbk)
ISBN: 9781138063037 (pbk)
ISBN: 9781315164038 (ebk)

Typeset in Bembo
by Swales & Willis Ltd, Exeter, Devon, UK

MIX
Paper from responsible sources
FSC™ C013985
FSC
www.fsc.org

Printed in the United Kingdom
by Henry Ling Limited

Dedicated to those who use the tools of business to make the world a better place.

Contents

Illustrations

Figures

Tables

A note on the references

The note indicators and their corresponding notes (found at the end of each chapter) provide web references that were active and checked in September 2017. To assist in following up references, a full and updated list is available as web links on the author's website: http://sector4focus.co.uk/company-citizen/.

Author biography

Tom Levitt has been a consultant on 'using the tools of business to create public good' since 2010, before when he was the Member of Parliament for High Peak for 13 years (and a school teacher before that). Never having been directly employed in the private sector allows him to be objective in his analysis of its role in society; an argument augmented by both a science degree and periods of attachment to major companies including Walgreen Boots Alliance, as well as working closely with businesses as a constituency MP. His recent research makes him an authority on how smaller businesses engage with their communities and he's been involved in setting up a successful business, the social enterprise Fair for You. He brings to the table comprehensive experience of charities and volunteering (he has chaired three national charities and the charities' All Party Parliamentary Group), community development, organisational governance, international development (as a junior member of the DfID ministerial team, 2003–7) and, of course, politics and government. His previous book, *Welcome to GoodCo*, was critically acclaimed.

Tom has an honorary doctorate from the University of Derby and is a season-ticket holder at Brentford FC.

Preface

For the sake of our planet, nation and communities we desperately need business to think and behave as good citizens do. The challenges that we face today, at every level, feel insuperable confronted with an approach of 'business as usual'; we need the powerhouse that is the private-sector economy to be more public-minded. Fortunately, it's in the interests of business to do just that, especially as longer term thinking (the one absolute essential in any formula for survival) makes business sense, even in traditional capitalist terms.

The challenges to the planet are climate change, resource depletion and the twin evils of hunger and poverty. All threaten the conventional predictability of the marketplace and challenge humanity on a truly global scale. Whilst once we thought that governments might come together and save the world today, their influence, relatively speaking, is less than it was – whilst that of the private sector is more. Only when the two address common goals together can our survival, literally, be assured.

At a national level the sixth richest nation in the world, Britain, is also one of the most unequal; this has consequences way beyond the mathematical. Again, the ability of governments to bring about change is not what we believed it once to be (writes one who spent 13 years in government) and the monolithic approaches of the past – to energy, health and care in particular – are not fit for tomorrow's purpose. Austerity and isolation are political choices Britain has made, collectively, but we don't know how to handle either of them.

Not only are businesses found in our communities but businesses *are* communities themselves. Neighbourliness and citizenship are based on values that should never die but deprivation saps moral fibre; statistical inequalities have very real consequences on the ground. Communities that lack capacity lack spirit; the Company Citizen has the power, position – and responsibility – to help address those capacity issues by using the skills it has to empower, protect and enhance its nearest and dearest.

Some will say that this book is negative, that there are too many horror stories in it, and I accept that the record of Company Citizenship as a culture is mixed. Yet those stories serve to remind us how powerful are the forces of business and how much better things could be, with the right approach – always based on a business case.

There are, fortunately, some companies – even major players – who do 'get it', and smaller ones to whom engagement with communities, both local and along the distant supply chain, is not second nature but first. We can learn, we must learn from them, that business doing good is doing good business. If we don't adopt that approach then our resources, our water, our climate, our food and even our human spirit are under severe threat of being reduced or even extinguished.

If *Welcome to GoodCo* was a history book, *The Company Citizen* is a manifesto, backed by evidence that just might help business engage better with the world of today and tomorrow, at every level.

Company Citizens unite! You have nothing to lose but your planet.

Abbreviations

APR	Annual Percentage Rate
BHRRC	Business and Human Rights Resource Centre
BITC	Business In The Community
BRIC(S)	Brazil, Russia, India, China (South Africa)
BSR	Business for Social Responsibility (US)
CR	Corporate Responsibility
CRS	Corporate Responsibility and Sustainability
CSR	Corporate Social Responsibility
DRC	Democratic Republic of Congo
DWP	Department for Work and Pensions (UK)
ESG	Environmental, Social and Governance
ESOP	Employee Share Ownership Plan
ETI	Ethical Trading Initiative
FSB	Federation of Small Business
GDP	Gross Domestic Product
GIIN	Global Impact Investing Network
GRI	Global Reporting Index
ILO	International Labor Organisation
MDG	Millennium Development Goals
NCVO	National Council for Voluntary Organisations
NGO	Non-Governmental Organisation
NMW	National Minimum Wage

OECD	Organisation for Economic Co-operation and Development
RE100	Renewable Energy 100 campaign
RSA	Royal Society for the encouragement of Arts, Manufactures and Commerce
SDG	Sustainable Development Goals
SEUK	Social Enterprise UK
TI	Transparency International
TUC	Trades Union Congress
UNDP	United Nations Development Programme
UNGC	United Nations Global Compact

Acknowledgements

Many people have helped me with this book: some through serial conversations, some one-off, some email responses to queries, others delivering lectures or taking part in debates . . .

I thank Michael Green of the Social Progress Imperative, fellow DfID alumnus and writer, for permission to use Figure 3.1. Antony Jenkins (formerly of Barclays) and economist Vicky Pryce were generous with their time and advice. Jonathan Norman, formerly my publisher at Gower, and Alex Atkinson at Taylor & Francis between them provided all the support that good publishers should. Naomi Baird proved adept at reading lots of my words and questioning many of them. Special thanks to Adam Craker, CEO of South Africa's IQ Business, for keeping in touch over a politically challenging year.

Talking with Lord Victor Adebowale is always good value and so, during the writing of this book, have been chats with Jerry Allen (Greenwich University) and Good People's good person Richard Tyrie. Honourable mentions go also to David Adair (PwC), Charlotte Alldritt (who thinks about inclusion for RSA), Zoe Arden and Rob Cameron (at SustainAbility, masters in the field), Jamie Audsley (ShareAction and Croydon Council), Sir Alan Budd, Gib Bulloch, James Butler (of SEUK) and Mark Cook (of Anthony Collins LLP) on Social Value, Richard Brophy (Thompsons/Reuters), Andrew Brown (a fellow Journeys for Change alumnus, now at Colaboratory, Colorado), Prof. Cary Cooper, Lisa Cunningham (BITC), Andrew Dakers (West London Business), Ed Davies (Centre for Social Justice), Ruci Fixter (Burston Marsteller), Sir Stuart Hampson (former Chair, John Lewis Partnership), Peter Harrison (Schroders), Catherine Howarth and Anne-Marie Williams (ShareAction), Martin Jervis, Neil Johnston (Paddington Development Trust), Isabel Kelly (Profit with Purpose), Mike Kelly (Living Wage Foundation), Beth Knight (EY), Michael Mapstone (CAF), Geoff McDonald, Sarah Mitchell (Heart of the City), Prof. Alex Murdock (LSBU), Chris Pond, Sarah Poretta (Lloyds Bank), Unilever's Paul Polman, Prof. Jeffrey Robinson (Rutgers University), Nick Sammons and Anita Longley (ICRS), Javier Santoyo, Michael Solomon (Responsible 100), Mark Spelman who introduced me to the Circular Economy, Alison Symmers (Willmott Dixon Foundation), Jake Tantram (Terrafiniti), Baroness Glenys Thornton (The Young Foundation), Owen Tudor (TUC/ETI), Julia Unwin,

Abigail Vickers (Alium Partners), Bevis Watts (Triodos Bank), Nigel Wilson and Graham Precey of Legal & General and others. Many of my conversations happen at the RSA where Matthew Taylor's influence keeps our thinking both focused and expansive.

The commitment shown by two teams of people to using the tools of business to create public good has been inspiring during my 'journey'. They are the team under Angela Clements and Ben Reid at Fair for You and the sustainability advisory panel at Walgreen Boots Alliance (Global Brands) under Mark Goyder of Tomorrow's Company. The WBA team includes Cheryl Hall, Nigel Hayes, Andrew Jenkins and Laura McGonigal (all WBA), Lisa Purvis (Boots Opticians) and my fellow independent members Yogesh Chauhan (Tata Consulting), Stephanie Draper (Forum for the Future), Oonagh Harpur, Alex Maitland (Tomorrow's Company/Oxfam) and Tobias Webb (Innovation Forum). The influence of Richard Ellis is never far away.

Other moral and practical support came from Hannah Anderson (Collaborate), Rick Benfield (ThirdBridge), Jim Bignall (Triple Purpose), Max du Bois, Vicky Browning (ACEVO), Tomas Carruthers and Colin Peacock of the Social Stock Exchange, Lily Chong, Dan Firth (Interserve), Sarah Foster (Good Economy), Bennett Freeman (Business for Social Responsibility, USA), Cathy Garner and team (The Work Foundation), Ann Heal (formerly of BT), Prof. Adrian Henriques (University of Middlesex), Loughlin Hickey and Charles Wookey at Blueprint for Better Business, Katie Hill (B Corps UK), Peter Holbrook (SEUK), Michael Jacobs (IPPR), the ubiquitous Prof. John Kay, Doug Mather, Ed Mayo (Co-operatives UK), Jeannette McKenna, Prof. James McCalman (Portsmouth Business School), Polly McKenzie, Colin Melvin, David Morris (London Business School/NewCo), Peter Neville-Lewis, Rosie Oglesby (Feeding Britain), Reema Patel (RSA), Robert Phillips (Jericho Chambers), Cosmina Popa (Rainmaker Loft), Sacha Romanovich (Grant Thornton), Hemma Varma (Marriott Hotels), Peter van Veen (Transparency International), Peter Ward (Telos Partners), Anne-Christine Wegener, Richard Williams (NCVO) and my fellow members of Third Sector magazine's Business Charity Awards judging panel under its editor, Andy Hillier. Thanks, too, to Liam Byrne MP for keeping the Inclusive Economy on the Parliamentary agenda. Apologies to anyone I've missed.

Regular email briefings from Edie, Impact Alpha, the Innovation Forum and the *Guardian*'s Sustainable Business were very helpful! Finally, I acknowledge the work of Tom Levitt at the Sustainable Business page of the *Guardian*. We share our name and talk the same language but we are, in fact, different people.

1 The case for company citizenship

In 1948 my parents got engaged to be married.

In other news, Land Rover and Alcoholics Anonymous were born and Mahatma Gandhi was killed, the Windrush arrived at Tilbury and Bradman was out for a duck in his final test innings. Steps were taken to create NATO and introduce the Marshall Plan whilst the British Parliament passed a Bill to establish the National Health Service.

Work started to construct the headquarters of the fledgling United Nations on a patch of Manhattan real estate donated by John D. Rockefeller Junior. That year the 58 members of the UN were busy: they approved its Convention on the Prevention and Punishment of Genocide, set up the World Health Organisation and adopted the Universal Declaration of Human Rights.

The optimistic era of world government had begun.

Despite vivid memories of world war this was an age of innocence. Of course governments and democracy were the way forward, legitimately elected powers should rule their nations, international co-operation between governments – who else? – was the way to tackle conflict, global injustice and hunger. In 1951 the UN adopted a convention on refugee status, still an issue six years after the war. Those who gathered that year, at that new, permanent UN Headquarters, were truly the powers that be, the wise, the diplomatic, the champions of peace, harmony and mutual success, the embodiment of universal citizenship.

How the world has changed in 70 years. If we were convening the United Nations today, who would sit around that table? Suppose we all agreed that climate change, hunger, poverty and the depletion of natural resources – and their consequences – were the issues that most threatened humanity globally, who should we call upon to address them? Would we believe, as they did in 1948, that governments alone could solve these issues?

Climate change and the depletion of natural resources weren't on the agenda back then because they weren't yet in crisis. That came later, as industrialisation gathered momentum, forests were laid to waste, fossil fuels were burned like there was no tomorrow: if you ran out of stuff, you just dug up more, at home or in the former colonies. And then came globalisation . . .

The downside of all of these issues, changes for the worse, are traditionally associated with (some might say 'blamed on') the activities of business. Business is accused, with some justification, of wasting our resources, exploiting our labour, poisoning our environments, never mind that they also produce the wealth we share, homes, jobs and purpose for countless millions.

If the UN were starting today global business would have to be at the table. Natural justice says so – 'you helped get us into this, you help get us out' – but so does the realpolitik of power. In 1948 those 58 nations *were* the powerhouse, the brokers, the world's wheelers and dealers; perhaps only the Rockefellers, whose family embodies both the extravagance of oil and all that's best in philanthropy, would have understood back then. Today, as we shall see, the world's biggest businesses are on a par in size and power with nations but without their democratic constraints. They must be at the table, in the game, as trustworthy partners in a common cause.

For our planet, as for our nation. The huge and barely accountable monoliths that government created back in the 1940s, the nationalised coal, steel, transport and utility companies, are today in private hands: few would turn all of those clocks back to exactly where they were then. A third of our public spending is now outsourced, for good or ill, largely to private companies. The National Health Service itself (where the proportion of private provision is, counterintuitively, far lower than elsewhere), is struggling to survive as a centralised, nationwide, bureaucratic 'sickness service'. Our government, which collects half of its tax revenue from businesses and their employees, has still not recovered from the world's showdown with those global banks that were 'too big to fail' a decade ago.

As economic inequality grows even within Britain, fatuously blamed on some inevitability of capitalism, the communities that suffer most are those that lack the services, skills and spirit that bring reality to words like 'cohesion' and such slogans as 'we're all in this together'. The cohort of 'just about managing' is one of only a few groups in society experiencing growth – but of the wrong sort.

At every level – planet, nation, community – we need the resources of business to be deployed positively to support our common causes of justice, sustainability and dignity; our tools must be carrots because sticks don't work. We also need business to keep doing what it does best, but better: providing us with the wealth we need whilst helping us to steward our resources, promote the purpose that sustains our mental health and supply the structures by which we regulate our days.

In this book I will argue that such positive and engaged behaviour is not only good for us, the people, it's good for business too. A business case can be built: business for good is good for business. I'll advocate a mindset which I call 'Company Citizenship'; it's not a badge, accreditation, sect or club but rather a way of thinking which applies to the multinational conglomerate, the independent hairdresser and every business in between, should they choose it. And they should.

This is the case for the Company Citizen.

***

A Company Citizen is a body corporate, owned and run by people.

Companies have purposes and, whilst they vary immensely, 'staying in business' is certainly amongst them. Alongside a task-orientated purpose – writing the best programmes, being able to retire in comfort, cleaning floors to the highest standard or developing the missing link – they have missions, visions and values, though not always explicit or well-defined: the owner may not even be aware of them. But if owners don't adopt values then others will define those values and labels for them, confer and incorporate them into the company's reputation – including those perceived as negative.

A Company Citizen respects and engages with others and plans for the long term. Aware of its environment, fiscal, market and physical, it responds to changing circumstances as guided by its judgment and values and as allowed by its resources.

It respects laws, rules and conventions but reserves the right to challenge and even work to change them, transparently, either alone or collectively with others.

It speaks out as the need arises.

A Company Citizen is accountable to . . . now, there's a question. To its owners, certainly, to its regulators, where appropriate, to the law. To its customers. And to the court of public opinion.

Good Company Citizens are 'responsible' in their actions; although they can be passionate, they're guided by rationality and those stated purposes and missions. A common (but not universal) value, often implicit, recalls the Hippocratic Oath: 'to do no [net] harm'.

Yet public confidence in business continues to fall; only half of the populations of 28 countries in 2017 trust business to 'do the right thing', says Edelman.[1] At 52 per cent that figure mirrors that for the voluntary sector (53) and is significantly higher than for government (42) and media (43), though faith in all four is falling. For the first time, 'peers' are ranked more trustworthy than 'experts'. There's a crisis of confidence in leadership generally, with only one in six believing that 'the system' is working. Job security is a major issue in the face of globalisation and technological change, so half the population favour protectionist trade policies. Edelman rightly regards this as an opportunity for business, not just a challenge. In a world where the public trust employees' views more than those of CEOs, the three greatest opportunities for building trust and restoring a 'licence to operate' are treating employees well, offering high quality products and listening to customers, all favoured by those whose confidence in 'the system' has been shaken. Every element of social responsibility is key to restoring trust: from paying taxes properly to ethical behaviour, transparency, honesty and environmental stewardship.

Edelman reports both massive public support for *better* regulation of business and that *greater* regulation is what business fears the most. The way to head off this 'threat' is to render it unnecessary, by getting ahead of any bow-wave push for laws on more responsible practices.

In short, every company should be a Company Citizen. But *why* should they? The herd mentality mitigates against boldness, breaking tradition or the sticking out of corporate necks. Business will only become more 'human', citizen-focused and environmentally positive through incentives. Each of these qualities can be justified by a business case but cultural change is a real challenge –especially amongst those with the largest workforces, where communication is most difficult and cynicism most deeply entrenched. Ultimately only conventional business drivers will drive large scale change: existing businesses need conventional business motives to make the idea of Company Citizenship sustainable.

At the clothing company Patagonia, their hearts told them to utilise only organic cotton but insecticides and pesticides were so ingrained in that industry that there was insufficient organic supply available for them to use. They decided to shrink the business for three years whilst they educated their supply chain. They came back with a strong USP and a niche market (plus great products, appreciated by the mainstream) and today they can claim both the ethical and commercial high ground. That principled stand couldn't have succeeded without turning it into a business case.

Citizens are decent people; they care about others and value the idea of working together in common cause. Company Citizens are little different from human citizens in those respects. Lord Victor Adebowale, a leading thinker in social business and public service reform, says: 'If you're not producing social value you're not a business, you're a gang.'[2]

Larger Company Citizens adopt a hierarchy of leadership, the managers may or may not be the owners, the owners may be individual or multiple, engaged or *laissez faire*, identified or anonymous. They may even be other Company Citizens. They employ people, assigning them responsibilities. They may be geographically concentrated or disparate, the business may have an established and explicit mission and values – or not. The smallest Company Citizens are companies in name only, legal entities with company status, barely distinguishable from the human sole trader behind the label.

The status of 'Company Citizen' is a state of mind, one that we might wish would inspire more in the humans that we unquestioningly describe as citizens. Nor does the mindset relate only to business leaders: two thirds of British workers think that their work makes 'no meaningful contribution to the world' but wish that it were otherwise.[3]

Some tell me that citizenship is too precious a quality to bestow on a mere corporate legal entity; if it doesn't breathe or defecate it can't be a citizen. Conventionally, we believe that citizens care, vote and interact through cooperating, volunteering, creating and maintaining communities. We try not to define or judge them by their thoughts. Companies do all of those things. Companies who care aren't hard to find: Unilever's ten-year sustainability plan is perhaps the most comprehensive and focused of its kind, reflecting the United Nations' Sustainable Development Goals (SDGs), an approach worthy of the most conscientious of citizens. (In 2014 at a community project in a São Paulo favela, Brazilian children were being taught the dangers of dirty water and the importance of rigorous hand washing. 'This looks like the Unilever Lifebuoy project,' I said. 'It is,' I was told, 'we've rebranded it.')

There are 1,600 companies worldwide that are B Corps, trading in traditional ways but with an avowed principal purpose which is social, at least as important as conventional measures of their business success. Mostly in USA, they submit to regular objective and comprehensive assessment of their progress. Almost all B Corps – including all of the 100+ in Britain – are small- or medium-sized enterprises (SMEs) of under 250 employees. The biggest is a giant, Natura toiletries and cosmetics of Brazil; the best known is Ben & Jerry's, part of the Unilever family.[4] Thousands of social enterprises use the tools of business to deliver a social or environmental object, not ignoring the need to be financially sustainable but not being dictated to by any perceived need to maximise dividends.

Companies engage in politics, as we saw in Britain's referendum on European Union membership, and that's fine when the outcome directly impacts on their operations, even their existence, as membership of the Single Market undoubtedly did for many UK companies. Most who spoke out favoured 'remain', whose campaign was chaired by a former corporate CEO; what's right for British business, they argued, was right for Britain. There are limits to political engagement: even people who could never be described as 'anti-business' find the incestuous, financially focused relationships between big business and the legislature of the United States beyond the pale. Others grimace at the UK's Lobbying Act, which imposes tighter constraints on campaigning by charities, where social purpose runs through their veins, than on business.

Business Fights Poverty works for justice and equity in developing countries. Its founder, Zahid Torres-Rahman, formerly of PwC, calls on business to focus ever more on changing our world, telling his corporate cousins: 'There's never been a more important time to be brave.'

Specifically, he calls upon them to mobilise (around the Sustainable Development Goals); drive action (citing Richard Branson's B Team's call for business to 'start working on issues they care about'); and speak up (praising Lego for ceasing advertising in those UK newspapers which adopted racist attitudes to migrants).[5] Plusnet, The Body Shop and Specsavers followed Lego in support of the Stop Funding Hate campaign.

Gib Bulloch, pioneer of Accenture Development Partnership, agrees: 'If we are to harness the power of business to change the world, we must first change the world of business.'[6]

Former head of Friends of the Earth, Tony Juniper, told a business conference: 'Population growth, climate change and resource scarcity have rendered social and environmental issues non-negotiable for the private sector.'[7]

Companies even vote. Although the general right of companies to vote in elections was banned in Britain as recently as 1969 certain practices are still allowed. The City of London had its maximum population in the early 1800s, although only a few of its 130,000 inhabitants, property-owning males over the age of 21, qualified to vote. The devastating bombardment of World War Two drove people away and only 5,000 lived there in the late 1940s. In the 1960s the Barbican estate boosted numbers but today's register, of just 9,000 human voters, is a non-viable democratic base – so businesses were allowed to remain on the polling register. Today, following 2002 legislation which increased the business franchise, 24,000 companies may vote in elections to the City of London Corporation (it's not called a council). In contrast, the right of British adult human citizens to vote is not universal: some prisoners (a controversial issue), some mental health patients and, for general elections, members of the House of Lords are denied the vote.

To be clear, I'm not calling for Company Citizens' franchise to be extended, merely pointing out that we have neither a universal ban on companies voting nor universal permission for people citizens to do so. Voting does not define citizenship. Nor does political engagement have to be Party political, though some companies do make donations to political parties which, where significant, must be transparent and open. Any company registered within the European Union and trading in Britain may donate to our political parties: gifts of over £5,000 per year must be authorised by shareholders, where appropriate. During the 2010–15 Parliament companies and associated individuals donated £73.6m to the Conservative Party and £10.6m to Labour.

One of President Trump's first acts in office was to rail against refugees in general and Muslims in particular, seriously offending American Company Citizens. On the day after the President signed the order to ban migrants coming from some countries those who took to the world's streets were joined in spirit by the corporate realm: Google and Apple declared the ban irrational, counter to the interests of companies that fished in global talent pools, whilst Microsoft identified those employees who would be banned from the US. The CEO of Ford, fresh from an Oval Office meeting, criticised the measure as 'against our values' and Muhtar Kent, Turkish-American CEO of Coca-Cola, used the same words. Starbucks promised to recruit 10,000 migrant baristas worldwide over the next five years. Mark Zuckerburg of Facebook spoke for many: '[The USA is] a nation of immigrants, and we all benefit when the best and brightest from around the world can live, work and contribute here.'

JP Morgan Chase, Netflix, Nike, Amazon, Twitter and the *New York Times* denounced the President's action as did others including Goldman Sachs, whose links to the administration are renowned, and BlackRock, whose CEO had been in line for a top job had President Hillary Clinton come into office. The stock markets stuttered as leading US businesses, half of them created by immigrants or their children, queued up to condemn.

Uber's Travis Kalanick resigned from the President's business advisory panel over the issue. Months later, when several more CEOs stepped down in protest against Trump's unwillingness to denounce violent far-right and white supremacist demonstrations in Charlottesville, he promptly disbanded both the

Manufacturing Council and his Strategy and Policy Forum, practically severing his formal links with business.[8]

When Marc Benioff of Salesforce quoted scripture when opposing the ban he was well outside the normal corporate comfort zone. Yet it's clear that, in this era of constant digital scrutiny, spurred by the softer values of the upcoming Millennial generation, businesses who claim to operate by sound values need to demonstrate this occasionally. In that sense, the proposed migrant ban was opportune, allowing companies to stand together, avoiding the risk of being picked off. Their stance was a statement of values with which the majority of Americans could identify (remember that Trump lost the popular vote) and, of course, companies that hired the best talent from wherever in the world certainly didn't want to lose that right.

Former US Treasury Secretary Larry Summers encouraged such moves:

> There are signs that quite a few business leaders are waking up to the dangers for their companies inherent in current trends. So maybe the business community, whose approval the administration craves, will start to pressure the administration rather than simply cheering on tax cuts and deregulation.[9]

It wasn't just in America: in UK the Institute of Directors and the British Chambers of Commerce both joined the chorus. The CEO of Anglo-Dutch Unilever, Paul Polman, said on Twitter that the 'Inherent worth and dignity of every world citizen [is] being challenged in US at the moment'.

These are the values of Company Citizens.

★★★

Citizens are subject to taxes: we'll revisit this controversial field. The contribution made by direct taxation of businesses, to both national exchequer and local coffers, is very significant; and many millions of individual taxpayers are only able to pay their due because they're private sector employees.

Citizens also volunteer. Volunteering, says the charity umbrella group NCVO, is any activity that 'involves spending time, unpaid, doing something that aims to benefit the environment or someone (individuals or groups) other than, or in addition to, close relatives'. Studies show that 14.2 million Brits volunteer in a formal context at least monthly and over 40 per cent of us volunteer at least once a year. Participation in informal volunteering is even higher: a third give time each month and two thirds of us do so at least annually. These figures have been stable, within five percentage points, for 15 years.[10] Within this army of unpaid workers we find some employer-supported volunteers: 2.7 per cent of employees do regular voluntary work in work time (a slow but steady climb from 2 per cent, eight years ago) and one in twelve employees has done so in the last year (this figure has doubled in eight years).

But hang on. These are paid employees and volunteers aren't paid, that's the essence of volunteering. Surely employer-supported volunteers aren't really volunteers?

Strictly speaking no, they're not. So who is volunteering? In the case of employees in work time it's the company donating its time, and the skills that it's paid for, to the good cause – whether digging a community garden, auditing a charity's accounts, creating a web site or staffing a cake stall. It's the Company Citizen, not the individual, that's volunteering here. Society needs Company Citizens to be better engaged in our communities: fortunately, it's in the interests of business to pursue this agenda. However, 'better' shouldn't mean 'more of the same'; business needs to rethink its role in society, at local and national levels.

There are moral, political and business arguments for this change and pioneers from whom aspiring businesses can learn. There's even a global framework for Company Citizenship – those Sustainable Development Goals – and ample evidence across the world that engagement works, in the interests of companies, beneficiaries, nations and communities.

So companies can regard themselves as citizens. Why should they?

The moral case

Those who exercise power should do so responsibly, not simply to mitigate the negative impacts of their activity on society or the environment, but in socially constructive ways. This collaborative spirit drove the formation of the United Nations, bringing together the world's economic and political powers – 20 nations in 1939, over 50 by 1945 and 193 today.

That the UN is the leading voice of global, secular, moral authority is generally accepted even if its impact often underwhelms. In 2000 it established eight Millennium Development Goals (MDGs), based on fairness, dignity and basic rights, surprising no one.[11] It set testing yet achievable targets and inspired the world's governments to make some moderate progress.

The MDGs' agenda was for developing countries but their 2015 successors, the 17 SDGs, challenge business everywhere to 'walk the walk'. By adding Goals on energy use, clean environments and the better management of raw materials, business has been irrevocably implicated in their implementation; no longer does responsibility fall only on governments, communities and the developing world.[12] Companies should decide which of the 169 measures contained in the Goals are most material to them, choose specific targets (such as percentage reduction in water use by such a date) and report annually on progress towards each.

Based on universal values the moral charge on business to accept some responsibility for achieving the UN goals is supported by a stark statistic: today 42 of the world's 100 largest economies are not countries but businesses.

How different is the 21st century from the mid-20th.

Let's reflect on the list to be found at the end of this chapter. The rank order of countries is unremarkable: based on GDP it's a narrow definition of economic development, with OECD countries and the oil-rich economies taking their senior places. If the pre-Brexit European Union were listed it would be second, behind the USA, with a GDP of $16.5tn. If California were independent it would rank in the top ten, alongside UK or France. Such figures are a snapshot: markets change, currencies fluctuate, crises happen and the list will vary, slightly, almost daily.

In 26th place we find the biggest company, the US retailer Walmart, with an annual turnover of almost half a trillion dollars. It's the only retail company in the top 100 economies: UK's Tesco, the American Costco and France's Carrefour, all around $100bn, don't make the cut. After Walmart the next three companies are Chinese state-owned energy monopolies and then Royal Dutch Shell is in 47th position. These are the five companies in the top 50 economies.

However, in the second batch of 50 we find no fewer than 37 companies. Within the total of 42, 13 are American, six are Chinese. The nine which are state-owned include all six Chinese plus the Brazilian and Venezuelan entries and the Japanese postal service. Only one, BP (56th), is British; a third of them are in energy. Many are not household familiars, trading under different brand names: Berkshire Hathaway (at 58) is the investment empire of Warren Buffett. Buffett's partner in philanthrocapitalism, Bill Gates, doesn't even make the top 100: in 2014 Microsoft's revenue was a mere $86bn. Apple is 54th at $234bn. Unilever is another relative minnow, well outside the top ranks at just $60bn.

The world's 100th biggest company, Royal Phillips Electronics of the Netherlands, is the same size, at $3bn, as the 100th largest country economy, Cameroon.

There's a moral imperative, one can argue, for the most powerful – don't let them tell you these figures don't describe power – to wield that power responsibly.

Given these relative strengths whatever the countries of the world decide to do together, through UN conventions, the Paris Climate Change Agreement or other accords, they can't achieve their goals without having business on board. Not only are 42 of the world's 100 most powerful economies corporates but that figure is growing. Where once it was enough for business to co-exist with global society, not standing in its way, today the SDGs, embodying decency, sustainability and fairness, absolutely rely on the active involvement of the corporate sector. This is a challenge that global Company Citizen pioneers have taken up with relish.

Paying fair levels of tax is another moral duty. People don't understand why, on modest incomes, they appear to be contributing more tax than some multinationals that palpably trade profitably in Britain. People are naturally suspicious when companies arbitrarily headquarter themselves offshore; they're 'up to no good'. Some make no net profits to pay tax upon: all of their surplus is redistributed as dividend, reinvested or, as with some coffee shops, paid to an offshore holding company for permission to use their name. In 1997 both the revenue and net income of Amazon were zero, whilst in 2016 it had revenue of $120bn and had a net income of . . . you guessed.[13] No profits means no taxes.

People are sceptical that business leaders merit being paid many multiples of the salary of Britain's most accountable person, the Prime Minister: shareholder revolts on top pay packages are growing, as we'll see. For the first time in half a century the level of profit that business gives out as dividends is growing faster than employee pay.

That the cost to business of a 'licence to operate' is partly measured in moral terms has never been more true, especially since 'the crash'.

The financial sector is almost unique in its capacity to act in an amoral way. The full depth of the loss of trust, devil-take-the-hindmost attitude and other aspects of the 'crash' of 2007–8 may never be known as its consequences still reverberate. Its perpetrators still rule their roosts and hold much sway over the rest of us. Their state of mind has not essentially changed as they undertake, for example, to dismember the American Dodd-Frank Act, intending to re-inflate that destructive bubble by removing some moral constraints. Key people move seamlessly between working for regulators, law firms or Government agencies before finding their ultimate reward on the boards of the very banks they were supposed to bring to heel. Or the other way round: several of the first Trump cabinet were Goldman Sachs alumni.

Globally banks have paid $275bn in fines for misconduct since the crash without batting an eyelid. Of that amount, $35bn of that was paid to the British government with several mammoth cases yet to be settled. In 2015 over 4,000 of Europe's 5,000 bankers on €1m-plus salaries were based in UK. Although knighthoods have been removed and future board prospects lost, ten years on very few bankers in Britain or USA have been charged with offences – even for laundering billions of dollars of illegal drugs money. Other EU countries have had the guts to prosecute, as has Iceland, where banks constitute a hugely disproportionate part of the economy.[14]

Businesses which behave outside accepted moral frameworks cannot be true Company Citizens.

There's a Biblical saying: 'if you're not with us, you're against us'. As we explore the politics of the case for greater business engagement with society, we'll see that case applying as much in local communities – if not more – as on the national or global stage.

The political case

Politics puts values into practice.

Britain is one of the world's most generous countries. Charitable giving, volunteering and corporate philanthropy are all at a high, if static, level. Over the last 60 years a growing, increasingly professional, voluntary sector has shared responsibility with government, public and private sectors for delivering services to meet people's basic and specific needs. Recently a number of trends have challenged the dynamics of cross-sector relationships: 'outsourcing' services has proved controversial; commissioning practices may have perverted charity missions and encouraged dependency on government funding; poor privatisation practice has allowed questionable profits to be made whilst vastly reducing the accountability (and sometimes quality and reliability) of such services.

On the other hand, there's no doubt that cross sector partnerships can increase the qualitative value of services and that business efficiency can make them more effective (and even cost effective). Although such positive virtues are not guaranteed, cross-sector working is here to stay. We've even seen businesses and charities voluntarily come together to work collaboratively without the need for the fine print of a government contract.

A decision on whether to outsource a public service to a 'for profit', or an inaccurately labelled 'not for profit', company is a question not wholly of economics but partly of values. Of course a so-called 'not for profit' company has to make a surplus or profit; if it didn't, it wouldn't survive. The American definition of 'non-profit' – reliant on external sources of funding – has it right: in Britain the only true 'not for profits' are charities dependent on gifts, public services dependent on tax revenue – and companies that have gone bust. How a company uses its profit tells us about its values. The term 'social enterprise' describes a business with a social principal purpose which does some combination of donating surplus profit to a good cause, reinvesting it in the company or using it to reduce the cost to service user or commissioner. Such businesses don't take a disproportionate amount out of the company to reward shareholders and aren't geared to maximise profit, but they're not 'not for profits'.

Southern Cross (see Chapter 4) was a private equity-owned company which grew to be Britain's largest private provider of care home beds before its spectacular collapse in 2011. This oft-quoted example is a case in point. How can a company whose mission is the maximisation of short-term profit be trusted with the long-term care of frail and vulnerable people? That's not to say that a different 'for-profit' company, with a caring ethos and more nuanced values, can't be trusted with such a duty; would such a service really look so different from one provided by a social enterprise with overtly social values, employing business tools to implement them?

This blurring of historic sector boundaries is permanent. So, it appears, are government austerity measures and their consequences, public spending cuts, the dependency of the voluntary sector on government funds and the flatlining of charity income in the face of growing demand on their services. So are rising levels of inequality and the 'poverty premium', the phenomenon whereby elements of the cost of living are higher for the poor than for the rich. Official figures show that more British people are in 'working poverty' than ever, despite legislation designed to tackle low pay. Such people are employed disproportionately in the private sector and on short-term, variable or zero-hours contracts (see Chapter 3).[15]

It's no surprise, therefore, that our poorest communities are often, literally, hopeless. Those least able to afford it have borne the brunt of spending cuts. Their imperfect appreciation of politics, combined with an understandable belief that the economy isn't fair, that the 'establishment' doesn't care and that nothing they do will make a difference, led to the rise of the far right in continental Europe. In Britain we've seen Brexit, the UKIP phenomenon and even the repositioning of the Labour Party from a party of government to a more populist opposition. Those who rallied to the standard of Donald Trump in the belief that you punish the establishment by forcing them to scrap 'their' spending on 'their' programmes will taste their own medicine. In this political reality it's not for business to take sides. All politicians want to help their country achieve stability in a sustainable way, according to their vision of priorities, what's fair and what's possible, following that global financial crash of ten years ago. Don't they?

But neither can business stand idly by. The economic case for being involved in the relief of poverty is that poor people are poor consumers, a challenge central to the evolution of the 'shared value' philosophy championed by Michael Porter and integral to the 'inclusive economy'. Economically inefficient too are people who are excluded because they are sick but curable, temporarily or even permanently incapacitated, and those who are isolated – geographically, digitally or socially. Those who lack dignity often lack capacity. Stressed and unfulfilled employees are suboptimal performers – as influenced by the world outside the workplace as much as by the one within. Any business that cares about sustaining productivity is a potential Company Citizen.

Decent citizens care for the welfare of their neighbours; they work with them to address common issues in the community; are generous with their time, skills and other resources. The Company Citizen is actively engaged, not in Party politics but in lobbying for what's right and helping mitigate what's wrong.

However, fewer employers are found in our most deprived communities than in even slightly more affluent ones. Ironically, research also shows that such places have fewer successful voluntary-sector organisations: these communities often lack the social capital necessary to cope with poverty and social exclusion, to withstand ongoing economic shock, even to organise at a basic level. Where business is absent, how can the Company Citizen help without taking the place of the voluntary sector, public services or community networks?

Ask community organisations and small charities what they need most and they'll probably say money, but they're wrong. They need skills to plan their operations, to strategise, to lobby. These are essentially business skills that can be donated by a company at little cost in the course of an ongoing and committed relationship with a community. Get these skills right and whilst the money won't necessarily look after itself at least it will go further. Better still, skills transfer is a two-way street and workers will become better employees, better people, through such involvement.

According to a report by Social Enterprise UK, one third of local authorities have chosen to fully implement the 2012 Social Value Act (see Chapter 7).[16] This says that in commissioning the supply of services over a certain value a council may insist that bidders demonstrate positive values towards the community and the environment: reducing carbon footprint, increasing apprenticeship levels, encouraging employee volunteering and more, they all count. Manchester, Croydon and Birmingham councils apply these values to all of their tendering for goods and services and can demonstrate benefits for the community as a result. In those cities a business that wants to trade with the council has to be a Company Citizen. And businesses engaged in this way, as partners to non-business players, as enhancers and facilitators of 'public' services, are inevitably behaving as political animals – every day, not once every five years as do some in the political zoo.

Tom Wilson runs Allstate, America's second largest insurance company, which recently raised its own minimum wage standard to $15/hour, more than double the Federal level and significantly higher than in any individual state. He also represents three million businesses as vice chair of the US Chamber of Commerce. He writes:

> The corporation of the next 100 years must take on societal problems. On their own, governments, social service and charitable organisations simply do not have the capabilities and resources to solve the problems of inadequate education, poverty or public fiscal insolvency . . . fully integrating social good into a corporation's purpose is also good for business. Helping communities raises a company's reputation among customers, which supports growth and helps them attract, develop, motivate and retain the best workers.[17]

The business case

If philanthropy is the unprompted and unconditional donation of resources to a good cause, usually cash or kind, then the business case for it is – minimal. 'Corporate philanthropy' is too often donor-focused (hence the word 'philanthropist'), paying little heed to the long term or net impacts on the funded project. This is why Martin Luther King said: 'Philanthropy is commendable, but it must not cause the philanthropist to overlook the circumstances of economic injustice which make philanthropy necessary.'[18]

Many businesses give big sums from corporate coffers to charity as a matter of course, boast about it and then forget it. In one recent year the biggest single donation of money (several million pounds) from a business to a charity was an endowment from a mining company to its own, newly established, charitable foundation. A worthy cause in the long term, perhaps, but that transfer had no impact on any beneficiary of the foundation and therefore was only preparatory to 'doing good'. Currently £6bn per year (that's £23 per week, per company) is given by businesses to charities in Britain, a figure which has fallen slightly in recent years. This not insignificant amount is, of course, welcome but could be utilised better, as more sophisticated corporate donors have discovered. Philanthropy can undoubtedly enhance reputations but this falls apart when a company acts in ways which undermine the values associated with their philanthropic gestures. This is 'greenwashing'.

Putting this admittedly narrow definition of philanthropy aside, what's the business case for a company behaving as a company citizen?

Many ways for business to engage with a community are more sustainable than simply writing cheques:

- employer-supported volunteering can transfer, boost and extend employee skills;
- a business with a sense of purpose better engages its employees, thus boosting productivity;
- a values-led, ethical and sustainable value chain enhances reputation and can drive sales . . .
- . . . whilst making sourcing practices more efficient and legally compliant.

We'll explore these ideas in other chapters. For now it's worth noting that engaging a company with its community is a powerful way of engaging employees with the company mission and vision: an engaged employee is more productive and loyal than others; stays in post longer, reducing recruitment costs; and is a better informal ambassador. Such an employee takes less time off work, thinking 'yes' on those 50:50 'shall I go in?' days. They're engaged in activity outside the mainstream of their work, in work time and otherwise, either developing new skills or honing existing ones in new contexts, often adding soft interpersonal skills to the harder professional ones of the workplace. A company with values integrated into mainstream activity attracts a higher calibre of graduates, especially amongst millennials, who seek purpose and meaning in employment; and also let's not forget the marketing benefits of the best charity partnerships that work on a common mission – like that of Boots with Macmillan Cancer Care.

Young social enterprises have a higher survival rate than other SMEs, due perhaps to their more realistic expectations, higher tolerance of failure and having qualitative as well as financial goals. Investment in companies focused on 'engaged', 'ethical' or 'responsible' causes produces higher long-term returns than do mainstream FTSE indices, as we shall see in Chapter 4.

There's thus a strong conventional business case for being a Company Citizen.

***

So far we've discussed the rights and opportunities of citizens and whether they could be said to apply to companies. But citizens have obligations too: laws that support the common good need to be observed by both human and corporate bodies. What responsibilities does citizenship bring? Figure 1.1 describes three duties, aligned with and supported by three pairs of responsibilities for business.

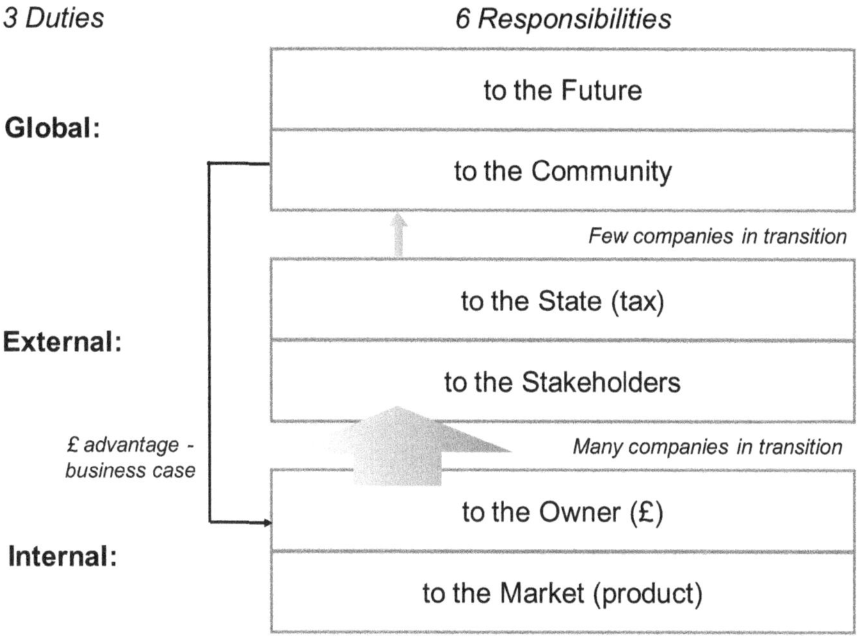

Figure 1.1 The three duties and three pairs of responsibilities of business

The internal duty – to owner and market

Companies have a duty to support the business itself. In the 18th century Adam Smith stated that a business could only sell what someone would buy and in the 1960s Milton Friedman argued that making a profit was the primary purpose of business. Essentially, both are correct: without a return on investment any business will fail whilst a company trying to sell a product that no-one wants is also doomed. But these are inward-looking responsibilities which don't completely reflect today's complex business world which, while not perfect, is in a state of flux. The Smith/Friedman axis is not wrong but it's far from the complete answer. Hopefully gone is the red-in-tooth-and-claw sentiment of Cousin Jonas in Dickens' *Martin Chuzzlewit*, pre-dating Friedman: 'Do other men, for they would do you. That's the true business precept.'

The external duty – to taxpayers and stakeholders

A company, like a citizen, has a degree of autonomy within the law but doesn't operate in isolation. Over recent generations business has come to appreciate its external responsibilities to all of its stakeholders and not just to its owners (see Chapters 5 and 6).

'From each according to his ability, to each according to his needs' is perhaps the most widely accepted, usually unwittingly, of Marxist principles. Company Citizens accept that paying tax is a moral obligation: it's right to help those worse off than ourselves through an element of redistribution. This price tag on their 'licence to operate' means that tax avoidance is frowned upon and evasion is illegal. Clearly not every company yet accepts this and some go to great lengths to minimise tax payments, to the extent of appearing to have no external accountability. At the accountants Grant Thornton, CEO Sacha Romanovitch says: 'If there are clients who are coming to us and their goal is to pay no tax, we don't work with them. We've walked away from a number who've wanted to work with us on that premise.'[19]

Contributing fairly through taxation is a hallmark of citizenship, not least as avoidance and evasion must logically increase the tax burdens on others. Accountants generally, as represented by their professional body, ICAEW, support the Fair Tax campaign and tax evasion has been the biggest public concern about big business in Britain since 2014, a real challenge to companies' licence to operate. Local authorities are permitted to refuse to trade with companies whose approach to Corporation Tax is not 'fair tax' compliant.[20] Many co-operatives and social enterprises voluntarily apply for the Fair Tax Mark; the first FTSE company to do so was Scottish and Southern Electricity.

Tax raises both practical and ethical questions. Sir Christopher Kelly is a former Chair of the Committee on Standards in Public Life, a body that advises the Prime Minister and Parliament. Writing to mark the 25th anniversary of the Institute of Business Ethics, he talks about the expectations of business stakeholders:

> The seven principles of public life – selflessness, integrity, objectivity, accountability, openness, honesty and leadership . . . describe the standards of behaviour expected of all politicians and civil servants who serve the public.
>
> The public might reasonably expect the same qualities in the behaviour of those they deal with elsewhere. They may realise that companies may not be selfless, or even perhaps completely objective about their products. But they increasingly expect them to show integrity, to be open and honest and to be accountable – not just to shareholders.[21]

Most companies accept the stakeholder argument and wouldn't dream of bending regulations to maximise their gains or, even worse, risk being found out – but the 'external duty' of company citizenship is not yet universally adopted. Look what happened when Volkswagen deliberately installed software in their cars which misreported emissions under test conditions, thus allowing their diesel engines to exceed legal limits on oxides of nitrogen (NOx) by up to 40 times. NOx emissions contribute to poor air quality, causing thousands of premature deaths across Europe (the diesel capital of the world) each year.

Although there are relatively few diesel cars in America, the US hit the company hard, fining them $2.8bn in 2017 plus civil penalties of $1.5bn for conspiracy to defraud the USA – with other jurisdictions likely to follow. Six VW executives were charged with criminal offences so the story didn't end there. The company, created in 1930s Germany to rival Ford as the world's biggest car manufacturer, set aside $7.3bn for making its cars retrospectively compliant, if such proves feasible. Its budget for compensating European VW owners for their misrepresentation was originally zero, though 10,000 British vehicle owners were each seeking over £3,000 compensation. VW could yet face legal challenge from its rivals for unfair competition; its excuses have been lame, even arguing, in behaviour reminiscent of tobacco companies of old, that NOx is not so lethal.[22] British sales of diesel-engine cars, of all makes, fell significantly in 2017.

The global duty – to communities and the future

Few mainstream companies yet adopt a philosophically global approach to citizenship. One of the two responsibilities enshrined in this duty is from history: it's to the future. In the era of family-owned firms companies were driven by the desire to pass a thriving business to the owner's children, obliging owners to consider the nature of the company 25 years hence. That generational perspective has been lost, short-term thinking has come to dominate business practice: witness the shrinking time spans of share ownership and CEO tenure, the growth of impatient venture capital, the dominance of quarterly financial reporting and the short-term focus of the bonus culture.

Only by appreciating our role in a world that's changing more rapidly than ever before in human history can we appreciate, for example, the prevention and mitigation work that must be done to reduce mankind's contribution to global warming to an absolute minimum. Written down over two years, investment in generating green energy is expensive; written down over 20 it's much less so. This is a particularly good example, as we're today paying the price for more than 50 years of reckless behaviour towards the atmosphere, justified at the time because the contemporary values of economic growth and the creation of wealth were deemed more important. The major, drastic measures we need to take today to combat the biospheric chaos of global warming will have no meaningful impact tomorrow, next week or next year. But by taking these actions we're casting a vote of confidence in future generations whose fortunes, even their lives, will be in serious jeopardy if we don't – see Chapter 2.

Peter Harrison, CEO of Schroders, told me at their 2017 AGM, as the company committed to the RE100 goal of using 100 per cent renewable energy by 2025: 'The reason we have a climate change problem is because so many people have taken so many short term decisions over so long' and 'We need to think long term, and that's what we advise our clients and investees'. Schroders is Europe's most responsible active asset manager according to ShareAction's 2017 holistic annual assessment.[23]

The other global duty is to 'community', explored in Chapter 7. The Company Citizen's a good neighbour, ready to help others in crisis or need; ready to work with others to improve the state of the local environment, human and ecological. Neighbourliness includes the obligation to respond reasonably and considerately when confronted with concerns that may otherwise lead to conflict or disdain. Never again should a company executive, pointing at a council estate from his sixth-floor window, say to me 'I know nothing about how they live down there'.

The beauty is that these six responsibilities together constitute a business case which feeds back (the anticlockwise arrow on Figure 1.1) to profitability.

When we talk of 'communities' we usually mean engagement with the social structures that unite, empower and provide for people: the grassroots, voluntary and social-sector players in what is colloquially called 'civil society', and their public-sector cousins.

Consider the relative strengths of business and charity: Britain has five million companies. Ninety-nine per cent employ fewer than 250 workers and most employ between five and ten. Two million companies employ no one at all, some being self-employed individuals whilst others may not be trading. The average company turns over £740,000 annually whilst the biggest, as we've seen, are mind-bogglingly large: a single supermarket store can turn over a million pounds each day, comparable with Manchester United or the international development charity, Oxfam.

Businesses, as some sector leaders are well versed in telling us, are not charities – so please indulge the author in a fantasy. Of 166,000 registered charities in Britain only 14 are bigger than Oxfam. Two thirds turn over less than £100,000 per year and of those half have an income of under £10,000. So big are the biggest charities – just 1,200 account for two thirds of the sector's income – that the sector's combined turnover is £46bn, says NCVO, and their mean income is £278,000.[24] (The Charity Commission's total of £73bn includes public schools, religious bodies and public-sector bodies with charitable status, such as universities.)

Let's say 75 per cent of charity income is spent on charitable causes whilst the rest goes on administration, fundraising and marketing. Assuming that this 75 per cent all delivers impact, quite an assumption, then charities as a whole produce £46bn × 75 per cent or £35bn of annual social value.

If every company focussed just one per cent of their turnover on creating social value this would generate £40bn of value in Britain for good causes (compared to under £6bn today), half from corporates, half from SMEs (assuming 100 per cent efficiency, with significant overhead costs being absorbed by the business).

In other words, one per cent of business effort (cash, goods, services or employee time and skills) could deliver a degree of social impact comparable with 100 per cent of charity effort. Adding it to charity output doubles the social impact. If it was not added but used instead to grow charity capacity – leveraging scale, making existing charities more effective – then the impact would be increased many-fold.

If only companies would focus just one per cent of their activity in this way.

Could it happen? 'We don't know what to do', wail smaller companies in particular. Yes you do. Many are already helping charities create capacity. Use your skills and develop your employees' experience by helping charities raise money, become more efficient, develop more effective business practices – in marketing, HR, planning, digital or retail skills, make sure you know what charities you're best able to assist, cost effectively, and what they really need. It would also help if people understood better the causes their partner charities represent, especially when they chime with the mission of the Company Citizen.

This is happening. Charities used to regard their relationships with business as 'arm's length' (albeit with the charity arm outstretched, palm upwards); in 2012 only 20 per cent of our largest charities agreed with the statement: 'By effectively harnessing our corporate partners' competences and non-cash assets [our organisation] can make much more of an impact on our mission delivery objectives than through cash-based relationships.'

In 2013 it was 34, 48 in 2015 and 60 per cent agreed by 2016. Over just four years there's been a sea change in the way big charities view the role of business partnerships in helping them deliver their mission.[25] At the same time businesses are growing more likely to regard their charity partnerships as strategic, acknowledging the contribution charities can make in helping businesses develop policies on sustainability, diversity and inclusion. In C&E Advisory's annual 'hit parade' the three partnerships consistently voted the most impressive by their peers are GSK with Save the Children, Boots with Macmillan and M&S with Oxfam (all featured in *Welcome to GoodCo*).

As a general rule, don't try to do it alone. Help the experts do what they do, even better.

Our poorest communities are in crisis. They feel ignored, excluded, exploited. They lack the social capital that a vibrant voluntary sector creates, which is why the otherwise worthy government initiative, 'Big Society', was always doomed to fail. Business can make the difference, partnering with others in the voluntary and public sectors, but only if it adopts the garb, practices and personality of the Company Citizen.

In doing so companies will become better places to work, better at what they do – and better citizens.

Table 1.1 The world's 100 largest economies

Ranking	*Country/corporate*	*Country*	*Market*	*Revenue/ turnover US$ (million)*
1	Country	USA		18,561,934
2	Country	China		11,391,619
3	Country	Japan		4,730,300
4	Country	Germany		3,494,900

(continued)

Table 1.1 (continued)

Ranking	*Country/corporate*	*Country*	*Market*	*Revenue/ turnover US$ (million)*
5	Country	United Kingdom		2,649,893
6	Country	France		2,488,280
7	Country	India		2,250,990
8	Country	Italy		1,852,500
9	Country	Brazil		1,769,600
10	Country	Canada		1,532,340
11	Country	South Korea		1,404,380
12	Country	Russia		1,267,750
13	Country	Australia		1,256,640
14	Country	Spain		1,252,160
15	Country	Mexico		1,063,610
16	Country	Indonesia		940,953
17	Country	Netherlands		769,930
18	Country	Turkey		735,716
19	Country	Switzerland		662,483
20	Country	Saudi Arabia		637,785
21	Country	Argentina		541,748
22	Country	Taiwan		519,149
23	Country	Sweden		517,440
24	**Walmart**	USA	Retail	482,000
25	Country	Belgium		470,179
26	Country	Poland		467,350
27	Country	Nigeria		415,080
28	Country	Iran		412,304
29	Country	Thailand		390,592
30	Country	Austria		387,299
31	Country	Norway		376,268
32	Country	UAE		375,022
33	Country	Venezuela		333,715
34	Country	Egypt		330,159
35	**State Grid**	China (SO)	Energy	330,000
36	Country	Hong Kong		316,070
37	Country	Israel		311,739
38	Country	Philippines		311,687
39	Country	Ireland		307,917
40	Country	Malaysia		302,748
41	Country	Denmark		302,571
42	**China National Petroleum**	China (SO)	Energy	299,000

43	Country	Singapore		296,642
44	**Sinopec Group**	China (SO)	Energy	294,000
45	Country	South Africa		280,367
46	Country	Colombia		274,135
47	**Royal Dutch Shell**	Netherlands	Energy	272,000
48	Country	Pakistan		271,050
49	**Exxon Mobil**	USA	Energy	246,000
50	Country	Finland		239,186
51	**Volkswagen**	Germany	Automotive	237,000
52	**Toyota**	Japan	Automotive	237,000
53	Country	Chile		234,903
54	**Apple**	USA	Consumer electronics	234,000
55	Country	Bangladesh		226,760
56	**BP**	United Kingdom	Energy	223,000
57	**Total**	France	Energy	212,000
58	**Berkshire Hathaway**	USA	Conglomerate	211,000
59	Country	Portugal		205,860
60	Country	Vietnam		200,493
61	Country	Greece		195,878
62	Country	Czech Republic		193,535
63	**McKesson**	USA	Pharmaceutical	192,000
64	Country	Romania		186,514
65	Country	Peru		180,291
66	Country	New Zealand		179,359
67	**Samsung**	South Korea	Conglomerate	177,000
68	**Glencore**	Switzerland	Commodities	170,000
69	Country	Algeria		168,318
70	**China Railway**	China (SO)	Transport	163,000
71	**Phillips 66**	USA	Energy	161,000
72	**Japan Post**	Japan (SO)	Conglomerate	157,000
73	**Daimler**	Germany	Automotive	157,000
74	Country	Qatar		156,595
75	Country	Iraq		156,323
76	**General Motors**	USA	Automotive	152,000
77	**General Electric**	USA	Conglomerate	149,000
78	**Exor**	Italy	Financial services	148,000
79	**Allianz**	Germany	Financial services	148,000
80	**AT&T**	USA	Telecoms	146,800
81	**Ford Motor Company**	USA	Automotive	144,000

(continued)

Table 1.1 (continued)

Ranking	*Country/corporate*	*Country*	*Market*	*Revenue/ turnover US$ (million)*
82	**Petrobras**	Brazil (SO)	Energy	144,000
83	**Lukoil**	Russia	Energy	144,000
84	**Honda**	Japan	Automotive	142,000
85	**CVS Health**	USA	Retail	139,000
86	**Chevron**	USA	Energy	138,000
87	**Industrial and Commercial Bank of China**	China (SO)	Financial services	137,000
88	**Amerisource Bergen**	USA	Pharmaceutical	136,000
89	**E·ON**	Germany	Electric utility	135,000
90	**Foxconn**	Taiwan	Electronics	133,000
91	**Eni**	Italy	Energy	133,000
92	**Valero**	USA	Energy	131,000
93	**United Health**	USA	Health care	131,000
94	Country	Kazakhstan		128,109
95	**PDVSA**	Venezuela (SO)	Energy	128,000
96	**Trafigura**	Switzerland	Commodities	129,000
97	**Verizon**	USA	Telecoms	127,000
98	**China Construction Engineering**	China (SO)	Construction	125,000
99	**Cargill**	USA	Food processing	120,000
100	Country	Hungary		117,065

Note: (SO) = State owned. Company figures refer to consolidated revenue, as available, November 2016. Country figures refer to GDP according to the International Money Fund, October 2016. The World Bank and United Nations use slightly different criteria to these but their rank orders are comparable: the World Bank would put slightly more corporates in the top 100, UN slightly more countries. All data are snapshots and will vary slightly, even daily, according to influences such as currency fluctuations. (Source: collated from data available on Wikipedia.)[26]

Notes

1 www.edelman.com/executive-summary/.
2 Private correspondence.
3 https://party.coop/publication/in-our-interests-building-an-economy-for-all/.
4 Both described in my book, *Welcome to GoodCo.*
5 http://community.businessfightspoverty.org/m/blogpost?id=2014886%3ABlogPost%3A243750.
6 https://twitter.com/gibbulloch/status/794466147718590464.
7 www.edie.net/news/7/Tony-Juniper--Sustainability-will-determine-business-survival-in-2050-/?.
8 www.bbc.co.uk/news/business-40952820.

9 Ibid. The ban was withdrawn after Supreme Court intervention and re-introduced, watered-down, though again delayed by Court action.

10 https://data.ncvo.org.uk/a/almanac17/. More recent figures suggest that a significant fall in volunteering may be happening: www.thirdsector.co.uk/volunteering-levels-fall-government-figures-show/volunteering/article/1440384.

11 www.unmillenniumproject.org/goals/.

12 www.un.org/sustainabledevelopment/sustainable-development-goals/ and http://sdgcompass.org/wp-content/uploads/2015/09/SDG_Compass_Guide_Executive_Summary.pdf.

13 http://evonomics.com/accounting-smoke-mirrors-makes-corporate-profits-rich-peoples-income-invisible/.

14 'In the City', *Private Eye* 1437, 10 February 2017. The first British prosecution of a UK bank related to the crash was announced in June 2017 (Barclays): www.sfo.gov.uk/2017/06/20/sfo-charges-in-barclays-qatar-capital-raising-case/.

15 www.jrf.org.uk/press/work-poverty-hits-record-high-housing-crisis-fuels-insecurity – see also Chapter 3.

16 www.socialenterprise.org.uk/procuring-for-good – see also Chapter 7.

17 www.washingtonpost.com/opinions/how-corporations-can-be-a-force-for-good/2016/09/29/08e99268-7ac4-11e6-ac8e-cf8e0dd91dc7_story.html?.

18 https://ssir.org/articles/entry/shifting_philanthropy_from_charity_to_justice.

19 http://vibranteconomy.grantthornton.co.uk/the-importance-of-purpose-and-business/.

20 https://fairtaxmark.net/take-action/local-council-campaign/.

21 www.ibe.org.uk/userassets/otherpdfs/25on25.pdf.

22 http://fortune.com/inside-volkswagen-emissions-scandal/ – see also Chapter 5. In 2017 VW, followed by Ford, introduced scrappage schemes for diesel and older petrol-driven cars.

23 https://shareaction.org/wp-content/uploads/2017/03/Survey-LiftingTheLid.pdf. In July 2017 RE100 reached its first goal of 100 corporates committing to 100 per cent renewable energy: http://there100.org/news/14257837.

24 https://data.ncvo.org.uk/a/almanac17/.

25 www.candeadvisory.com/sites/default/files/headline_findings_Barometer%20 2016.pdf.

26 https://en.wikipedia.org/wiki/List_of_countries_by_GDP_(nominal)#cite_note-GDP_IMF-5 and https://en.wikipedia.org/wiki/List_of_largest_companies_by_revenue. Please note: my list uses 2016 data. Wikipedia's 2017 list shows minor changes in rank order but includes only the 25 biggest companies by revenue, those worth more than $140bn. Wikipedia also lists the quarterly top ten (only) based on market capitalisation (MC) and dominated by Apple, Alphabet (Google), Microsoft, Amazon and (to a lesser extent) Facebook. MC is a volatile measure, revenue has more in common with GDP. Since mid-2015 the only non-American businesses in the MC top ten are both Chinese, TenCent and AliBaba.

2 The world is ready

Is our planet ready for Company Citizenship? Yes, desperately so.

We know that 42 of the world's 100 biggest economies are corporates, not countries. Just 500 companies control two thirds of world trade and 3 million new companies (globally) emerge every year.[1] Whilst today one third of global GDP comes from 150 cities in the western capitalist world, half of all new GDP between now and 2025 will come from 450 cities in the developing world.[2] These statistics should prompt an outburst of humility, responsibility, calls to action and offers to help from those who control that most powerful weapon on the planet: the global economy. Is it realistic to expect the same players that helped to cause so much environmental damage, allowed so many to starve, produced ever greater inequalities, to become a force for good? Yes. It's essential.

Those 17 Sustainable Development Goals, more business-focused than their predecessors, represent a road map for business doing good, even though 54 per cent of sustainability professionals rank our progress towards them as 'poor'. Generally those on human health, energy, industry, climate and partnership are most on course, whilst reducing inequalities, responsible consumption, protecting life in water and on land are least.[3] Although extreme poverty and child mortality are falling and vaccination, basic education, literacy and even democratic participation are significantly up, none are yet at an acceptable level globally.[4] Their interconnections throw up secondary issues such as population growth and mass migration. Our problems can no longer be solved by nation states acting either alone or even together. It's vital that companies, global Company Citizens, act with them.

Perhaps economic globalisation led to or exacerbated many of today's problems, but globalisation itself was both inevitable and value-free. It was, and continues to be, the consequence of trade, the quest for new markets, new sources of materials; it reflects a world of instantaneous movements of cash and data; it includes the aspirant 'developing' nations, aligning themselves ever more closely to wealthier lifestyles. No one was ever going to stand in its way.

Though globalisation may be consequential on what went before, its detail has been manipulated, engineered, exploited; it's been painted as socially damaging. As companies grew in size they became multinational, then supra-national, now even a-national: those dealing especially in virtual or digital products are readily divorced from any geographical identity – for tax purposes, at least. Through globalisation we allowed corporates of obscene size and power to emerge, so big that we must question their ability to even know what's happening in the far-flung parts of their own empires, let alone be held meaningfully accountable. This too was not inevitable; we let it happen.

Food and hunger

> We have the ability, as members of the human race, we have the means, we have the capacity to eliminate hunger from the face of the earth in our lifetime. We only need the will.

President Kennedy was right. His lifetime lasted only a little while longer and the promise is long overdue. One in nine people, including one in four Africans, suffer from hunger or malnutrition, together a more immediate threat to life than malaria, tuberculosis and AIDS combined.[5] Yet in 2012 the World Wildlife Fund stated that we're already scheduled to use 1.5 times the resources of the planet and three planets will eventually be needed. Those clever people at NASA are on the job, though once Mars is colonised they fear it will take 120 more years to make it habitable, and by then . . . ?[6]

Food production and affordability have made progress, as has population control; absolute global poverty fell by a third between 2005 and 2010. Today progress is still evident but it's slower, restrained by competition from growing consumption in many parts of the world, especially the east, and the damage to agricultural land and water supplies caused by climate change, of which more later.

Say 'agricultural technology' and many think 'Monsanto' as the conversation turns to genetically modified (GM) crops. As a scientist I maintain an open mind, believing that the private-sector-led crusade behind GM food is potentially beneficial as long as safeguards are maintained. It can improve crop yields, enhance resistance to disease and drought, reduce fertiliser use and make land more productive, though we must be ever aware of 'unforeseen consequences'. Some GM soy beans are neither more nor less 'natural' than a green pea, an orange carrot or the modern chicken, none of which existed just a few of our generations ago. The World Bank calculates that if current consumption continues humanity will need to increase cereal production by half and meat by 80 per cent by as soon as 2030.[7]

That the food revolution hasn't happened as promised is often blamed, at least in part, on private companies. Innovative plant genotypes have become secretive, expensive, the focus of espionage. Companies have declined to develop perennial strains, obliging subsistence farmers to buy seed every year rather than allowing their plants to propagate themselves. Monocultures protected by chemicals have been created, damaging biodiversity. Disproportionate profits are made. The merger between Monsanto and Bayer isn't reassuring; it will further concentrate clout and reduce diversity in the market.[8]

Such operations have fomented public hostility to 'Frankenstein farming', contributing to an anti-boffin, anti-expert culture and the consequent reluctance of governments and regulators to back opportunities for progress. Sceptical public opinion holds back the potential for good.

Business is in the driving seat on agricultural reform. If the quest to feed the world were led by Company Citizens it would be more diverse than the seed and chemical lobby allows today, incorporating broader technologies. We'd grow biofuels in salt water, perhaps in unproductive brackish areas, releasing land for food production. We hear of protein-rich locust flour, but where's the investment to take this to scale? Most deforestation and habitat destruction in South America is to rear cattle to serve American burger bars, feeding the most obese on earth with products of which they need to eat less; deforestation in Brazil jumped by over a quarter in 2016, capitalising on political instability. Major players in cattle, palm oil, soy, cocoa and timber itself are trying to address sustainable forestry issues but, lower down the supply chain, coordination is poor and unregulated, and illegal activity is rife.

Such issues arise and threaten because the market allows them to.

In the last few decades we've realised that the best way to help the African subsistence farmer is to create an effective market so that he can both feed his family and trade his surplus to achieve an income, and thus afford to buy nutritious foods. Making the market work effectively means making it biologically and economically sustainable – 'dumping' excess food from elsewhere disrupts those goals. Such changes reflect a movement from 'aid' towards 'development'. A very significant contribution to making the market work in East Africa was M-Pesa, a Vodaphone project backed by Britain, which brought mobile telephony to places which had never seen copper telephone wire and henceforth would never need to. The beauty of M-Pesa was that it was both a communications tool – the farmer driving his cattle to market could check the prices cows were fetching in different villages and vary his route accordingly – and a source of basic telephone banking. It was revolutionary and continues, ten years on, to make an impact. Today 33 million of Kenya's 47 million people have mobile phones and half of them have M-Pesa accounts; it's in a dozen other countries and growing. Ten per cent of sub-Saharan Africans use it.[9] All of Tanzania's mobile networks offer compatible money transfer services to the extent that the country's 18 million active users put half of the country's GDP through M-Pesa each year.[10] As an MP I was attached to the Department for International Development when we gave a grant to develop M-Pesa. If that had been a loan, an equity investment or a joint venture then the impact would have been as positive but the money could have been recycled to support other development projects.

Anyone who's ever flown over Zambia will have marvelled at its wide open spaces, rich soil and sparse multi-acres of scrub punctuated by occasional, green, circular, automated sugar-snap pea farms, each with its own landing strip. Zambia's climate and rainfall give it huge agricultural potential and it's claimed that the country could feed the whole of Africa . . . with the right investment. It needs infrastructure, rail, road and air links, irrigation: in short, everything except biopotential, which it has in excess. That investment won't come from the impoverished government nor from the international community, unless other funding lines are sacrificed. The country is a long-term opportunity ripe for private-sector investment by benevolent – and patient – Company Citizens.

It's not easy to answer a child's question 'where does our food come from?' We live in a global marketplace where every vegetable aisle can generate a formidable geography lesson. Mass transport may have a price in carbon terms but scale reciprocates unit cost and major food stores have many suppliers to call upon. Roses grown in Kenya are cheaper than from Holland, despite the cost of air freight, as they don't require intense cultivation or heating. Such flexibilities are relatively new; the world is truly smaller than it was.

Global markets have proven volatile, especially in recent years. Whenever the price to the African smallholder goes up, often for reasons outside his control such as currency fluctuation, there's a risk that the supermarket will take their custom elsewhere. When that happens the farmer's income goes down and he's less able to afford nutritious food or send his daughters to school.

Company Citizens have allowed Fairtrade to flourish.[11] Supply chains that guaranteed minimum incomes for growers in developing countries found favour in the west and were promoted by charities and religious groups from the 1960s. Although the arguments for moral limits to markets were around before then, mainstream Fairtrade labelling only began in the 1980s. The market diversified within and beyond food and grew ten-fold, to $4.4bn, by 2014 (a third is in Britain). In recent years the family of certified producers growing Fairtrade products has reached a million and growers are more directly involved in the international bodies which certify them. Increasingly the model is seen as a basis for continuous improvement in the social progress of grower communities, often now dominated by self-governing co-operatives. Today it's difficult to find a banana that isn't 'Fairtrade', ethical chocolate has broken into the mainstream consumer space and demand is outstripping supply in many Fairtrade food products; yet this remains very much a minority activity within global markets. Sainsbury's is UK's largest Fairtrade retailer and has championed the cause – until now? Their plan to instigate 'fairly traded' tea involves no longer paying the price premium to growers automatically but distributing it strategically through the Sainsbury's Foundation. Working with growers and campaigners, this could broaden the positive impact of pro-poor trade; the jury is out.[12]

One third of the food that comes out of the world's farms, intended for human consumption, is dumped as a billion go hungry. Why? Over-ordering, rejection of 'substandard' yet edible vegetables, artificially low prices. Today's sophisticated supply chains need to be much more sensitive to the needs of communities at all stages. Company Citizens must always be aware of the consequences of their purchases, especially on the poorest and most vulnerable, knowing that solutions are in their hands.

Climate change

Frequently painted as controversial, despite its basic truths being at least 97 per cent certain, according to at least 97 per cent of informed scientists, climate change affects us all now and will, even more, in the future. Twentieth-century global industrialisation was the main destroyer of climate equilibrium. Business not only has the power but shares the responsibility to correct this imbalance.

Many elements of this debate are beyond argument:

- the planet's natural cycles of cooling and warming are beyond our influence, being dependent upon, for example, the sun;
- we're in an historically warm period, though throughout human history variations in global temperatures have been small. We had a warmish period about a thousand years ago and a relatively cool 16th/17th century. Fifteen of the 16 hottest years ever recorded were in the period 2000–16;
- certain naturally occurring gases, principally carbon dioxide (CO_2), methane and water vapour, enhance the atmosphere's ability to retain heat rather than radiate it into space;
- burning fossil fuels creates excess CO_2 whilst deforestation restricts the environment's natural ability to remove it from the atmosphere;
- any impact on the atmosphere is global, not local, as gases move and impacts dissipate; and
- our ice caps and glaciers are melting.

Ever since the industrial revolution was followed by the era of internal combustion we've been increasing manmade CO_2 production whilst restricting the environment's ability to maintain a balance. As a result, the amount of CO_2 retained in the atmosphere increased significantly during the 20th century, mostly in the second half, and is still increasing. Ice-core sampling has shown that global CO_2 has risen by 36 per cent since 1750 and methane by 148 per cent, both to levels unprecedented in 800,000 years. A quarter of manmade CO_2 emissions come from the USA and a tenth from China. The latter is growing fast, though China has recently scrapped plans for 85 coal-fired power stations in favour of a £300bn investment in renewables.[13] In 2015 atmospheric CO_2 reached 400 parts per million for the first time and it's not expected to fall below that level again in our lifetimes, even if drastic action is taken now.

Nine tenths of the excess energy released into the atmosphere by burning fuel is absorbed by the oceans, causing three major effects:

- melting the ice caps increases sea levels and releases frozen reserves of greenhouse gases such as methane;
- reducing the ocean's ability to dissolve oxygen, threatening the microscopic life which powers marine food chains; and
- warmer oceans interact with the atmosphere, disrupting weather systems.

Fossil fuels account for 87 per cent of carbon emissions caused by human activity but only 4 per cent comes directly from industrial processes. The remainder of the carbon equation is accounted for by changes in land use, principally cutting down trees, burning forests and damaging carbon sinks such as peat. Throughout the world reserves of peat are being destroyed. Burning peat either deliberately as fuel or, in places like Indonesia, through literal 'scorched earth' policies, the CO_2 that the biosphere has stored over millennia is released and adds unnecessarily to atmospheric CO_2. The world's largest reserve of peat was recently discovered in Congo; let's hope it remains intact. Amongst fuels coal releases more CO_2 by weight than others; it accounts for 43 per cent of the fossil fuel account, oil 36 and gas 20.

As a greenhouse gas the methane released by melting ice caps is more powerful than CO_2 but methane has another major source: ruminants. Cattle belch methane-rich air from their stomachs in massive quantities. Beef production is now the main reason for cutting down forests around the world, accelerating the growth of greenhouse gases. In 2006 Greenpeace brokered an agreement – with food manufacturers, supermarkets, commodity traders and fast food giants, including McDonalds and KFC[14] – which has reduced by 99 per cent the loss of virgin Amazon forest due to soya farming for cattle feed. Unfortunately other crops, and other locations, have not achieved the same level of co-ordinated success. Almost 500 procurers are today pledged to avoid unnecessary and illegal deforestation.

The sea is predicted to rise by up to a metre over this century. Most people in Bangladesh, one of the world's poorest countries, live close to sea level and the world's atoll communities are similarly vulnerable: to them climate change is very real. London, Mumbai, Shanghai and New York are also threatened.

Meteorological disruption isn't just weather becoming wetter or windier. Combinations of relatively small changes to weather patterns can cause catastrophic storms, hence those that make the news are more frequent and more intense; even our seasons misbehave. Interaction with changing ocean currents produces longer-term effects: drought is more than an inconvenience, it damages vulnerable crop production in poorer countries. This leads to food shortages, migratory pressures and the growth of cities through the accretion of slum communities in which abject poverty, disease and civil unrest can all take hold.

Somewhere in the 1970s the planet stopped being able to take everything we could throw at it. Since then human activity, not solar or 'natural' cycles, has been the dominant cause of global warming: in recent years sea-level rises and Arctic ice cap shrinkage have been faster than predicted. The task now is to prevent a further calamitous rise in global temperature, which can only be achieved through a massive reduction in emissions over a relatively short time.

Rio '92 was the first climate summit. The Paris COP21 meeting of 2015, bringing together 55 countries responsible for over half of our carbon emissions, finally produced a ratifiable agreement, which came into force in 2016.

When a country says it will reduce emissions it means 'our businesses will reduce emissions'. The European Union has committed to reduce CO_2 output by 40 per cent by 2030, having already reduced it by a quarter since 1990 (whilst growing its economy by half). Reducing CO_2 stimulates economic activity through new technology – witness how solar energy production has grown cheaper as it's grown in scale. The investor climate has also changed considerably, as we shall see, increasing the focus on clean energy and low-impact business.

Since COP21 business has focused on the challenge of sustainable energy: in Europe 77 per cent of big businesses rated the agreement as important in 2016 (up from 69 just a year previously). Even in the USA more than half of all businesses agreed (55 per cent, compared with 41 in 2015), suggesting that Trump's regressive plan for a resurgence of coal will have little impact.[15] The supply chains of 3,000 global companies have reduced their emissions by half a billion tonnes of CO_2 – think France – in just a year. However, fewer than a quarter of companies engage with their supply chains on carbon emissions (and only a sixth on conserving water).[16] Within hours of Trump's declaration that the US would join Syria and Nicaragua as the only countries outside the Paris Accord, and against the advice of his influential daughter, Tesla's Elon Musk and Disney's Robert Iger quit the President's Business Advisory Council. Then California, New York and Washington states, a fifth of the American population, announced they would stick with COP21. They were cheered on by a once unlikely alliance of China, Russia, business leaders, investors ($17tn worth), the UN and the European Union. France's President Macron defiantly parodied Trump, 'Let's make our planet great again', whilst former New York Mayor Michael Bloomberg offered to pay the $15m Trump was withdrawing from UN climate programmes. Those closest to business and the people will play their part in combating climate change, whatever the President's wishes.[17]

The Oil and Gas Climate Initiative's mission is to prove that it's no oxymoron: seven leading oil companies have contributed $1bn over ten years to promote innovative low emission technologies, though that's a fraction of the $61bn spent by BP cleaning up after the Deepwater Horizon oil spill. 'The energy mix of the world will evolve', said Total's Patrick Pouyane, implying that more investment would follow.[18]

Companies can generate their own zero carbon electricity. Bywater operates London's biggest reclamation and recycling plant: its solar array produces enough electricity for 100,000 homes whilst saving 500 tonnes of carbon emissions each year – significantly more than anticipated.[19] Belfast Airport's solar plant saves them £10,000/month and water treatment in west London is powered by the world's largest floating solar array on a reservoir near Heathrow.[20]

Electricity generation produces more CO_2 than any other industry and fossil fuels account for two thirds of energy production in all but two G8 countries, Canada and France, thanks to hydroelectric and nuclear power respectively. After electricity, transport is both the next biggest sector and the fastest growing: Network Rail is UK's biggest electricity consumer. Within transport 72 per cent of CO_2 comes from our roads, 11 from aviation and 14 from shipping, though shipping produces more per kilometre than any other mode – and it's growing.[21] Despite its poor reputation – possibly because of it – there are strong currents within commercial shipping to respond to COP21 by setting tough standards to reduce the industry's carbon footprint. Fifty sector leaders including Maersk and Cargill support the Sustainable Shipping Initiative to make the industry sustainable by 2040.[22] Their goal requires them to cut carbon emissions by 90 per cent; without this initiative, shipping's carbon emissions could double by 2050.[23]

On Britain's roads 483,000 heavy goods vehicles worked for over 36,500 transport businesses in 2015, transporting comparable quantities of goods with the pre-2007 era.[24] Whilst car and van numbers are stable, heavy road freight numbers have fallen, partly reflecting more efficient practices. One in five new cars in Britain now have hybrid or electric engines (as do all new London buses) but not lorries, which, like black taxis, are mostly diesel-powered with its additional pollution issues.

The cement industry is disproportionately represented on the league table because the heating of limestone releases additional CO_2. Our homes account for a large element of domestic carbon emissions: the value-for-money zero-carbon house is perfectly feasible but housebuilders aren't delivering. A UK Government target of all new homes being zero carbon by 2016, set in 2006, was quietly, and inexplicably, abandoned in 2015.

Many strategies to combat climate change involve an upfront cost. Business must rethink its approach to long-term investment and be more relaxed about accounting for returns over 20 years. Actions which businesses of all kinds do consider, and many now undertake, include:

- sharing haulage;
- replacing older vehicles with fuel-efficient ones;
- reducing energy use;
- purchasing electricity from renewable energy providers or creating their own;
- replacing some transport costs with video conferencing;
- encouraging home working and flexible hours, reducing transport demands;
- using recycled building materials, reducing the need for virgin cement; and
- raising energy awareness amongst staff.

In July 2017 RE100 reached its initial goal of 100 major companies committed to achieving zero net carbon. IKEA, a founding member, is investing €2bn to achieve carbon neutrality across its 336 stores in 28 countries.[25] Sharing their 2020 goal are Aviva, BT, Sky, Coca-Cola and AstraZeneca; others are targeting 2025 and Tesco is aiming at 2030. Ninety six per cent of all the energy Apple uses globally is already from renewable sources and they're helping their manufacturers achieve the same. Microsoft has been net zero carbon since 2014,

Heathrow now uses only renewable energy and Unilever is carbon neutral in USA and Europe.[26] Lego reached its target three years early. Whitbread (Premier Inns, Costa Coffee) achieved 100 per cent renewable energy, including solar panels on the roofs of 88 hotels, in 2017. Two thirds of Fortune 500 companies are working towards clean energy or climate change targets.

The low-carbon, green-energy business in Britain is already worth £46bn. Coal usage in Britain is at its lowest for 150 years, falling by half in 2016 alone (abetted by a steel works closing), helping the UK reduce CO_2 emissions by six per cent – but it's not enough.[27]

It can be done, if not always very well.

I visited South Africa in 1999 when the poorest communities still had little access to electricity. In 2016, driving along sleek motorways around Johannesburg, I was impressed to see a huge investment in low-cost housing. Typically South African, the bungalows were brick, small but homely. On top of each was a black cylinder and a black screen; a water tank and a solar energy collector. Excellent! Then I realised . . . I was travelling north in the southern hemisphere so the screens should also have been facing vaguely north. But they were facing every which way, including south. A great idea made less efficient, it appeared, by poor execution.

Frankly, whether carbon emissions directly cause global warming or not (and they do) it makes no sense to continue our dependence on hydrocarbons. They're going to run out. They're unsustainable. Once used they're gone. As a source of chemicals and plastic they're too valuable to burn. The scarcer they get the higher their extraction costs – and risks. Many hydrocarbon sources are in politically unstable regions; it's eminently sensible to source energy which can't be held hostage.

Access to sunlight has never yet been a reason for war.

Water

Ninety seven per cent of the world's water is in oceans. Of fresh water, 70 per cent is locked in ice caps and glaciers and just 1 per cent is in rivers, streams and lakes. The rest is in the ground. Annual human demand for water globally is rising and will top 5,000km^3 before 2025.

Conflicts over access to drinkable water have existed for 5,000 years. In the Middle East, where 5 per cent of the world's population enjoy just 1 per cent of the planet's drinkable water, the rivers Jordan, Euphrates and Tigris have all been controversial. Yemen's current unrest started in 2009 with water riots and the state of Jordan, wholly dependent on aquifers, cannot for that reason alone host its half a million Syrian refugees in perpetuity. One of many objections to the Israeli construction of a wall around the West Bank is that, in straying from the internationally acknowledged border, it has reallocated water sources from Palestinian farms to Israeli territory. Many Chinese rivers rise in Tibet, perhaps explaining the superpower's interest in controlling its neighbour?

Two of the world's biggest cities, Beijing and Jakarta, are subsiding due to over-extraction from aquifers. Shanghai and Mexico City have the same problem whilst parts of California's Central Valley have fallen by an incredible 8 metres. Deeper boreholes are expensive to drill and they release mineral-rich barely potable water. In many places leaky elderly pipework, superficial investment in water infrastructure and a liberal approach to wasting it haven't helped. The UN predicts that drinking water will be in global deficit by 2030, prompting a fall in the planet's GDP of 6 per cent.[28]

Two thirds of fresh water extracted from aquifers is for agriculture. Normally, nature slowly replenishes water taken from the ground but that can no longer be taken for granted, partly because of climate change but mostly because extraction has increased beyond a sustainable level. Massive investment in water technology in Saudi Arabia has literally turned the desert green with fruit and vegetable farms – temporarily.

Some water shortages are exacerbated by business. Excluding agriculture, industry consumes 22 per cent of fresh water compared with 8 per cent for domestic use.[29] Each year fracking for shale gas requires two million gallons of water per well, yet half of American fracking is in areas of high water stress.[30]

In 2002 locals claimed that a new bottling factory in India would take an unfair share of water from the local watershed, leading Coca-Cola to abandon its development. Other companies have cancelled similar plans for the same reason. Coca-Cola saw the light: they spent $2bn over a decade to make their water usage sustainable. A Japanese nuclear energy company spent $10bn cleaning up groundwater pollution following the 2011 tsunami and BG Group $100m to pipe treated fresh water from an Australian gas field to local communities. RTZ and its allies invested $3bn on a desalination plant and pumping facility in Chile, allowing them to operate a mine using treated seawater rather than competing for the scarce fresh water with local communities. Two thirds of mines owned by the big six mining companies are in areas of high water stress. Due to a stark consequence of climate change at an Alpine hydroelectric station, EDF has spent €20m constructing a new tunnel to bring glacial water to its power plant – because the old tunnel no longer reaches the retreating glacier. Between them, big corporates spent $84bn between 2010 and 2015 on infrastructure to conserve, recycle and source water.

But more is needed. Water wasn't in the World Economic Forum's top five risks to business prior to 2011 but it's been in the top three in every year since. Between 2015 and 2016 the negative impact on business of droughts, floods and water pollution rose five-fold to $14bn globally; good water management and reducing carbon emissions complement each other.[31]

In 2014 the Governor of California regulated the pumping of ground water in drought-hit Central Valley, a major producer of fruit and vegetables where aquifers provide 60 per cent of potable water. Aggressive, unregulated and unreported extraction by private landowners over generations, combined with historically low rainfall, have created a crisis. Communities are already bringing in expensive tankers of water for domestic use. The Head of the Pacific

Institute has said: 'Whoever has the most money, the deepest wells and the strongest pumps has been able to take this public good and turn it into a private commodity.'[32]

The new law gives local agencies powers to restrict pumping, close wells down and impose penalties for illicit extraction. It obliges local agencies to produce groundwater sustainability plans . . . by 2040. The plans aren't popular amongst environmentalists ('too little, too late') or those Americans who believe that access to water is as much a right as that of bearing arms.

Manufacturers of bottled water in California are under pressure. Nestlé has been obliged to point out that their total water extraction at a controversial plant, 700 million gallons a year, is the same as that required to maintain just two golf courses (of which the region has many). Whatever the morality of bottled water, for some in California it may soon be the only source of safe and affordable drinking water locally available.[33] Another Californian bottling plant facing calls for closure provides Starbucks with its own brand water: with every bottle sold a donation is made to help . . . people suffering from water shortage.[34]

War

In the 1960s Edwin Starr sang that, of all businesses, war was 'friend only to the undertaker'. Those American companies who, between them, received $138bn of taxpayers' money for work in Iraq in the ten years following the 2003 war might disagree. A third of that sum went to a single company, KBR, a former subsidiary of Dick Cheney's Haliburton, for reconstruction work, outsourced security functions and facilities such as water supplies.[35]

Over the last decade Britain has become the world's second largest arms exporter. Our recent portfolio has included sales to 39 of 51 countries not regarded as 'free' and 22 of the Foreign Office's own list of 30 countries where human rights issues are problematic. These latter sales were worth £8bn and include BAE Systems' fighter jets wreaking havoc in Yemen under Saudi colours.[36] Whilst the arms industry may take a benign view of conflict, business and war are generally unhappy bedfellows. The 'peace dividend' benefits the purses of both private sector and other organisations.

The days are largely gone when businesses employed armies, as the Dutch East India Company did 400 years ago, yet armies do employ businesses. Wherever there's a conflict there's supply and demand for mercenaries. They might be provided by security companies such as Academi, which has a training facility in North Carolina. At one point it could call upon 20,000 soldiers, 20 aircraft and a fleet of armoured vehicles ready to deploy wherever the price was right. Formerly known as Blackwater, Academi changed its name after being embarrassed by 'wrongful shooting' scandals in Iraq. They patrolled the streets of New Orleans to prevent post-hurricane looting, protect Japan's missile defence systems and support operations against drug cartels in South America. There's little transparency in the operation of such companies because of 'commercial considerations'.

Armed conflict within a country is often associated with a dysfunctional society, extreme poverty, weak government or scarce resources; such factors mitigate against the political stability and economic growth that support a prosperous and successful business community. There's evidence that local conflict is a powerful recruiting sergeant for groups such as ISIS. The impact of war on businesses and communities depends on whether you're aggressor or defender, winner or loser. In all cases, public resources are diverted to arguably non-productive use and there's a degree of civil disruption. Whether a country is under attack or merely losing fit citizens to conscription, forward planning by businesses is made more challenging and supply chains become disrupted. More directly, investment and trading opportunities disappear, infrastructure is damaged and employees may be killed. There's a business case for avoiding armed conflict.

In Syria the disruption to trade is well documented. As early as 2013 the complex conflict between three parties, namely the Syrian government and its allies (including Russia), the insurgent Islamic State terrorist organisation and a loose coalition of groups (generally supported by the west, Turkey and Iraq) was taking its toll. In two years the cost to the country was over $48bn or four fifths of GDP, half caused by a loss in trade and half 'capital damage': under-production and loss of industrial capacity, reduced investment and physical damage to buildings and equipment. The country was poorer by the equivalent of 20 years of human development, its GDP plummeting. The SME sector, the biggest employer of the lowest paid, had been hit hardest and income from tourism had fallen by 90 per cent in just two years.

In October 2011 the world imposed sanctions on the Syrian regime, which cut oil production by half as manufacturing output fell by three quarters. Public investment halved as Assad's government focused on shorter-term needs, public debt doubled and the currency was devalued by two thirds. Over 1.5 million jobs were lost, the black market grew and a quarter of the adult population was unemployed.[37] The Syrian economy has been devastated; little wonder its remains are in hock to the Russians.

All of the above happened in the first two years of the conflict and nothing has improved since then.

Business cannot defend against war. But it can assist with peace building, help avoid war and contribute to recovery in the aftermath. The mining industry often finds itself near the front line – the phrase 'conflict minerals' didn't arise by accident.

The ground under the Democratic Republic of Congo (DRC) contains three quarters of the world's coltan (a source of niobium and tantalum used in mobile phones), half of the planet's cobalt reserves and significant amounts of copper and zinc, as well as a quarter of the global diamond supply. It ought to be a rich country; it's not.[38] A sixth of the population depends on small-scale mining.

Early in the 20th century Belgian forces took over this huge country in pursuit of slaves, rubber and ivory. Joseph Mobutu, the first leader of independent Congo from 1965, renamed it Zaire for a generation; he crushed rebellions in the name of unity but then succumbed to corruption. War in neighbouring Rwanda spread into DRC, toppling Mobutu in 1994. The ten years of domestic conflict that followed cost five million lives.

In the last decade order has gradually replaced anarchy in much of the country. Some mines are still exploited by gangs and 'informal groupings', neither companies nor government forces, who manage to feed the minerals into supply chains which western companies have continued to access. Lacking both national infrastructure and skilled labour, costs are low and opportunities exist to profit – though the 'conflict minerals' stigma keeps prices down.

Terrible things still happen in DRC despite the war being formally over. Child soldiers fight for both sides and some government forces have worked in cahoots with militias; low level conflict and corruption persist. Both sides have used mass rape, informal executions and massacres and rebel leaders are wanted for war crimes; 20,000 UN peacekeepers have been there for 30 years.

The UN Guiding Principles on Business and Human Rights state that companies should respect human rights through responsible operations, observing relevant national and international laws and standards. Where sources are 'not under legitimate control' four minerals – cassiterite (a tin ore), coltan, wolframite (a tungsten source) and gold – are designated 'conflict minerals' and their use in supply chains is strictly monitored.[39]

Three hundred and fifty electronics companies came together as the Conflict-Free Sourcing Initiative to identify and certify conflict-free content of smelters around the world. Smelters are important because minerals reach them from identifiable sources while downstream they're untraceable.[40]

Amongst the provisions of America's 2010 Dodd-Frank Act is s1502, requiring businesses to declare the country of origin of all conflict minerals used in their products and processes. Prior to this transparency rule rebel militia in DRC were receiving $180m/year from illicit sales from unlicensed mines. Within four years the number of mines under illegitimate control was reduced by two thirds.[41] Businesses may complain about the $140m/year cost of Dodd-Frank compliance but the industry is worth over $3bn/year; the Trump administration's desire to scrap s1502 has been described as 'a gift to companies wanting to do business with the criminal and the corrupt'.[42] The slow pace of progress led to loss of confidence, falling incomes and demand moving elsewhere; undoubtedly some miners lost money, others jobs, some even joined the rebels in protest. But the militias, sometimes aided by corrupt army officers, have either gone underground or moved on to other trading niches.[43] By 2017 most of Congo's minerals, apart from gold, were close to being 'conflict-free'.

Mining is not just the victim of strife: it can create it. There were local conflicts, rioting, even deaths in over 200 locations related to mining in 2016 in South and Central America alone.[44]

Although the mining industry is often on the front line it's taken a stand in addressing conflict, complemented by operations such as the electronics industry's Conflict-Free Sourcing Initiative. Larger mining operators, with economies of scale, access to investment and more to lose if it all goes wrong, can usually guarantee better working conditions than smaller ones. Across Africa the former practice of housing men working at remote sites in makeshift camps has been replaced by investment in community development and the encouragement of family life. This reduces stress, violence, substance abuse and industrial unrest and boosts productivity accordingly. Anglo American alone has built 20,000 homes in South Africa and invested nearly $400m in improving communities.[45]

Peace is not just an absence of war and the risks that it poses to business. A community at peace generates lower insurance premiums, longer employee life expectancy, and a lower risk of crime to company and worker. People with a stake in their local economy are less likely to disrupt it.

In Sri Lanka co-operation between businesses was the starting point for post-conflict reconstruction. In Colombia private-sector employment programmes are helping reintegrate former guerrillas into society. After the recent Russian adventure in Ukraine an early initiative to get the two countries talking to each other happened under the business auspices of Richard Branson.

The global cost of violence in 2015 was $13.6tn, more than one dollar in every eight of the world economy; unproductive spending.[46] By 2030 half of the world's poor could be living in fragile, conflict-affected states with their associated high risk of chaos. Business needs consumers and workers who are safe, free, aspirational and secure, both financially and physically. Harriet Lamb, CEO of International Alert, is clear that peace should be a joint enterprise: 'History shows that the task of building peace can never be left to governments. With conflict on the rise globally, there can be no more urgent time to recognise that peace is everybody's business.'[47]

The Company Citizen agrees.

Migration and refugees

Migration has always happened: leaving one's home to seek a better life elsewhere is a difficult decision for individuals and families but understandable when the prompt is conflict, human rights violation, environmental degradation or the age-old concept of voluntary or economic migration. Most of the world's human migration is within countries, as economic forces push despairing rural dwellers towards shanty towns in the mega cities of Africa, China and elsewhere. The second largest group – including most Syrian refugees today – migrate from their country to its neighbour to seek relief, whilst only a tiny minority choose, or feel obliged to seek, or are inveigled into seeking, betterment on another continent. One new migrant was created every 2.5 seconds in 2015, that's 65 million that year, equivalent to the population of Britain and a 40 per cent increase in this century.[48] A third were classed as refugees. Only 1.3 million headed for Europe (2 per cent), compared with 13 million moving between Asia and Africa.[49] By 2050 environmental damage caused by climate change in vulnerable countries could add 200 million international migrants, doubling the current toll.

War, conflict and terror split families and create psychological scars which make survival anywhere an ordeal. Migrants believe that life might be better elsewhere, not that it will be; they don't assume that there are opportunities to be had and they don't believe in 'pots of gold'. Nor do they take welcome for granted, as I learned from talking to Afghan and Syrian refugees in Greece: a future of uncertainty is preferable to a present of fear and peril.[50] Where employment opportunities are scarce tensions arise – we know how readily economic stress can generate racist attitudes and a 'blame the immigrant' culture. Even to the economic migrant, relative poverty in London is preferable to abject poverty in Mogadishu; inequality generates magnetism.

Supported by the Foreign Office, I visited Poland three times in 2003–4 to campaign for that country to vote 'yes' to joining the European Union. Their assent led to significant economic migration from Poland to Britain, joining older generations who'd largely arrived as refugees before, during and immediately after World War Two. They arrived in an economically strong Britain and in the following years made a net contribution – don't let the sceptics tell you otherwise. But they also added to their home economy, sending money home to a relatively poor country at the end of each month. This practice of 'remittances' is a highly significant element of migration: in 2012 individual economic migrants, the global diaspora, sent home over $400m to their families in developing countries, more than the sum of worldwide aid from governments.[51] In 2016 global uncertainty and weak oil prices caused the grand total of remittances to fall, by over 1 per cent, for the second year running.[52]

Economic migration only works where there are jobs. In the Gulf over 40 per cent of employment is migrant labour – in Qatar it's 90 per cent. Migrants are prone to exploitation and abuse; where this happens at scale it becomes a threat to the working and living standards of the endemic population, especially in low skilled occupations. Multinational companies employing migrant labour often do so through third-party employment agencies, allowing them to pretend that they have no responsibility for practices at the base of their supply chains. In the 21st century, 24/7 scrutiny and the growing belief that top-order companies should take responsibility for their entire value chain are moving both opinion and practice in favour of transparency (see Chapter 6).

Both Britain and France have tried permitting economic migrants to work for specified periods when the needs of particular countries (in the case of Britain, the Balkans) coincided with the economic strength to support them. Whilst immigration needs to be and can be planned and catered for, countries suffering from emigration have less control over their fates. Britain's policy of not hiring nurses from sub-Saharan Africa, after countries complained that such recruitment was causing a domestic shortage, looked effective until nurses realised that they could still sell their skills in Britain if they came via a third country. Taiwan tries to attract former emigrants home to boost their economy: in 2003 there was one for every three leaving to seek their fortunes elsewhere.

In pre-Trump United States, a country built on immigration like no other, any migrant with a million dollars to invest could have a preferential visa whilst

Panama takes a green view, offering permanent residence to incomers who buy five hectares of land in a government reforestation programme.

In the USA labour unions work with migrant communities to prevent employers exploiting them, as poor practices for one group lead to exploitation for all; Hewlett Packard requires companies in its supply chain to provide translation and other services to help prevent threats of deportation. Other companies and campaigns clamp down on illegal trafficking and even the financial bond industry is urging investors to take migrants and migration into account in their pursuit of inclusive products.

In 2016 I attended AstraZeneca's AGM on behalf of the shareholder activist organisation, ShareAction, asking their Chair, Leif Johansson, about his company's engagement with refugees. 'Companies work and live in the societies they serve', he said. So could AstraZeneca provide medicines and kit to help organisations serve destitute refugees? Would they recruit appropriately skilled and properly settled refugees? Specifically, would the board engage positively with a UNHCR initiative to coordinate corporate responses to the challenge that those fleeing Syria presented? 'Yes.' The Chairman told us that his country, Sweden, had accepted more refugees per head than any other in Europe and that AstraZeneca was already finding work for skilled refugees, including pharmacists (of which there are many) in Sweden, Canada and France.

This is the approach advocated by Richard Branson's B Team. When they argue that refugees shouldn't be allowed to be a problem, far from turning their backs they're saying that engaging with refugees presents opportunities for business, as described in a joint publication by the UN High Commission on Refugees and the Global Compact.[53] Amongst those opportunities are creating low-cost versions of products for those in abject poverty, developing technology to help them rebuild their lives, employing refugees where legally permitted, encouraging refugee-friendly supply chains and developing employee-volunteering strategies that work with refugees alongside local civil-society organisations.

Business should speak up for refugees, says Branson, lobbying government to cut the red tape that hampers integration, fighting discrimination against them, being generous and helping raise awareness about refugee issues by telling stories in the workplace and elsewhere.[54] One business that's done its bit is IKEA, winner of the Design Centre's 'Design of the Year' in 2016 for its flat-pack, solar-powered refugee shelter. It comes in two boxes, can be built by four people in four hours and provides a robust alternative to tents, say the judges. It's big enough to stand up in, unlike alternatives, has light enough for a child to do their homework and spacious enough to run a small enterprise.[55] Sixteen thousand 'Better Shelters' have been deployed in two years – in post-earthquake Nepal, Djibouti (for Yemeni refugees), Iraq and Greece, which is today not so much a crossroads for refugees as a *cul de sac*.

IKEA has taken working with refugees to a new level, planning to create 200,000 jobs for them in its global supply chain. In 2017 they launched this initiative with a social enterprise production centre in Amman, where 200 Syrian refugees and 200 native Jordanians will make yarn and handcrafted woven goods.[56]

The British Red Cross reported in 2015 that the biggest corporate donors to its Syrian Refugee Appeal were Tesco, HSBC, Barclays, GSK, AstraZeneca and Thomas Cook.[57]

Other global issues

Despite years of education about ingredients in food, toiletries and cleaning materials, brand labels are gobbledygook to most of us. 'Palm oil' looks innocuous, but does it come from a sustainable source? Are orangutans or even the wellbeing of people being sacrificed to create space for growing it? The oil itself is benign, used widely in food and toiletries – but industrial growing practices, especially in south-east Asia, leave much to be desired. Palm oil production destroys habitats, rainforests, biodiversity and carbon sinks, threatening animal species with extinction. In Indonesia land clearance generates significant air pollution and in 2016 Amnesty International accused the world's biggest vendor of certified environmentally sustainable palm oil, Singapore-based Wilmar, of exploiting slave and child labour in their supply chain.[58]

Wilmar welcomed the Amnesty report and ordered a full audit of the sources named. They, their major customers and fellow members of the Roundtable on Sustainable Palm Oil – including Nestlé, P&G, Kellogg, Unilever – confirmed that they would never knowingly use oil from unethical sources and called for business and governments to work ever harder together on this issue.[59] (Previously Wilmar had suffered divestment by the Norwegian Sovereign Wealth Fund for its deforestation practices, subsequently addressed.)

The voluntary system of certification of palm oil sustainability was established over a decade ago. IOI, a Malaysian company supplying it to over 300 manufacturers, a founder member of the Roundtable, was suspended from membership in April 2016 on the grounds of habitat destruction, irresponsible burning and breaches of labour conventions. Unilever, one of the world's biggest consumers, immediately cancelled its IOI contracts followed by Kellogg, Mars, Colgate-Palmolive, Johnson & Johnson, P&G and Nestlé.[60] Within six months IOI had reformed and repaired sufficiently to rejoin the Roundtable – though not without taking a financial hit, making a second quarter loss of $15m compared with nearly $30m profit in the equivalent period a year earlier.[61] It's been up to Company Citizens to take the lead where governments prove equivocal or disunited, and some less responsible businesses (such as biodiesel) are continuing to increase demand for palm oil at a level that sustainable production methods cannot meet. More needs to be done: whilst companies genuinely want sustainable and ethical supplies there's clearly insufficient certified palm oil to go round – producers are not responding to this demand fast enough. Forty per cent of palm oil production is ultimately by smallholders, who don't have access to investment with the scale or urgency needed. The Roundtable itself struggles to command the level of confidence that consumers, purchasers and others expect – it needs reform. Today, only a sixth of world palm oil production is certified sustainable; growing that figure, not berating those that try to respect certification rules, is where campaigns need to focus.

Where governments have acted reasonably quickly, alongside Company Citizens, is in banning the use of plastic microbeads in toiletries. These are scouring agents used in shower gel and shampoo, exfoliation cream and toothpaste, before being washed down the plughole. As small as 6 microns across, the beads give 'cosmetic products unique flow properties and a soft touch feel', according to a Norwegian manufacturer. Hard and inert, polyethylene seemed, at first, to be an obvious choice but alarm bells rang when these invisibly small non-biodegradable particles were found concentrated in sea creatures, both in ocean depths and on restaurant plates. Almost all Norway lobsters (scampi to you and me) contain them.[62] In 2015 America announced a rapidly implemented ban on microbead use in toiletries and the EU wasn't far behind, halving this 1,700-tonne market in just one year. The global demand for microbeads in personal care products should end during 2018 although major manufacturers reached zero in 2016 (Unilever, Colgate-Palmolive, Tesco) and 2017 (Johnson & Johnson, L'Oreal, P&G, Boots and Superdrug). Biodegradable alternatives are being developed using products previously regarded as waste – walnut husks, apricot kernels, silica, pumice, even sugar.[63]

Unfortunately, personal care accounts for only four per cent of microbead use. A ban on their use in household cleaning products, as Tesco and Greenpeace have demanded, would create a far greater benefit to the oceans.[64] Scampi eaters don't really care whether the plastic inside it came from someone else's toothpaste or from scouring the floor.[65] The same problem arises with the microscopic fibres of man-made material that are washed from our clothes every day, for which no one appears to have a solution. Eight million tonnes of plastic accounts for 80 per cent of ocean litter; only 1 tonne in 7 is recycled, a $100bn opportunity going begging.[66] Unilever is developing open-source technology to recycle 'single use' plastic sachets.[67] With demand for plastic set to double, the Ellen MacArthur Foundation has launched a $2m prize to promote collaboration in raising plastic recycling five-fold.[68] The way the oceans are treated as a dump for all manner of waste is completely unsustainable, leading to loss of biodiversity and productivity; much of this damage is caused by the half of all manufactured nitrogenous fertiliser, intended to enrich agricultural land, that's leached instead into our watercourses and thence the seas.

Powdered mica, 'immediately dangerous to life and health' when in the air, is found in cosmetics and much of its world production is deemed unethical or unsafe. In 2014 Lush stopped using mica as it couldn't guarantee that its supply chain was free of child labour.[69]

The idea of sustainable certified timber production has been around for many years but neither demand for ethical timber nor the policing of the industry have yet tipped the global balance in the direction the planet needs to go. Legal timber production in the Amazon basin, one of the world's most sensitive environments and our biggest 'green lung', has fallen by almost half in a decade due to concerns about its environmental credentials. Over 95 per cent of production there is illegal, exploiting lower costs, zero taxes, weak enforcement. Reliable data management in South America would make it easier to identify legitimate sustainable timber.[70]

Another environmental concern is chemical pollution. Although highly regulated in the west, production has moved to developing countries where costs are lower and regulatory 'impediments' fewer. In 2000 three quarters of chemical manufacturing was in OECD countries but this fell to 63 per cent, of a $4tn market, in 2009. Common air pollutants include ammonia, hydrogen sulphide and formaldehyde, with nitric acid, manganese, methanol and formaldehyde polluting water. In Africa 50,000 tonnes of dangerous obsolete pesticides are stockpiled on a continent where chemical damage to humans is measured in billions of dollars. Much disposal of harmful chemical waste worldwide isn't even recorded, leading to suspicions that business isn't always as responsible as they'd like us to think; global targets to reduce illegal pollution by 2020 are way off course.[71] A specific problem in India and China is pharmaceutical waste in watercourses, including antibiotics, hastening the development of resistant bacteria and posing a huge risk to us all. Campaigners for responsible antibiotic use claim that the unwillingness of the pharmaceutical industry to act collectively gives bacteria the upper hand.[72]

Business collectively can respond to environmental and social issues quickly and effectively when guided by a Company Citizen outlook. Nevertheless, many problems start with irresponsible business practices and ignorance, wilful or otherwise, of long-term impacts. Today the emphasis is on not creating problems in the first place, though it's far from universally accepted and the law of unforeseen consequences still applies.

One international issue with great consequences for business continues to dominate British life.

Brexit

In May 1975 the British public took a momentous decision: to remain in the European Union, the international club which they had joined three years earlier, the world's largest trade alliance. In June 2016 they voted to reverse this decision and to go . . . where? Legally, the plebiscite was 'advisory' but the 52 per cent who supported British exit – 'Brexit' – weren't going to let go. Although all of UK's major parliamentary parties had supported 'Remain' the United Kingdom Independence Party (UKIP) joined forces with hardline Conservative Eurosceptics to deliver a profound impact on politics, and on traditional Labour heartlands in particular. Brexit is the one issue which no Government can slip into the 'too difficult' box – despite it patently qualifying.

The 2017 election, billed as focusing on the 'how' of Brexit, barely addressed it; it will dominate the agenda of the hung Parliament that resulted for the foreseeable future.

In the years before Britain establishes a new world role public scrutiny will fall on business as never before. Companies' 'licence to operate' will need to be more obviously earned and any thought that business was somehow above the tawdry world of politics must be reassessed. Brexit will change everything.

Big business was clear about Europe: international trade requires maximum market access with minimum trade barriers so support for continued membership of the EU single market was a no-brainer. Smaller companies, less dependent on foreign trade though similarly dependent on foreigners' skills, better reflected public equivocation.

Business and its allies failed to convince enough people that their profits and voters' jobs shared a common cause in 'Remain'; business leaders had no more credibility than politicians or erudite journalists. Major employers wrote to employees begging them to back 'Remain' in areas which subsequently returned large Brexit majorities. Whereas the City, much of the broadsheet media and big business were seen as pro-Europe the leafy home counties – home to the captains of those industries – voted 'out'. Did they not believe their own rhetoric? Or were they exercising, as the Labour Party Leader was alleged to have done, their right to say one thing in public and another in the privacy of the polling booth?

Two groups were depicted as pariahs during the referendum: immigrants and, less predictably, 'experts'. Anyone who knew what they were talking about was, bizarrely, not to be trusted. Leaders of multinational corporations suffered three-fold: they were 'experts', who associated with Johnny Foreigner and their interests were those of 'the establishment'. They were criticised for daring to contribute, yet it was clearly right that Company Citizens should express their opinions. Indeed, where the collective national interest is at stake, and by any reckoning the health of the economy and the creation of jobs are national interest issues, companies have a duty to speak out.

Business was blamed for recruiting foreign labour at the expense of natives and immediately after the referendum hate crimes rose significantly, with Eastern Europeans and Muslims bearing the brunt of a brief racist tide. Some Eastern Europeans whose parents had arrived in Britain as refugees before the EU even existed suffered verbal abuse for the first time. In America the election of Donald Trump, equally shocking to the establishment, produced a similarly unnerving response. Company Citizens are vigilant to prevent such attitudes poisoning their workplace.

A sense of powerlessness and alienation contributed to the Brexit vote: a third of the population felt that the outcome left Britain more divided whilst only 12 per cent thought that communities had 'rallied round'; business doesn't thrive in divided societies. Capitalism itself, however, didn't appear to be at fault: both those who felt it was a force for good and those who disagreed broke

50:50 on remain/leave. Brexiteers blamed multiculturalism, globalisation, immigration, even feminism and the green movement for their alienation.[73] Inflated top salaries in business, growing levels of working poverty and the apparently 'optional' approach to taxation of some multinationals all reinforced the view that the UK and EU 'establishment' was uninterested in 'ordinary people'. (However, two thirds of the Leave campaign's £24m budget was funded by just five 'establishment' businessmen.)[74]

Most intellectual leaders were stunned by the unexpected and irrational nature of the referendum outcome – the strongest of all correlations to voting 'leave' was with low educational attainment (as it was with supporting Trump). Prime Minister Cameron jumped ship rather than take responsibility for calling the referendum or its outcome: business cannot do the same. Business has to find a new identity, less distant, a more human approach to the bottom line, one that promotes inclusivity not just in the workforce but alongside others in local communities. In doing so they must work in partnership with the state but not expect the government to put its hand deeply into its pocket; austerity will be compounded by the huge and unplanned cost to the Exchequer of Brexit itself.

Early indications are that threatened corporate departures to the mainland may be fewer than was feared. However, the Brexit rubber has barely hit the road and the financial sector is clearly vulnerable. Any 'deals' that are done have to be fair and must comply with EU state aid rules, at least until the decree is absolute. If Theresa May's insistence that 'no deal is better than a bad deal' comes to pass then UK industry faces annual EU tariffs of £6bn in order to maintain our export profile, adding 10 per cent to the price of British cars and doubling the price of our sugar beet.[75]

This story isn't over: social and economic conditions could get worse before they get better. Certainty and stability are gone, compounded by the outcome of the sudden 2017 election; even Brexit itself is unlikely to gain clarity until towards the end of the Article 50 period, perhaps three years after the referendum. As this book is published we may still not know whether there will be any semblance of membership of the single market or the customs union, or at what price, or whether there will be free movement of some labour or of none. The absurdity of expelling from Britain a million European nationals, productive taxpayers in the main, and replacing them with a million repatriated suntanned UK pensioners, net users of public services, cannot be discounted.

Some regard the Single Market as Margaret Thatcher's greatest legacy. It represented a common approach, a market big enough to make a difference and small enough to be flexible; agreement on rules and conventions, the reduction of barriers to trade to an absolute but agreed minimum, perhaps a model for the world. Its standards are those of common decency – environmental impacts, food standards, working conditions: the very word 'standards' describes thresholds below which, in or out, we should not demean ourselves to fall. Its partial destruction is a real concern. Britain's been a minority player in that market for two generations, but punching above our weight. Both Britain and the remaining market will be the worse for our departure. We have influenced the direction of that market (despite Brexiteers' protestations) and kept at arm's length both the democratic and 'democratic at one stage removed' institutions of the European Union on matters not strictly concerning the Market. We've even helped to keep bureaucracy at bay; the headcount at the entire European Commission is similar to that of the recently diminished British Home Office. And Brexit itself, this unnecessary and masochistic programme, will push social and other priorities off the parliamentary agenda.

Without the protection of that regulated market – the prime purpose of which is to facilitate trade based on consensus and agreement – we face a world not of double standards, in both direct and implied meanings of the phrase, but of multiple standards. Our manufacturers and service providers will have to conform to buyer's demands in many markets, at many levels. The only logical ways for companies to avoid this avalanche of bureaucracy is either to remain in the Single Market by taking themselves physically out of Britain and over to (or back into) mainland Europe, or by agreeing that the new world market shall be one with few common rules. Such a 'Devil take the hindmost' approach is contrary to the direction generally labelled 'responsibility'.

The phrase 'better together' has never rung more true as we turn our backs on the biggest single market in the world and 40 years of associated social and environmental progress. Business must be part of 'together' without being arrogant or lofty; the quality of our future somehow outside political Europe depends – to some extent – on the Company Citizen stepping up to the mark.

This is a good time to say that Company Citizens must help make post-Brexit Britain a better place.

Notes

1 www.purposeofcorporation.org/en#how-this-affects-companies.
2 www.mckinsey.com/global-themes/urbanization/unlocking-the-potential-of-emerging-market-cities.
3 http://10458-presscdn-0-33.pagely.netdna-cdn.com/wp-content/uploads/2017/03/gss-evaluating-progress-towards-the-sustainable-development-goals.pdf.
4 www.weforum.org/agenda/2017/01/ricardo-hausmann-why-governments-act-on-their-lies.
5 www.wfp.org/hunger/stats.
6 http://motherboard.vice.com/read/we-need-three-planets-to-keep-the-human-race-alive-nasa-scientist-says.
7 http://innovation-forum.co.uk/analysis.php?s=whats-the-acceptable-use-of-tech-in-agriculture.
8 www.dw.com/en/monsanto-shareholders-approve-merger-with-bayer/a-36754523.
9 http://news.mit.edu/2016/mobile-money-kenyans-out-poverty-1208.
10 http://documents.worldbank.org/curated/en/340591491579331322/pdf/114125-NWP-P156957-PUBLIC-add-series-9th-TEU-April-7-2017-reduced.pdf.

11 www.fairtrade.org.uk.
12 www.independent.co.uk/news/business/news/sainsburys-fairly-traded-tea-own-brand-fairtrade-foundation-farmers-producers-a7753561.html.
13 www.independent.co.uk/news/world/asia/china-scraps-construction-85-coal-power-plants-renewable-energy-national-energy-administration-paris-a7530571.html.
14 www.theguardian.com/world/2006/jul/24/brazil.foodanddrink.
15 www.bsr.org/reports/BSR_GlobeScan_State_of_Sustainable_Business_Survey_2016.pdf. See also Note 46.
16 www.edie.net/news/6/CDP-Big-businesses-are-driving-huge-cuts-in-supply-chain-emissions/34374.
17 www.linkedin.com/pulse/10-ways-support-climate-champions-sarah-finnie-robinson. See also www.americaspledgeonclimate.com.
18 www.telegraph.co.uk/business/2016/11/04/oil-chiefs-under-fire-over-pathetic-new-climate-investment-fund/.
19 www.edie.net/news/10/London-s-largest-solar-retrofit-generates-large-carbon-savings/?.
20 www.theguardian.com/environment/2016/feb/29/worlds-biggest-floating-solar-farm-power-up-outside-london. China now has a bigger, sea-based array.
21 http://whatsyourimpact.org/greenhouse-gases/carbon-dioxide-emissions.
22 www.theguardian.com/environment/2016/oct/19/shipping-progressives-call-for-industry-carbon-emission-cuts?CMP=Share_iOSApp_Other.
23 'Sea Change Needed', by Casey Aspin, *ESG Magazine*, Winter 2016.
24 www.gov.uk/government/uploads/system/uploads/attachment_data/file/546346/domestic-road-freight-statistics-2015.pdf.
25 www.forbes.com/sites/paulmartyn/2016/12/14/supply-chain-sustainability-the-new-green-lean-money-machine/#5eec98712f7e and http://there100.org/news/14257837.
26 http://there100.org/companies and http://there100.org/news/14257837.
27 www.carbonbrief.org/analysis-uk-cuts-carbon-record-coal-drop.
28 http://news.nationalgeographic.com/2016/07/world-aquifers-water-wars/.
29 www.ft.com/content/8e42bdc8-0838-11e4-9afc-00144feab7de.
30 www.coal-seam-gas.com/environment/water.htm#.WQiSplLMyRs.
31 www.cdp.net/en/research/global-reports/global-water-report-2016.
32 http://news.nationalgeographic.com/news/2014/09/140917-california-groundwater-law-drought-central-valley-environment-science/.
33 http://fortune.com/2015/11/04/nestle-shared-value-water-paul-grimwood/.
34 www.theguardian.com/vital-signs/2015/apr/30/california-drought-bottled-water-nestle-arrowhead-starbucks.
35 www.ft.com/content/7f435f04-8c05-11e2-b001-00144feabdc0.
36 www.independent.co.uk/news/uk/home-news/britain-is-now-the-second-biggest-arms-dealer-in-the-world-a7225351.html.
37 www.al-monitor.com/pulse/business/2013/02/economic-impact-syrian-crisis.html.
38 www.gov.uk/guidance/conflict-minerals.
39 http://ngm.nationalgeographic.com/2013/10/conflict-minerals/gettleman-text.
40 www.conflictfreesourcing.org.
41 www.enoughproject.org/special-topics/progress-and-challenges-conflict-minerals-facts-dodd-frank-1502.
42 www.theguardian.com/us-news/2017/feb/08/trump-administration-order-conflict-mineral-regulations.

43 www.theguardian.com/world/2014/dec/02/conflict-minerals-law-congo-poverty.
44 www.economist.com/news/americas/21690100-big-miners-have-better-record-their-critics-claim-it-up-governments-balance.
45 www.angloamerican.com/~/media/Files/A/Anglo-American-Plc/media/releases/2007pr/2007-08-09/2007-08-09.pdf.
46 http://community.businessfightspoverty.org/profiles/blogs/philomena-blees-can-and-should-enlightened-global-businesses-solv.
47 http://community.businessfightspoverty.org/profiles/blogs/harriet-lamb-building-peace-is-everybody-s-business.
48 'Migration Watch', Heather Hachigan, *ESG Magazine* 6, Winter 2016, and other sources.
49 www.nature.com/news/what-the-numbers-say-about-refugees-1.21548.
50 http://sector4focus.co.uk/blog/greece-is-the-word-for-refugees/.
51 https://unchronicle.un.org/article/migration-sustainable-development-and-role-business.
52 www.worldbank.org/en/news/press-release/2017/04/21/remittances-to-developing-countries-decline-for-second-consecutive-year?.
53 https://business.un.org/documents/business_action_pledge_refugee_crisis_illustrative_examples.pdf.
54 http://bteam.org/announcements/new-report-refugees-are-an-opportunity-for-humanity/.
55 www.theguardian.com/artanddesign/2017/jan/27/why-ikea-flatpack-refugee-shelter-won-design-of-the-year.
56 www.dezeen.com/2017/04/18/ikea-massive-social-sustainability-drive-production-centres-refugee-camps-jordan/?.
57 www.redcross.org.uk/About-us/Media-centre/Press-releases/2015/October/Red-Cross-overwhelmed-by-UK-publics-generosity-towards-refugees.
58 www.amnesty.org/en/documents/asa21/5243/2016/en/.
59 www.channelnewsasia.com/news/asiapacific/concerted-effort-required-on-labour-rights-wilmar-on-amnesty/3366276.html.
60 www.theguardian.com/sustainable-business/2016/apr/09/ioi-malaysian-palm-oil-company-unilever-mars-kellogg-rspo-deforestation.
61 https://innovation-forum.co.uk//analysis.php?s=investors-push-palm-oil-to-act-on-deforestation.
62 www.dailymail.co.uk/news/article-3768050/Superdrug-Boots-order-firms-ban-toxic-beads-Retailers-offer-ultimatum-cosmetic-companies-remove-plastic-poison-products-removed-shelves.html.
63 http://blog.euromonitor.com/2016/10/plastic-not-fantastic-industry-responds-to-us-microbeads-ban.html.
64 www.independent.co.uk/life-style/health-and-families/health-news/tesco-bans-microbeads-from-all-products-a7437316.html.
65 www.theguardian.com/environment/2016/dec/20/ministers-explore-extending-microbead-ban-household-products.
66 www.ellenmacarthurfoundation.org/publications/the-new-plastics-economy-rethinking-the-future-of-plastics.
67 www.independent.co.uk/news/business/news/unilever-plastic-sachets-recycle-stop-enter-ocean-creasolv-process-billions-cosmetics-food-products-a7728396.html.
68 www.edie.net/news/5/Ellen-MacArthur--Businesses-must-collaborate-to-make-circular-economy-mainstream/?.
69 www.theguardian.com/sustainable-business/lush-removes-mica-child-labour.

70 http://community.businessfightspoverty.org/profiles/blogs/pedro-moura-costa-big-data-bold-moves-combatting-illegal-logging-.
71 www.reuters.com/article/chemicals-environment-idUSL6E8K4FPL20120905.
72 www.theguardian.com/sustainable-business/2016/oct/25/antibiotic-waste-pollution-india-china-rivers-big-pharma-superbugs-resistance?CMP=ema-1706&CMP=.
73 www.cafonline.org/about-us/publications/2016-publications/a-stronger-britain-how-can-charities-build-post-brexit-britain.
74 *The Sunday Times*, 23 April 2017.
75 www.theguardian.com/uk-news/2017/feb/20/no-deal-brexit-would-mean-6bn-in-extra-costs-for-uk-exporters?CMP=share_btn_tw.

3 Britain is ready

What does the way we treat our poorest and most excluded people say about Britain today?

We're the fifth richest country in the world; we're not poor. We have huge assets: our English language, our convenient time zone, a finance sector of global significance and a spirit which once ruled all the pink bits on the globe. We were on the winning side in two world wars and yet our virtues include humility, diffidence, modesty, sticking to the rules and 'getting by'.

Britain's also the world's fourth most unequal country. In *The Spirit Level* (Wilkinson and Pickett, 2010) the measure of inequality in the 23 most developed nations for which data is available is 'how many times richer is the top fifth of earners compared with the bottom fifth?' In Japan, Scandinavia and the Germanic countries the answer is between four and five. For much of the rest of Europe, Australasia and Canada, it's five to seven. Then comes UK at just over seven, with Portugal and USA higher and tiny Singapore topping the league at almost ten.

That's life. Why does this matter? There's no easy answer in absolute terms, but that it does matter is beyond doubt, given how strongly social indices correlate with economic inequality. Wilkinson and Pickett, comparing data from the UN Development Programme, found that countries with high levels of economic inequality also had relatively high levels of mental illness, infant mortality, obesity, teenage pregnancy, imprisonment and homicide; and lower than expected levels of educational attainment, life expectancy, trust, social mobility – and happiness. They then looked at these same criteria against the average income of each country, finding this correlation either weak or absent in every single case. The relationship was with inequality, not with national wealth.

An oft-quoted figure is that in Fortune 500 companies the top earning director earns 400 times their average worker's pay; he surpasses his firm's average annual salary during the afternoon of New Year's Day. Ridiculous, but true.[1] In Britain the equivalent figure is 150×. In 2017 the average FTSE CEO received £4.3m (including bonuses) compared with his average employee's £28,000; only Switzerland and America pay their top bosses more.

In 2016 Portland, Oregon, became the first administration to levy an inequality tax: 500 companies in the city in which the CEO earned more than 100 times the average for workers in their employment saw corporate taxation rise by 10 per cent. Dismissed as a 'stunt' by business leaders, the measure would raise $2.5m/year, ring-fenced for tackling homelessness. Raising the pay of the lowest-paid workers reduces the ratio and thus the levy.[2]

'Governments are not powerless' is the optimistic message from Sir Alan Budd, an economist who has influenced many of those with their hands on the economic levers over many years. Without committing to a figure, he told an event organised by Blueprint for Better Business: 'We can't just say that excessive salaries are "natural", the question of a cap should be explored.'[3]

An absolute cap on top pay would release funds for investment, worker pay, price reduction or even tax for the public good; it would force that capital to work rather than be stashed away in the bank, be gambled in the casino of the financial markets or generate property price inflation. What if we limited top salaries in British companies to a maximum of 40× the mean in that company (£1m top whack compared with a £25,000 average)? This would impact relatively few outside financial services. Rationally, 40× wouldn't knock back ambitious people (footballers excepted) and wouldn't appear to be extreme. A 20x ceiling would release much more money into play, a realistic end target, though it might take ten years to bring it down from 40× to 20×. In the 1980s Ben & Jerry's instigated an 8× rule but scrapping that was a condition that Unilever insisted upon in their otherwise friendly buy-out, 20 years later. Twelve times was rejected by a 2013 referendum in Switzerland not because the principle was wrong (I believe) but because they put up an Aunt Sally, a formula designed to be rejected, setting back the cause of tackling inequality.

Bonuses also need review: they should be transparent, accountable, linked to long-term performance and available outside senior management. However such money released by the cap is distributed, inequality would be reduced significantly and the community would be happier, healthy, more productive as a result, if the *Spirit Level* hypothesis applies. It's worth testing.

Whether we measure inequality in the way favoured by *The Spirit Level* (top:bottom quintiles), Portland (top:mean), OECD (top:bottom deciles), by the complex Gini Coefficient or even whether we measure before or after tax, the rank order of countries (companies, communities) remains roughly the same. Inequality is rising across all OECD states because, they conclude, tax and benefits are failing to restrain it, top pay is racing ahead of what productivity can justify and employment patterns are changing.[4]

If top salaries have become disengaged from productivity then the pay of most workers has been held back by the lack of it. Between 2003 and 2014 median salary for Britain's top 350 CEOs (at £1.9m) almost doubled while their companies' productivity rose by around 1 per cent. UK productivity hasn't recovered from the 2007–8 crash: between 2008 and 2014 it rose by 5 pence in every £1,000 per year, way behind most comparable economies, compared with £23.80/£1,000/year over the 16 previous years.

Over at Grant Thornton the incoming CEO or senior partner, Sacha Romanovitch, caused a stir in 2015 when she announced a substantial cut in her own pay, to 20 times the firm's average salary, and extended the company's profit-sharing scheme from its 185 partners to all of its 4,500 staff.[5] As a privately owned company with no shareholders, Grant Thornton isn't obliged to conform to external codes of governance. However, Romanovitch believes that linking pay more clearly to performance, consulting colleagues more widely, sharing profits and even opening up board meetings all generate staff confidence, create a sense of common cause and foster collaborative instincts. Surely she is correct; these are admirable qualities to have.

A perhaps unlikely champion of executive pay restraint is BlackRock, the world's largest independent fund manager. BlackRock wrote to Britain's top 300 companies to call for executive pay rises to reflect those of other grades proportionately and for bonuses to reflect reality, threatening to vote out non-executive directors who don't conform. Bearing the brunt of their criticism was Imperial Brands, the world's fourth largest cigarette manufacturer, who were apparently so struggling to retain their Chief Executive, Alison Cooper, on £5.5m that they suddenly had to award her an additional £1m.[6] Imperial scrapped its proposal. As the *Evening Standard*'s Simon English says: 'BlackRock is going to get some stick . . . since its own top brass are doubtless very well paid. But it has picked a good fight and the right time to have it.'[7]

Indeed, BlackRock's Larry Fink was paid $26m in 2016. Even though the investor had backed 92 per cent of pay settlements in companies where it held shares during 2015–16, their threat was real.[8] The Local Authority Pension Fund Forum, with 72 members and assets of £175bn, also weighed in, calling for shareholder votes on top pay to be binding.[9] The worm is turning.

It's sometimes argued that 'bad' wealth should be more heavily taxed than 'good'. 'Good' wealth arises from innovation, providing a valuable service, activity generally, whilst 'bad' wealth is lazy, passive, the product of rents, property price hikes, parasitic professions and that traditional cash cow, inheritance. If only things were so simple. There must be an absolute level of income above which no one needs to rise and where penal levels of taxation are legitimate. We came close to a cap, with income tax at 98 per cent on top earners, when Wilson and Healey were making the pips squeak 40 years ago. Taxation is rightly a tool of equalisation and justice, but not egality. Taxing 'bad' wealth differently raises many questions around consistency, applicability and a basic fundament of tax, fairness.

As *The Spirit Level* shows, it's not wealth, not even modest inequality, that corrodes our society, it's when inequality is perceived as extreme, unfair and immutable that the most damage is done. Tax must be part of the way we tackle that. And yet although there's a popular consensus in favour of better services there's another supporting lower taxes: the irresistible force meets the immovable object.

We've seen evidence of polarisation within Britain not simply along the traditional lines of the poor resenting the rich and the exploited resenting the exploiting, but the less educated resenting the more so, the 'others' resenting the 'elite', the lay people the 'experts' and those who've learned to be without hope resenting those with clear opportunities. Some of those doing the resenting take it out, irrationally, on those eternally convenient scapegoats, migrants, often doing the jobs the resenters don't actually want to do.

A natural and positive consequence of resentment is a desire to 'take back control' but details of from whom and to whom are best left to others. The electoral danger of this is that it's always easier to campaign against something than in favour. A result may arise that reflects the power of 'down with the establishment', such as Brexit or Trump, but when that fails to satisfy who do they vote for next?

The Social Progress Index (SPI) was developed by Professor Michael Porter. It rejects the idea that Gross Domestic Product (GDP) alone is a measure of a nation's worth, arguing that GDP is only an economic measure and a partial one at that, taking account of neither investment in social good nor the negative impacts of economic progress, such as on the environment. Taking 50 established categories of development, divided into 'Basic Human Needs', 'Foundations of Wellbeing' and 'Opportunity', the SPI ranks each country for each quality, allocating the most developed 100 points and the least 0, giving all the others a value in between according to their degree of development. In 2017 the list included 128 countries with an average score of 65.[10]

The SPI data for the 23 *Spirit Level* countries is fascinating. There's a strong correlation between social progress and inequality: all of the Scandinavian countries in the top five in *Spirit Level* terms are in the top eight on the SPI. Only diminutive Iceland (joint third) is in the SPI top 20 in 2017 but not listed in *The Spirit Level* (SPI has insufficient data on the world's most unequal country, Singapore).

Britain's weaknesses relative to that basket of richer countries, says SPI, are in criminality, premature death from non-communicable disease (such as smoking), obesity and religious and racial tolerance. Our two relative strengths, compared with the rest of the world, are reducing death from traffic accidents and the controversial issue of access to higher education.

On this data Britain is the 12th ranking SPI country (down from 9th in 2016) and USA the 19th: we should both be doing better. The SPI also enables us to show an interesting relationship between 'social progress' and GDP *per capita*, as illustrated in Figure 3.1.

Of course there's a link between social progress and economic development, why else would the world's poorest countries aspire to become better off? But that's the point: that very strong positive relationship between social and economic progress in the poorest societies gets weaker as they become more affluent, such that as the richest third of all nations become even richer still they make less and less further social progress. Chad and Sierra Leone need money for schools, immunisation and feeding programmes and every little helps. Because infant mortality is so low in UK, targeting a further reduction requires disproportionate investment and would make little

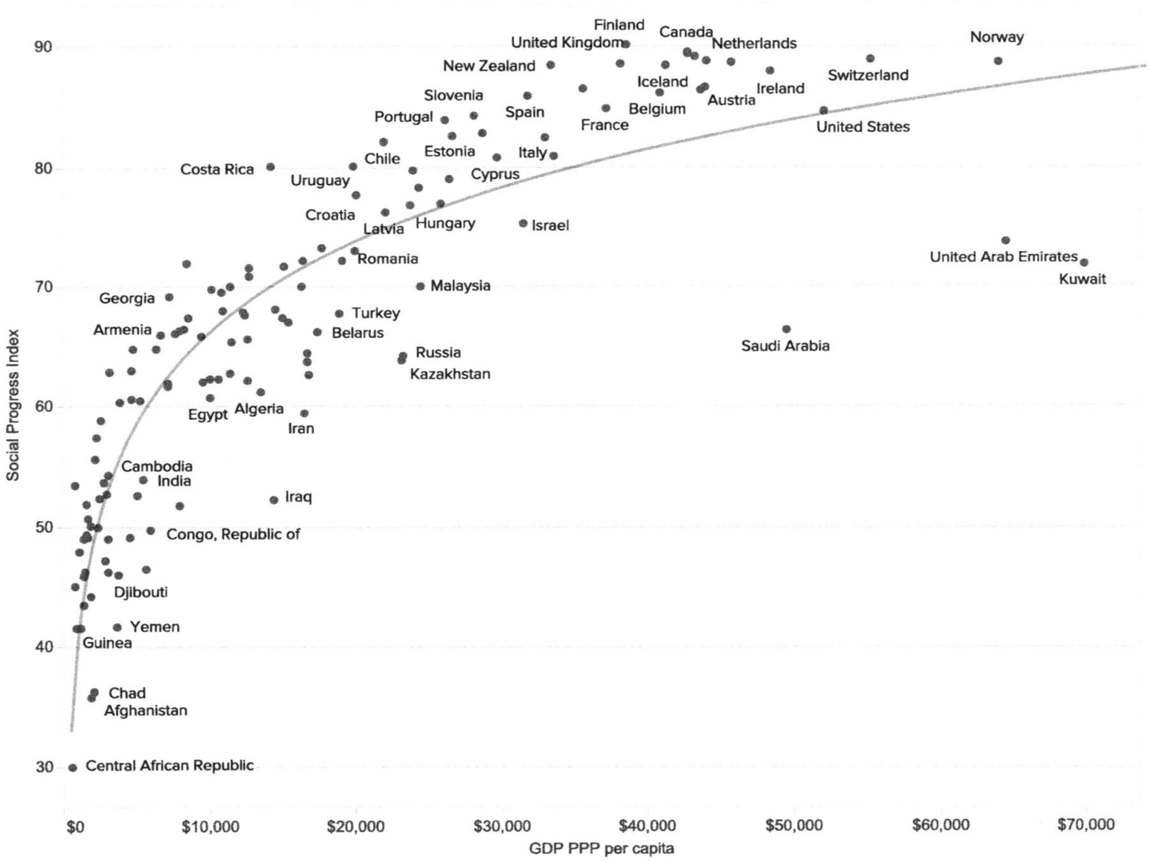

Figure 3.1 Social Progress Index vs GDP per capita (2016) (Source: SPI, with permission)

statistical difference. The GDP advantage that UK has over some countries indicates only that our rich people are relatively richer than theirs – it doesn't reflect proportionately better services, nor does GDP growth provide a uniform boost to our living standards.

I attended the London launch of SPI in 2013. Since then it's improved its data, become more sophisticated – and is revised annually. Paraguay, Costa Rica, Peru and Brazil were quick to take it up as a tool to give focus to development programmes. In Brazil they use it to compare sub-national regions, a feature now being exploited by the European Union and India. I spoke to a conference at York University in 2015 where I predicted that SPI could be extended to assess the social health of smaller, sub-city or rural communities. A few weeks later Bogota became the first city to publish just such a community analysis and Rio followed.

Poverty in Britain

Functioning markets need consumers to buy stuff. Poverty is the enemy of business because it deprives consumers of choice and companies of sales. Both poverty and inequality are getting worse in Britain with no evidence that this trend will peak any time soon.

Our problems are difficult to grasp if you're not on the receiving end. After the 2008 crash the incoming government of 2010 put 'austerity' at the heart of its economic and, consequently, its social programme.

Inequality doesn't get worse by accident and what's happening to British household incomes is unusual.

- Whereas living standards recovered following the 1979 and 1989 recessions (up 5 per cent in four years, on both occasions) the damage of the post-crash recession still hasn't been repaired; in fact, living standards fell by 1 per cent over seven years.[11]
- Between 2007 and 2015 UK's 'real' earnings fell by 7.7 per cent; of OECD countries only Mexico (7.8) and Greece (17.8), whose economic crisis was infamous, did worse.[12]
- The top 1 per cent of earners received about 4 per cent of the nation's income through the 1960s, 1970s and 1980s. Since then their share has doubled.[13]
- The number of households in poverty fell by half between 1996 and 2004, since when it's flatlined at about 20 per cent.[14]
- Today, half of all manual workers and unemployed people couldn't meet an emergency £500 household bill, perhaps for a replacement heating boiler, without borrowing.[15]
- Pensioners have seen the biggest fall in poverty (from half in 1996 to under a fifth in 2010 and 1 in 8 in 2015) whereas the rate for children, also 50 per cent in 1996, fell below 30 per cent in 2010 but rose again thereafter.[16]

Across the whole economy wage growth averaged +2.9 per cent over the 1970s and 1980s, +1.5 in the 1990s and +1.2 in the 2000s. In the first few years of the 2010s it was negative, at -0.1 per cent, for the first prolonged period ever, and this figure hid a bigger contraction for people on lower incomes.[17] The group of people for whom living standards fell most were low-income families with more than two children.[18] The decade 2000–10 was the first ever in which the share of profit that British companies spent on dividends rose whilst, at the same time, the proportion spent on wages fell.

Previously every twist of national economic fortune was shared, rich and poor experiencing both booms and busts. Since the crash things have been different; the 'bounce' has gone out of the economy. Britain now mimics the sort of income inequality traditionally associated with the USA, where wages at the top have grown faster than others and the top 1 per cent take home 60c in every dollar of all new growth. After inflation, average pay in Britain in 2015 was no higher than in 2003; 102 of 111 countries fare better than us in that respect.[19] The Institute for Fiscal Studies has projected that in the period to 2020 these trends will continue unless there are major changes in policy.[20]

At the same time unemployment hasn't shown the significant rise that followed previous downturns. Ministers never tire of reminding us that record numbers of people are employed today, there are jobs for people to do: yet the benefits of higher levels of employment have been countered by reduced incomes at the bottom of the earnings scale. 'Being in work', said Lloyd George after the General Strike, Beveridge in his plans for the welfare state and every PM since Attlee, 'is the best way of escaping poverty.' For the first time in a century that's no longer guaranteed in Britain.

Supporting households in poverty costs the UK taxpayer £78bn/year in services and a further £70bn in the payment of benefits, according to the Joseph Rowntree Foundation.[21] Governments resent ever-increasing spending on income-related benefits; it's a sign of failure, best hidden, an unproductive use of resource. Furthermore, governments ideologically committed to the market, to a 'hands-off' economy, a 'small state', need to spend less, not more, on everything. Hence an arbitrary cap on the total amount of poverty-related benefits a family with children can receive, set at £26,000 in 2010 (average pay), was summarily reduced in 2016 to £20,000 (£23,000 in more expensive London).[22] Those receiving housing benefit in areas of high rental cost are most affected (home rents in London rose by 8 per cent in 2014–15). Half of those hit by the cap live in South East England, 300,000 children were affected and some families lost over £100/week.

Nigel Wilson, CEO of the insurer/investor Legal & General, laments the fact that globally $10tn is invested in financial markets, serving no socially valuable purpose, whilst housing, regeneration and social care are all critical and economic regeneration is desperately needed. The affordable zero-carbon house can now be built, but isn't. UK housebuilding has failed to match need for more than a generation. British pension funds alone have £1.3tn of assets and sovereign wealth funds another trillion, yet an extra investment in housing of only £150bn would do the trick. Why isn't it happening, Nigel asked the 2017 annual investors' meeting of the Social Stock Exchange, why don't all big investors follow L&G's example of investing their paltry £900bn of assets into small businesses, regeneration, homes and clean energy?[23]

As a cost to the taxpayer welfare benefits are a concern to the Company Citizen. Over half of all annual spending by the Department of Work and Pensions goes on non-means tested pensions leaving about £74bn per year for the relief of poverty through family benefits, income support and tax credits, housing and unemployment benefits. Reducing this budget sustainably, which means reducing poverty rather than simply cutting subsidies to poorer households, is clearly in the interests of both government and taxpayers, both human and corporate.

Creeping into that list is 'tax credits'. Working Tax Credit increases the income of low-paid workers by redistributing tax income towards them whilst the eponymous Child Tax Credit is less focused on the poor. Both were introduced by Labour in 1999 in an anti-poverty drive aimed at families, whether in work (more than two thirds of recipients) or otherwise. As we've seen, such policies reduced child poverty significantly over the following years. Forty per cent of working families with children receive tax credits and there are concerns that they may discourage part-time workers from raising their weekly employment above 16 hours.

Working Tax Credit has become embedded both in the Exchequer and the national psyche; it's now accepted that the taxpayer should subsidise employers who pay staff at levels which cannot sustain families (plus some who are slightly better off). Parliament has resisted government attempts to restrain the tax credit budget because so many voters enjoy the help that it brings. Even when I voted to introduce tax credits I hoped their need would be temporary. I supported, too, the National Minimum Wage (NMW) and envisaged this rising faster than inflation over the years to come, to decrease reliance on tax credits and shift some responsibility for decent incomes from taxpayer to employer. Calculating NMW is an art, not a science; it's not based on objective assessment of what households need to survive (thus it misses that target) but rather its affordability is negotiated between companies, unions and government.

The 1999 NMW was criticised as a potential burden on business and some maintained that it would cost jobs, though employers can mitigate additional costs of NMW through inspiring greater productivity. Job losses didn't happen to any significant degree and a relatively large rise in NMW in 2016, raising the income of 1.25 million people, mostly women, passed with little comment – other than on the political shenanigans of the Government rebranding the measure as a 'National Living Wage' to spike the guns of the 'real' Living Wage campaign. This well-established movement wants to see a higher level of minimum wage, linked objectively to living costs. In recent years it's gained traction with employers, especially in London – where it started and where the calculated figure is higher than elsewhere. In 2017 there were 3,500 accredited Living Wage employers though many are small or, like Lloyds TSB, Barclays or KPMG, employ a relatively small proportion of people who benefit from it.[24] The volunteers include one third of the FTSE500. The British Library is a public institution that's signed up and so have several relatively small employers; among London's football clubs only Chelsea subscribes.[25]

The retail sector pays less than many other business sectors. In 2015 the Living Wage campaign reached a significant milestone when Lidl, with 15,000 employees, became the first supermarket chain to adopt it. Lidl's small size and culture, in which employees frequently move from one role to another, may make it easier to afford to pay the Living Wage by helping employees become more productive – as they tend to be multi-skilled already. In bigger supermarkets a shelf stacker is a shelf stacker, once the shelves are stacked they can't increase their productivity further so opportunities are restricted. This highlights an issue with low pay and social mobility generally, which the British Retail Consortium has identified. There are, they say, three career paths for people who start work on low pay: a few climb the ladder to the top, as recent leaders of Tesco, Boots and M&S have done, leaving low pay well behind; some move to a 'comfortable' level in the hierarchy, where family costs can be met, and stay there; and some become trapped at the bottom, often lacking both skills and opportunities to progress. Breaking that low pay trap – which is not just a wages issue – is the key to greater flexibility and productivity.

Home care agencies are also renowned for low pay. Of over 1,000 in London in 2014 only four were Living Wage accredited yet 74 per cent of the public believe that those charged with looking after their loved ones should receive the Living Wage. The sector has many issues which keep pay rates down, including zero hours contracts and questions over whether periods between domestic visits constitute working time. Another low-paid sector is hospitality: some big Living Wage-accredited corporates will only use hotels that pay the Living Wage. In the year after Adnams brewery introduced the Living Wage into its hotels staff turnover amongst low-pay grades fell from an incredible 200 per cent to just 30 (high churn is a major issue for hotels). The contract-cleaning company ISS says that levels of employee engagement and satisfaction are 8 per cent higher on Living Wage contracts than those in companies which don't insist on it being paid.

More than nine out of ten Living Wage employers report a positive impact upon introducing it, including lower absenteeism, higher productivity, greater job satisfaction throughout the organisation and reputational benefits.[26] Some report that investment in employees prompted further investment in their training, increasing productivity further, creating better relationships with trade unions and attracting a higher calibre of job applicants.

Accreditation as a Living Wage employer obliges companies to pay at least the Living Wage to all on-site workers, including subcontractors such as cleaners employed indirectly, within three years: Aviva, Barclays, KPMG, Nationwide, HSBC and Nestlé all comply, the latter a year ahead of schedule. One hundred thousand people have benefited from the Living Wage to date and the company with the greatest number of these is IKEA. The John Lewis Partnership is not so accredited, surprisingly, as even though its employees are all paid above Living Wage it declines to include contract cleaners.

Mike Kelly, formerly of KPMG, now chairing the Living Wage Foundation, observes that privately owned companies like IKEA and Adnams may find it easier to implement a Living Wage policy than those who must justify the expense to shareholders; and small businesses appear to be more relaxed about implementing it than larger ones because 'fairness' is a more persuasive emotion when a personal relationship exists between employee and employer. New SMEs, in particular, find it easy to design in the Living Wage at start-up, confirming my experience with the social enterprise Fair for You.

Between 2013 and 2017 over 1,000 companies failed to pay the legal minimum wage, resulting in arrears of £4.5m plus £2m in fines. Debenhams, the highest profile recalcitrant in 2017, blamed a technical error affecting 11,000 workers (John Lewis and Tesco have had similar problems), whilst others blamed misunderstanding of rules relating to travel time in domiciliary care. One even said 'I thought it was OK to pay foreigners less'. During 2016 a further 350 companies were 'named and shamed' and, presumably, came into line; at the end of the year 1,500 potential breaches were under investigation.[27]

The 'original' or voluntary Living Wage is designed to take people out of poverty, being slightly above 60 per cent of median earnings, a standard definition of poverty, and determined by the cost of a basket of goods needed for a 'decent standard of living'.[28] The Government's intention is for the rebranded National Living Wage to reach that decency level by 2020 – after when it will be benchmarked to rise with median pay. Today, some six million people in Britain earn the legal minimum or more, though less than the Living Wage.

When an employee is raised from the National Living Wage (the former NMW, £7.50/hour for those over 25 from April 2017) to the 'proper' Living Wage (£8.45 for those over 18 or £9.75 in London) certain savings are made, principally by the government through reduced demand on tax credits and housing benefits. Such savings are shared by payers of tax, including business. In this way businesses are, in theory, automatically partially compensated for paying their lowest-paid employees more.

And yet, a fifth of the population believe it's legitimate for high-earning individuals, corporations and others to dodge tax, putting the burden of spending on welfare and other services on others less able to carry that burden. It's a minority, but an uncomfortably large one.[29]

Self-employment

Recent years have seen a huge rise in self-employment in Britain. Whilst half such workers are in stable, traditional, entrepreneurial and skilled professions, described by the Resolution Foundation as relatively privileged, many are bogus and many have a precarious status.

Self-employment is often portrayed as an expression of pioneer spirit: it can be, and used to represent convenience for the artisan, opportunity for the entrepreneur, release for the hobbyist. But that rise, from 3 million in 2001 to almost 5 million today, is far from unalloyed good news about a vibrant economy. Today the average self-employee earns up to £60/week less, in real terms, than the comparable figure for 2001.[30] He's not entitled to sick, holiday, redundancy or overtime pay, employer's pension contributions or the National Living Wage; nor is an employer's National Insurance contribution paid on his behalf, saving a contractor perhaps £2,000/year per worker; nor is notice of termination obligatory. How tempting it must be for a company to engage an army of piece-rate workers reminiscent of the old construction industry 'lump', disorganised labour that's cheap, free of commitments, ultimately flexible . . . think Deliveroo, Boohoo, Sports Direct.

As the online taxi service Uber discovered, in a landmark 2016 court case, contracts cannot tie a self-employed person to a single employer and restrict his or her rights to trade – that's a scam. Self-employed status was used, at that company's insistence, to disguise a relationship that's really one of employee/employer but devoid of the commitment, care or paternalism that family concerns would have regarded as natural and fundamental not too long ago. A Company Citizen doesn't turn its back on commitment, responsibility or the idea that a company's relationship with its workforce is precious and based on mutual respect.

Unfortunately some businesses shy away from just that. In the construction industry half of the workforce is self-employed. Often this is legitimate; craftsmen need to work for multiple employers because a single employer may not have full-time ongoing demand for their specialist skills. However, in no other country's construction industry is this figure so high: it's not unknown for businesses to transfer their whole workforce from employment by the firm to being managed by a 'payroll company', sometimes without the employees even being told. In 2013 the construction union, UCATT, exposed the seedier side of payroll companies in an undercover report. The UK's largest such company had claimed that businesses could save 20 per cent of labour costs using a scheme which the courts had apparently ruled legal.[31] The employee's contract with the payroll company specifically states that the employee has no contractual obligations to the former employer and the fee for the new arrangement, typically £12.50/worker/week, is deducted from the former employee's pay. (The report stresses that not all payroll companies are this unprincipled: some refuse to accept that whole staff transfers can be legitimate.)

The loss of rights and payments involved in the transfer aren't made explicit but the worker's rights to claim expenses against tax are spelled out. Such expenses create a tax allowance of about £1,300/year, per person, possibly costing the Revenue £500m. Four hundred thousand people may be falsely self-employed in the construction industry alone, depriving HMRC of a further £1.2bn in unpaid employers' National Insurance Contributions (NIC).

Self-employed people pay a lower level of NIC compared with employees, creating a further loss to the Treasury. It's easy to see how £2bn is kept out of the Chancellor's coffers each year. To compensate for this he has to levy higher rates of tax on you, me and every Company Citizen – or make more cuts.

The Government's ham-fisted, unsuccessful 2017 attempt to reform self-employed NICs was nevertheless on the right lines: something needs to change. Charging self-employed people the equivalent of employees' NIC and that of employers would kill genuine self-employment, unless its threshold is raised significantly. Humanity and dignity argue that sick pay and paid parental leave ought to be available to the self-employed but who'd pay for it? Would holiday pay be included? A transaction tax, where a hiring company pays the same NIC whether the worker is an employee or a contractor, would work in a way which VAT-registered companies would recognise; or maybe the public would accept higher levels of tax on 'unearned' income in order to keep NIC levels low.[32]

Meanwhile, those self-employed workers who believe they have no option but to freelance are known by some as the precariat, reflecting their precarious employment status.[33] For up to 7 million people work is a matter of finding what opportunities there are, doing them for as long as required, possibly working for more than one employer in a single day and moving on. Alternatively it means being more or less loosely tied to an employer, such as a delivery company, but only working and being paid when there's work to be done. Nine hundred thousand of the precariat are on zero-hours contracts with no guaranteed minimum working time: up by 21 per cent in just a year they earn, on average, half of what equivalent payroll employees earn (and have fewer benefits).[34] Some even face fines for unplanned sickness absence. Their vision of work doesn't include training, progression, career planning or commitment to a particular employer; they may need to work long unsocial hours to make ends meet. Despite government initiatives, half of all those working for micro-enterprise, or self-employed, are without a pension, adding to the social challenges of decades to come.[35] Crowd labour is volatile, superficial, disorganised and it drives pay rates down through competition; two million of the precariat earn under £8/hour and that number's rising. Many are over-qualified for their menial work; think of graduates delivering pizzas. In agricultural Lincolnshire a quarter of all workers could be 'self-employed' by 2020.[36]

The precariat suffer disproportionately from 'anxiety, alienation, anomie and anger' according to alliterative academics, who know that 'anomie' means 'lacking normal ethical and moral guidance'. These emotions lead to a greater propensity to stress, depression and other mental health problems amongst the false self-employed. British members of the precariat often feel themselves to be in direct competition with struggling migrants in jobs that may be dominated by foreign-born workers, giving rise to skewed views about the 'damage' that immigration does to our country. Politically they're ill-informed, disinterested, minimally involved: they may find angry politics seductive. They're unlikely to depend on benefits because the benefit system is slow and unsupportive for people with variable and unpredictable incomes; they'd rather stay below the radar. (Tax credits, in particular, are notorious for being rigid, unable to respond to claimants' changing circumstances, so variations in income can result in big demands for repayment.)

In any normal workplace, a line manager gets to know those immediately below them in the hierarchy; over time they share a relationship of sorts, maybe a friendship, some knowledge of each other's family. Such social interactions are an important part of the workplace dynamic from which value can be obtained, but they're lacking where those relationships are transient, brief, necessarily superficial and providing no basis upon which to build. American research shows a huge contrast between people who are voluntarily self-employed and those who are obliged to be independent. The former are buoyed by working with autonomy, values and flexibility. They largely enjoy what they do and believe that they 'make a difference'. The precariat, on the other hand, lack routine, career prospects, benefits and, above all, control over their own destiny. They pay a price in terms of self-esteem, confidence and ability to respond positively to new challenges.[37]

Such is life in the precariat.

Foodbanks

Today's young people could be the first generation to earn less in total than their parents did. As we've seen, half of the children currently living in poverty in Britain live in families where at least one person is working, a situation not observed here previously. Some are users of foodbanks.

The Trussell Trust operates through 400 franchises, more than a third of Britain's foodbanks. Starting in 2008 with 29 outlets, their numbers doubled each year for three years and usage has continued to rise to the current rate of 1.2 million clients/year. A growing number of users are the in-work poor including, controversially, some nurses and other public-service workers.[38] The UK Government claims that this growth is caused by tapping into previously unmet demand whereas the Scottish Government believes that demand is actually growing, not least due to changes in the benefit system since 2010. The Trussell Trust agrees. We know that the period 2010–15 is the first five-year period on record in which UK living standards fell.[39]

Essentially a conventional foodbank collects donated non-perishable food, divides it into balanced parcels and distributes it to those in need as identified by agencies – police, social services, Citizens Advice – who issue vouchers of entitlement. Typically a person is given three days' supply for their household, which may be repeated only once in any six-month period (to discourage dependency). Foodbanks are generally run by volunteers. Variations on this essentially transactional model exist, with many foodbanks going beyond the fundamental: hot drinks, counselling, befriending and signposting to other services have been introduced, so too courses on low-budget nutrition and debt advice services. Many now encourage donation of tampons as a lack of affordable sanitary protection is, today in Britain, a significant reason why some girls miss school.[40] Delivering such initiatives taxes both the business acumen of managers and the demands on their volunteers.

If foodbanks are a crisis measure, a step towards food security, then they're justified as 'needs must'. There's no danger that they'll become so effective that sources of surplus food fall short of what's needed. Nevertheless, foodbanks aren't a long-term alternative to establishing food security or the sustainable relief of poverty.

Fareshare was established over 20 years ago. The charity sources around 7,000 tons of food per year from manufacturers and major retailers which would otherwise go to waste. They reduce companies' landfill costs (and associated methane emissions) as well as feed the hungry. From around 20 distribution centres they service almost 2,000 other charities who provide over 15 million meals yearly to clients who are homeless or otherwise vulnerable.

Feeding Britain coordinates pro-poor services in the most vulnerable communities. FoodCycle runs 20 projects in which teams of volunteers with surplus kitchen capacity and fresh vegetarian food donated by supermarkets provide a weekly, free, communal meal for a disadvantaged community.[41] Company Shop claims to be the UK's biggest purveyor of surplus food and has a Queen's Award for Enterprise for its 40-year record of operating from manufacturers' premises, where its members-only clientele is restricted to employees of the host business plus workers in the NHS and the emergency services. Members can access cheap food and there's a small financial return to the manufacturers. Company Shop's partners, including most major supermarkets and department stores, attest to its professionalism and its lack of competitive threat. If this membership model is not targeted at the poorest then its 2013 offshoot, Community Shop, certainly is. Working through community centres initially in Rotherham, Barnsley and Lambeth a similar model to Company Shop is emerging with a broader purpose: 'Members of Community Shop can shop for good food at great prices – easing pressure on family budgets – but also gain access to professional, personal development programmes, to kick-start positive change in their own lives.'[42]

Members of Community Shop must live in a specified local area of high deprivation, receive certain poverty-related benefits and want to change their lives for the better. Community Shop isn't a budget store (though prices are about one third of retail), nor are they a foodbank. Community Shop and Company Shop are businesses with employees and infrastructure, social enterprises in that profit is used to deliver a community service and reduce food waste rather than as an end in itself.

All these models use the tools of business to deliver a social purpose. Traditional 'for profit' businesses are not generally established with a focus on community needs but why should they not adopt a social purpose, above and beyond their commercial raison d'être?

There's every reason why they should: the Company Citizen has a conscience.

Markets are the lifeblood of business and there's no better-understood market than that of food. We know the market is failing when more children are starting school underweight (up 16 per cent between 2012 and 2015) whilst others are obese, growing numbers of infants and pregnant mothers are anaemic (the highest level in 20 years) and increasing numbers of people admitted to hospital are malnourished (up 43 per cent between 2010 and 2014), according to a Parliamentary report.[43] Today the poorest tranche of households spend 41 per cent of their income on food, fuel and housing compared with just 17 per cent for the wealthiest families. Today a quarter of a million British households skip the occasional meal for fear that they will run out of food or money before their next pay day or benefit receipt.

Supermarkets are often at the forefront of public campaigns to feed the hungry in Britain and most of them work with Fareshare. Aldi has recently joined the Company/Community Shop network, the Co-op has more than trebled its donations to Fareshare (to 300 tonnes in 2015) and Tesco has a 'zero edible waste' policy. Waitrose stores donate almost £1m of food to local good causes each year. Both Waitrose and Sainsbury's support FoodCycle whilst every Sainsbury's store has at least one local charity partnership into which surplus food is donated.

Today households waste a third of all the bread they buy, a quarter of the vegetables and a fifth of fruit, totalling a sixth of all food and drink purchased.[44] Not all waste from the food industry is suitable for human consumption: safety regulations that apply to selling food also apply to those giving it away. Two thirds of the food industry's 6.5 million tons of waste is food (much of the rest is packaging) and less than 2 per cent is currently redistributed to charities for human consumption.[45]

About two thirds of waste from food industries comes from manufacturers rather than wholesale or retail sources, although the industry is reducing waste by about 5 per cent per year. Half of all such food waste is recycled and a third is spread on land.

In Ohio, Walmart smartly dropped its support for a local foodbank when it emerged that some of the beneficiaries were their own employees.[46] What lesson did they learn? Companies don't normally know when their employees visit foodbanks; most managers would be concerned to hear that they did and rightly too. We think highly of those who donate the milk of human kindness yet we seem to think less of those obliged to use those services – and how we allowed them to get that way.

The Company Citizen focuses on solutions.

Public services

Public services are provided for the benefit of all directly by central government or local government or through agencies in other sectors. They're paid for largely from taxes, half of which income is collected directly from companies and their employees. Everyone uses them – education, roads, health – and having effective and appropriate services in every community is a concern of citizens of all types.

Although 17 of 21 Government departments saw cuts in spending between 2010 and 2015 the austerity axe hasn't fallen evenly. Communities and Local Government (CLG) saw the biggest proportional cut, slashing council funding by half and making them more reliant on the locally levied Council Tax and Business Rate, which are politically difficult to increase significantly. The non-benefits element of DWP's budget has taken cuts of a third. The Home Office, covering both police and the Border Agency, has lost a quarter as have Environment, Culture and Justice, including prisons; Transport, Defence and Business cuts have also been significant. Protecting the massive schools budget means that cuts elsewhere in Education (like Further Education) have been harsher than that Department's overall figure of 10 per cent suggests. Except for Health, bowing to public pressure and patently inadequate resources, the only departments to see spending rise have been tiny.[47]

Total government spending is around £600bn, of which over half goes on health or benefits (including state pensions); at 1.7 million people the NHS is the planet's fifth biggest employer. Though most of their funding comes from CLG, councils collectively raise about £28bn/year through local taxation and receive about £70bn from other government departments including Education, Health and Culture. On top of any charges councils may levy their services cost us £2,437 each in 2013–14.[48] Total council expenditure has flatlined at around £158bn, though the proportion which councils can choose how to spend has fallen.

We saw in Chapter 1 that charities' combined spending is £46bn, though their 'voluntary' or 'unrestricted' income from public donations has been static for a decade. Much comes through outsourced contracts so the rest can be added to the cost of services provided for the use of the public. The principle of 'full cost recovery', whereby charities delivering services on contract to the public sector should not have to subsidise such services from their charitable income, seems to have been abandoned in recent years, threatening charity sustainability. The fact that two thirds of charities delivering 'public' services on contract now claim to be subsidising that work from donated funds is of concern.

Put these figures in the context of demand. Services for children and elderly and vulnerable adults cost more per user than those provided for fit and healthy people of middle age. Recent statistics illustrate the changing demands on public services.

- UK population rose from 59 million in 2001 to 63 million in 2011 due to longer life expectancy and migration.
- Birth rates are up: in 2000 the average mother had 1.64 children (a historic low) but 1.92 in 2010.
- Death rates have been falling for some years, adding to population pressures, though the age-standardised mortality rate in 2015 jumped by 4 per cent.

- 40,000 people were registered homeless in 2010, a historic low, but this rose to 60,000 in 2016.[49]
- People from the lowest incomes are one third more likely to be admitted to hospital for both elective and emergency purposes than those at the top; the cost of this difference (over £4bn) is not offset by their lower life expectancy and is made worse by rising numbers in poverty.[50]
- 1.4 million British people had diabetes in 1996; in 2016 it was 3.6 million with perhaps another million undiagnosed.[51] One tenth of NHS spending already goes on managing diabetes – or the consequences of not doing so.

These statistics ring many alarm bells. On population alone we conclude that while spending on services has diminished, demand is rising. That 2015 rise in death rate correlates with the ongoing crisis in funding for elderly care. A quarter of us are over 60 (more than are under 18) and this will rise to a third in the 2030s. By 2040 there will be twice as many over 85s (3.4 million) as there are now.[52] Allied to this trend, exaggerated as the 'baby boomer' generation moves out of the workplace and into retirement, the ratio of taxpayers to those requiring care will fall. It's this, as much as people preparing to cater for themselves in retirement, that will force us to work for longer – if we can.[53]

Within health those bells toll loudest. The over 60s spend more time in hospital; 40 per cent of people over 65 have a long-term life-limiting illness. Most people over 80 have a disability. Despite the growing elderly population, spending on social care fell between 2010 and 2015. A third of elderly people deemed in need of some care at home receive nothing. Half a million NHS bed occupancy days each year are due to 'bed blocking' caused by inadequate access to social care. One in three pensioners will require high levels of care for dementia. Cancer and circulatory diseases (half of all adult deaths), together with diabetes, are often lifestyle-related conditions which employers could help to prevent.

Social care pays low wages and the rise in the minimum wage in 2016 caused budgets to tighten. By 2020 the extra price of paying what's intended to be a dignified level of pay could cost the industry £382m, a third of the funding gap of £1.1bn identified by the Conservative-leaning think tank Res Publica, who say that this shortfall will see 37,000 more beds lost.[54]

Age UK calculates that the poor quality of housing inhabited by many elderly people generates costs to the NHS of £1.6bn/year. Other areas of government spending are under similar pressures: the number of looked-after children in local authority care has risen from under 50,000, 20 years ago, to over 70,000.[55]

In short, the public sector is frail and vulnerable. Yet business needs strong public services to serve it and its employees. Some councils have developed innovative means of providing services at reduced cost but, whilst welcome, many of these are yet to prove scaleable or sustainable.

Elderly care has long been delivered or enhanced by charities and voluntary organisations. Such care demands a supportive infrastructure and access to professional services, things that charities generally don't have the scale, capacity or statutory duty to provide. The private sector also has a role, though companies that prioritise profit are often viewed with suspicion in this field. Whilst they usually behave ethically and co-operatively, alongside statutory and voluntary providers, the Southern Cross story is often cited to justify scepticism.

John Moreton made money from North Sea gas at a young age. In 1996 a Government shake-up of care, including a tougher regulatory regime and funding cutbacks, prompted many existing, smaller, private providers of elderly residential care to leave the market and sell their properties cheaply. Moreton saw an opportunity and created Southern Cross Healthcare in the belief that a lean and slim operation could provide a good service whilst making a profit. By 2002 the company had 140 sites – and a good reputation. Then a venture capital firm invested £80m in a management buy-out and Moreton departed.

Two years later an American private equity company, Blackstone, bought the growing concern for £160m. Until then the Southern Cross model was to operate in rented accommodation but Blackstone bought their largest landlord and more than doubled their number of care homes to 700, with 40,000 beds.

By 2006 Southern Cross was Britain's largest operator of private care homes. The company was floated on the stock market, doubling its share price within a year, before Blackstone sold it once more. Meanwhile, homes continued to close even though demand for residential care was rising as the elderly population grew.[56]

The 2008 global crash undermined the Southern Cross business model. Unable to meet debt repayments they issued a profits warning; the then CEO, who'd recently sold £37m worth of shares at 550p, saw them plunge, at one point from 300p to 130p in a single day. He quit.

Despite the efforts of restructuring experts, in June 2011 Southern Cross ceased to be.

Orchid View was opened by Southern Cross in 2009 and closed in 2011. An inquest later ruled that five residents had died from natural causes 'contributed to by neglect'. An enquiry found that warning signs had been ignored: not least that only one of the six managers who ran the home over two years had been properly qualified. Ambulance crews, relatives and pharmacists had expressed concerns about what they'd seen there but scrutiny had been scant, new residents were admitted even a few weeks before the home was known to be closing, allegedly 'filling up beds to make money'. Although five people were investigated there was insufficient evidence to prosecute.[57]

Southern Cross is not an example of poor outsourcing of public services because it wasn't commissioned to provide services (although public sector bed numbers had fallen over the period). It was a commercial provider, selling a service on the open market; although the principal buyers of such services were local authorities they also sold to individuals. There's a long history of private provision of care which today accounts for 90 per cent of Britain's 430,000 care beds.

In its report *Tomorrow's Business Forms* Tomorrow's Company argues that the character of a company, its nature and values, often determine both its success and its sustainability, reflecting its capacity for collaboration, responsibility, integrity and even ability to care.[58] The problem with Southern Cross, they argue persuasively, was not that it was a private company driven by profit, nor even that it was a private company operating in a role often associated with public or voluntary sector providers; it was that it had become a company with the ruthless, cash-driven, acquisitive and short-term values of a private equity investor operating in a market place where such values were simply inappropriate.

What looked like a strong and viable entity was built on sand; its focus had been on cash and not customers, who happened to be vulnerable and were probably reluctant to complain. Maybe therefore its catastrophic demise was inevitable, merely hastened by the global crash. And perhaps every public sector commissioner or procurer, indeed every family concerned, should ask 'What are the values of this company? Do they match the values of the service they seek to provide?' As Tomorrow's Company suggests, *caveat emptor!* . . . buyer beware!

The story of BHS, where Sir Philip Green sold the retail company for £1 just months before its new owner closed it down, shows a similar ruthless and mechanistic approach. The sale went ahead despite a half-billion-pound hole in BHS pension finances, after Green had taken out of the company dividends worth a similar sum for himself and his family. In this case the asset-stripping pillage of the retail chain, the abandonment of 11,000 workers and 20,000 pension-fund members, was deliberate, a clear case of the owner being guided by values that a Company Citizen would find inappropriate. In this case a reluctant and pompous apology was followed by a public promise to 'put things right' against the background of possible prosecution.[59]

If business with the wrong character can wreak such havoc, surely business with the right, citizenship-orientated character can do much more than simply set the pendulum straight?

Outsourcing

Even though it wasn't an outsourced service, Southern Cross is a parable of what can happen when a private company is asked to deliver a caring service, tending to legitimise public concern about the extent to which such services are privatised or outsourced. In 2013–14 the UK public sector spent £242bn procuring goods and services, over a third of all public-sector spending, the vast majority with the private sector. With public expenditure under continued pressure, government must utilise what third parties offer in terms of innovation, diversity of provision, cost reduction and the sharing of risk. In practice, much of this spending is with a small number of super-large companies designed to win contracts, costed competitively to meet compliance criteria, putting huge pressure on public-sector commissioning officers to do their jobs well – a matter on which the jury is still out, to put it politely. Although successful outsourcing – the majority – tends to avoid publicity, there are too many worrisome ones to feel comfortable. Parliament's Public Accounts Committee (PAC) reminds us of several:[60]

- the performance of G4S in failing to supply security guards for the Olympics;
- Capita failing to deliver court translation services and losing NHS records;
- issues with Atos' work capability assessments; and
- G4S and Serco overcharging for the electronic tagging of prisoners.

The committee put the blame squarely on poor commissioning and enforcement:

> These high profile failures illustrate contractors' failure to live up to standards expected and have exposed serious weaknesses in Government's capability in negotiating and managing private contracts on behalf of the taxpayer.

For political reasons service outsourcing within the NHS is much less, under 10 per cent, than many perceive it to be. In a subsequent report the PAC went further with scathing criticism of a 'grossly irresponsible' £800m contract between the NHS (Cambridgeshire and Peterborough Commissioning Group) and Uniting Care Partnership, which went belly up in just eight months:

> The deal went ahead without parties agreeing on what would be provided and at what price – a failure of business acumen that would embarrass a child in a sweet shop . . . with far more serious consequences.[61]

On closer examination, Uniting Care was a consortium not of private companies but of two health-service bodies. The report said: 'The case is a further demonstration of the lack of commercial skills in the NHS to procure patient services effectively.'

This wasn't a failure of the private sector: this was a gross failure of the public sector to exhibit the very skills that the private sector ought to bring to the table to ensure a sustainable model of service delivery for a fair price. As it is, a hard-pressed local NHS is paying £16m of consequences of this 'mismatch' from a highly stretched NHS budget.

In 2017 HMRC terminated a contract which outsourced investigations into tax credit fraud. By this point they had halved their estimate of the operation's savings, found that a third of Concentrix' actions against clients were unjustified, criticised the contractor's customer service and paid out £87,000 in customer compensation. Concentrix made a loss on the aborted contract and HMRC issued a sweeping statement saying that it doubted that private companies could understand the 'subtleties' of public service.[62] The French company Atos had previously walked away from a large DWP contract which, it claimed, was unworkable. The DWP select committee said the problems with the computer-led points-based assessment 'lay firmly with the DWP', adding that the department was failing to apply 'sufficient rigour or challenge to Atos'.[63]

A lack of skills for large-scale commissioning has dogged our public services for years; this has been exploited by the five main outsourcers who have simply grown too big to cope. In G4S, with 900 business units, and Serco, with 600, efficiency is stretched beyond credibility. With the rise in minimum wage, Brexit causing contract negotiations to pause and Government squeezing costs this sector's in crisis: four of the five big companies saw their share prices fall by half in 2014–16, three have recently lost their CEO and confidence is ebbing away.[64]

Perhaps 'big' is not 'best'. Perhaps decisions are being taken at the wrong level. Perhaps the mixed economy of service provision only works when it's genuinely mixed, and that can't happen at the level of government department and private sector equivalent. Although a small organisation can achieve economies of scale through growth there's a limit to that efficiency if the contract mission is to be maintained: there's growing evidence that at 'mega' level scale generates diseconomies, as lines of accountability are stretched to breaking point.

Successive governments' wish, that a quarter of all outsource spending should go to SMEs, is a distant pipe dream. It can only be delivered by pushing decision-making and contracting much closer to the communities they serve. It won't happen through using ever bigger providers which lose flexibility and nuance as they extend. Indeed, the New Economics Foundation has declared: 'The government's review of social care must set out how we can support a network of smaller care providers, putting dignity back into . . . services.'[65]

The alternative was to see £115m of a proposed £2bn rescue deal for social care pass directly to the investors in the five companies that provide the bulk of the service nationwide.

As Tomorrow's Company said in that 2016 report:

> It would be very helpful if those carrying out procurement on behalf of the public sector were able to make a wider assessment of the character and reliability of the companies bidding for work, alongside the important but narrower specifying of financial and operational objectives.

Hence the idea of a 'Trust Test'. The aim of such a test could be to reconcile the interests of companies, service users and taxpayers by ensuring that outside contractors, of whatever scale, have values which match those required of the service. Tomorrow's Company is working on this with the British Standards Institute and others.

The picture of Britain painted here is depressing but true. We can do so much better than this.

Whilst government may have chosen austerity there is no lack of resources across business. Yet the choices that are being made by many in business, to increase dividends at the expense of wages, whisk profits offshore, increase inequality through rampant levels of top pay, hold back on investment (aided and abetted by the banks) are all making things worse and Brexit creates further uncertainties. Tax rates might not need to rise if productivity could reach the European average – and companies who work to reduce the demand their employees make on health and care services would reap benefits themselves, as we'll see in Chapter 7.

Company Citizens, either independently of government, operating as partners in delivery or simply as citizens in sympathy with the broad goals of government, can contribute to a better, fairer, more inclusive Britain. Company Citizens can appreciate the business case for such a goal and increasingly they know how to help achieve it.

Notes

1 http://tomorrowscompany.com/wp-content/uploads/2016/08/An-opportunity-to-lead-post-Brexit-Tomorrows-Company.pdf.
2 www.theguardian.com/us-news/2016/dec/08/portland-oregon-ceo-pay-tax-passes-income-inequality?.
3 Speaking at a showing of the film *The Divide*, about inequality (http://thedivideddocumentary.com).
4 www.bbc.co.uk/news/business-32824770. The UK gap narrowed slightly in 2016.
5 www.standard.co.uk/business/sacha-romanovitch-sharing-profits-capping-her-salary-grant-thorntons-chief-is-transforming-city-life-a2945486.html.
6 www.independent.co.uk/news/business/news/tobacco-imperial-brands-chief-executive-alison-cooper-pay-rise-shareholders-gauloise-winston-a7547161.html.
7 www.standard.co.uk/business/simon-english-forget-football-the-real-top-pay-scandal-is-in-the-boardroom-a3442606.html.
8 www.ft.com/content/5c031f44-13a5-11e7-80f4-13e067d5072c.
9 www.ft.com/content/6df9902a-f8fc-11e6-9516-2d969e0d3b65.
10 www.socialprogressindex.com/results.
11 www.ifs.org.uk/publications/8375 – figures are for absolute poverty, after housing costs, except where stated.
12 https:// twitter.com/d_blanchflower/status/807325669730324482 – Blanchflower is a former member of the Bank of England Monetary Policy Committee.
13 Ibid, Note 11.
14 www.ifs.org.uk/uploads/publications/conferences/hbai2016/rjoyce_living_standards2016.pdf – absolute poverty is 60 per cent of 2010–11 median income; relative poverty is 60 per cent of contemporary median income.
15 www.dailymail.co.uk/wires/pa/article-3628805/Two-fifths-people-need-borrow-pay-shock-500-bill.html.
16 Ibid, Note 11 and www.theguardian.com/society/2017/mar/16/child-poverty-in-uk-at-highest-level-since-2010-official-figures-show.
17 Office for National Statistics, *An examination of falling real wages, 2010–13*, January 2014; and Labour Market Statistics, February 2016.
18 *Poverty in the UK*, House of Commons briefing paper 7096, November 2016.
19 http://touchstoneblog.org.uk/2017/02/uk-103rd-112-global-ranking-real-wage-growth-since-crisis/.

20 www.ifs.org.uk/uploads/publications/comms/R114.pdf.
21 www.jrf.org.uk/report/uk-poverty-causes-costs-and-solutions.
22 www.mirror.co.uk/news/uk-news/what-new-benefit-cap-affect-9173739.
23 Nigel Wilson was speaking at the SSE annual investors' meeting, London, February 2017.
24 www.livingwage.org.uk.
25 www.standard.co.uk/news/mayor/sadiq-khan-demands-londons-top-football-clubs-pay-living-wage-a3442441.html.
26 www.bitc.org.uk/system/files/living-wage-employer-case-studies.pdf–www.livingwage.org.uk/news/BusinessBenefitsPR.
27 www.retailgazette.co.uk/blog/2017/02/debenhams-tops-list-of-minimum-wage-offenders.
28 www.resolutionfoundation.org/app/uploads/2016/10/Living-wage-calculations.pdf.
29 http://ipsos-mori-almanac.co.uk/2016-favourite-facts/.
30 www.theguardian.com/society/2016/oct/18/self-employed-earn-less-than-2001-hit-welfare-cuts.
31 http://ucatt.infobo.co.uk/sites/default/files/uploaded/publications/greatpayrollscandal.pdf.
32 www.thersa.org/discover/publications-and-articles/rsa-blogs/2016/11/the-uber-ruling-reminds-us-that-sometimes-tax-does-have-to-be-taxing. In 2017 The RSA's Matthew Taylor explored 'Good work' in a report for the Government, reaching conclusions on the 'gig' economy compatible with those described here. See www.gov.uk/government/groups/employment-practices-in-the-modern-economy.
33 www.guystanding.com/files/documents/Fabian_Soc_Changing_Work_Precariat_Dilemma_2016.pdf (in Cooper, 2016).
34 https://worksmart.org.uk/news/problem-zero-hours.
35 www.professionalpensions.com/professional-pensions/news/3003678/aca-ae-to-exclude-12-million-people-by-mid-2018.
36 www.theguardian.com/uk-news/2016/nov/15/more-than-7m-britons-in-precarious-employment.
37 https://dupress.deloitte.com/dup-us-en/topics/operations/heros-journey-landscape-future.html.
38 www.trusselltrust.org/2017/04/25/uk-foodbank-use-continues-rise/.
39 www.tuc.org.uk/economic-issues/public-spending/labour-market/economic-analysis/living-standards-suffer-first-five.
40 www.theguardian.com/society/2016/dec/16/boots-support-campaign-end-period-poverty-paula-sherriff-tampons.
41 www.fareshare.org.uk; http://foodcycle.org.uk; and https://feeding-britain.org.
42 http://community-shop.co.uk/company-shop/ and http://community-shop.co.uk/community-shop/.
43 https://feedingbritain.files.wordpress.com/2015/02/food-poverty-appg-evidence-review-final.pdf.
44 www.gov.uk/government/uploads/system/uploads/attachment_data/file/567502/Digest_waste_resource_2016_rev4.pdf (also 2015 data).
45 www.wrap.org.uk/sites/files/wrap/Estimates%20of%20waste%20in%20the%20food%20and%20drink%20supply%20chain_0.pdf.
46 www.forbes.com/sites/causeintegration/2017/01/16/choosing-social-causes-that-make-sense-for-your-company/#1e9454131c51.
47 www.ifs.org.uk/tools_and_resources/fiscal_facts/public_spending_survey/cuts_to_public_spending.

48 www.gov.uk/government/uploads/system/uploads/attachment_data/file/444993/2904001_LGF_web_accessible_v0_2__final_.pdf.
49 www.gov.uk/government/uploads/system/uploads/attachment_data/file/555808/Statutory_Homelessness_and_Prevention_and_Relief_Statistical_Release_April_to_June_2016.pdf.
50 http://jech.bmj.com/content/70/10/990.
51 www.diabetes.org.uk/professionals/position-statements-reports/statistics/diabetes-prevalence-2016.
52 www.ageuk.org.uk/Documents/EN-GB/Factsheets/Later_Life_UK_factsheet.pdf?dtrk=true – the source of many statistics in this section.
53 www.resolutionfoundation.org/publications/live-long-and-prosper-demographic-trends-and-their-implications-for-living-standards/.
54 Quoted in http://tomorrowscompany.com/delivering-value-in-government-outsourcing/.
55 www.gov.uk/government/uploads/system/uploads/attachment_data/file/556331/SFR41_2016_Text.pdf.
56 www.theguardian.com/business/2011/jun/01/rise-and-fall-of-southern-cross.
57 www.theguardian.com/society/2014/jun/09/financial-strategy-southern-cross-care-homes-blamed-deaths-old-people.
58 http://tomorrowscompany.com/wpcontent/uploads/2016/05/tomorrows_business_forms_final__L__5294bdecb6f84.pdf.
59 http://uk.businessinsider.com/sir-philip-green-bhs-pension-fund-2016-7.
60 www.publications.parliament.uk/pa/cm201314/cmselect/cmpubacc/777/777.pdf.
61 www.parliament.uk/business/committees/committees-a-z/commons-select/public-accounts-committee/news-parliament-2015/unitingcare-partnership-contract-report-published-16-17/.
62 www.ft.com/content/f421092e-dbfd-11e6-9d7c-be108f1c1dce.
63 www.theguardian.com/society/2014/mar/27/atos-quite-work-capability-assessment-contract-early.
64 www.ft.com/content/3dfd0c3a-0590-11e7-aa5b-6bb07f5c8e12.
65 www.thetimes.co.uk/article/investors-will-get-100m-of-social-care-funding-jnrdvjgmp.

4 Business is ready

Business is like a toolbox.

Capitalism is a network of processes serving a market through which businesses navigate using that box of tools. The tools include employment, investment, accounting, sales, procurement, project management, risk management, human resources, marketing, logistics and the rest. Each resembles a Swiss army knife: tools within tools. Not every tool is used by every business: when a business employs no one and operates from no fixed premises the tools associated with employment and premises remain in their box. 'Citizenship' is amongst the arsenal available to business practitioners.

In some cases the tools are used for no discernible purpose other than to maximise profit. Some people have learned how to do this effectively: within the regulatory environment 'the system' allows us to get on with it whilst exacting a 'social price' for doing so, principally taxation, which pays for much that benefits business. At one extreme end of the business spectrum, dominated by the financial markets, huge short-term profits are possible which exaggerate the inequalities of outcome we've observed elsewhere and which, as a reward system, often appear to bear little connection to real life. Let's call this the 'mechanical' end of the spectrum, which gives low priority to its social 'licence to operate'.

At the other end of the spectrum, the 'human', identical tools are put to very different purposes. Here companies serve an essentially social mission, far removed philosophically from that of profit maximisation. This is the social economy: people are employed, things utilised and profits generated from the market in order to deliver a social mission or purpose, sustainably. Social enterprises plough profits back into the company or donate them to a cause in order to create social and environmental impacts – rather than taking them out of the business to benefit a few individuals.

At this end of the spectrum 'licence to operate' again isn't an issue: the licence is valid because the organisation is providing a socially positive function.

Most companies exhibit neither absolutely 'human' nor irrevocably 'mechanical' characteristics but some blend of the two (the spectrum is simplified in Figure 4.1). Businesses regard their workforce as somewhere between an asset to be cherished (a 'human' value) and a resource to be managed like any other, at

'Human' values	*← Mainstream business →*			*'Mechanical' values*
Social enterprise	**Socially responsible business**	**Compliant or neutral**	**Lip service**	**Exclusively profit-driven**
Business run with a social purpose, profits retained or donated, behaves only ethically.	For (private) profit but committed to ethical, responsible and sustainable mission.	Occasionally goes beyond level of responsibility required by law or regulation.	Pays lip service to socially responsible practices, e.g., superficial or minimal CSR.	Maximises profits at all costs, operates close to legal/ moral limits.
← Mission-driven business →		**← Profit-driven business →**		

Figure 4.1 Perceptions of business categories according to purpose

minimum cost ('mechanical'). Mainstream companies rightly have no guilt about making reasonable profits for their owners and are aware, to some degree, of their place in society, not just in the economy. Increasingly, a broad range of corporate characters has mainstreamed their ESG (Environment, Social, Governance) activity and in some circles there's been a deliberate shift away from talking about CSR (Corporate Social Responsibility, so 'twentieth century') as it's too often regarded as a superficial, optional, box-ticking, non-mainstream activity. Companies with more human values see CSR or CRS (Corporate Responsibility and Sustainability) as a key responsibility of senior management or of a major department such as HR rather than as a 'nice to do' communications and motivation exercise. A growing number of businesses place themselves towards that 'human' end when integrating triple bottom-line sustainability, relating to people, profit and planet, into everyday business activity. If you ask the owners of these businesses why they exist they may talk about 'mission', 'purpose' and 'values'.

In the middle, issues around 'licence to operate' are discussed and yardsticks are employed, though not all yardsticks measure the same things.

Barclays Bank is best known for its 'mechanical' activities. Whilst Barclays had avoided being publicly bailed out after the 'crash' in 2008 they had stinks of their own, not least the fiddling of the London Interbank Offered Rate. The London Interbank Offered Rate (LIBOR) is a published daily average of the rates at which 18 banks in the City lend to each other. Not only does this figure, first published 30 years earlier, guide financial institutions but derivatives worth trillions of dollars are based on LIBOR figures. Early in 2012 some Barclays employees were exposed for deliberately reporting inaccurate data to create consequences that worked in the bank's favour. This clearly fraudulent activity occurred on Bob Diamond's 18-month watch. These misdemeanours only became specific crimes in legislation the following year but the unsubtle boss was long gone by then.

In 2012 the bank with Quaker origins recruited a new CEO to replace the PR disaster that had been the brusque American. Apart from a few years in Citibank the new man, Antony Jenkins, was a lifetime Barclays insider known as 'the nice guy of banking'. He was recruited for his broadly 'human' values, which he summed up in a 2014 interview: 'We're in business to make a profit, of course we are, but we make a profit by serving our customers, by fulfilling our obligations to society and by providing great work environments for our colleagues.'[1]

In July 2015 he was dismissed from his post precisely because of these values; the men in suits decided that the priority given to maximising profit had slipped and they wanted it restored.

I met Antony Jenkins in January 2017 when he was establishing a new career setting up 10x, a fintech company designed to disrupt retail and commercial banking in order to restore its original purpose of facilitating relationships between borrowers and lenders. Banking had moved steadily away from this role over the years, he said, developing an overriding and self-serving purpose of its own. 'Finance doesn't really work these days', he went on, citing unacceptably low levels of customer satisfaction and suggesting that only regulation is preventing another lurch into a 2008-style crash. Will 10x wreak Jenkins' revenge on mainstream banking? By utilising the best that information technology offers it could certainly challenge current banking practices. He foresees the 'unstoppable' rise of ever cheaper and more sophisticated technology leading to the fragmentation of the big banks through greater personalisation of services, alongside the democratisation of finance through peer-to-peer lending. Cryptocurrencies, greater access to big data and the rapid evolution of artificial intelligence will add to the disruption. This belief will be proved, he believes, not by his building of a new empire but by copycat companies making the most of the same opportunities: having 1,000 flowers bloom.

So what of the behemoth Barclays? Jenkins came into office with the bank's reputation at an all-time low. Although he left three years into what should have been a five- or ten-year journey, he feels that he'd made some progress in addressing the 'self-serving, aggressive short termism' he'd inherited.

In the years leading up to the crash the public had tolerated ever higher executive pay in banking and elsewhere, in part because they perceived their own lot improving. However, once their personal progress had stalled, following 2008, the 'just about managing' became rightly concerned about runaway salaries. Banks were singled out for scorn because they were both familiar and appeared to see themselves as in a league of their own, where 'normal' rules didn't apply. Pay that reflects effort and genuine responsibility together with reasonable pay differentials are important symbols of a fair and just society, Jenkins states, though absolute caps on top pay won't work because imposing them will merely encourage firms to find a way around them.

He argues for two reforms that would better align the interests of executives to those of shareholders and society: relating the pay of top executives to a multiple of the median within an organisation and eliminating cash bonuses in favour of equity, or other ways of securing longer-term commitments. Although these are sensible, pragmatic, evolutionary proposals, as we saw in Chapter 3 the median may not be the best comparator because raising the pay of the lowest paid wouldn't change the ratio in the way that using the mean would; and if the ratio doesn't change there's no incentive to pay the lowest paid more (and thereby helping to end poverty pay).

'Personal motivation, purpose and values are incredibly important', says Jenkins, describing the culture of an organisation as 'an alliance of individual and organisational values'. In 2013, under him, Barclays published 'The Barclays Way', an excellent code of conduct, a corporate and personal guide to employees both in their work and in their relations with each other.[2]

Since leaving Barclays the former CEO has become the chair of the Institute for Apprenticeships and continues to chair Business In The Community. He acknowledges that BITC focuses almost exclusively on big business, with half of the FTSE100 amongst its 900 members, but passionately believes that it needs to grow, working with and for businesses of all sizes.

In our concluding moments Jenkins impressed me as a leader with a cause which goes wider than business alone. I'm pleased that he's putting his 30 years of experience at the heart of business at the disposal of the wider community. I hope his influence, frustrated by inertia and the self-interest of others at Barclays, will now spread far and wide. 'It's the job of business to serve society, not the other way round. That's not just the right thing to do, it's good for business', he says.

Business needs consumers to buy its products and skilled workers to power its metaphorical engines. Only with the right culture, values and capabilities will business thrive, deliver the best benefits available to society and win back its trust.[3]

There needs to be a debate about how to determine bonuses. Traditionally, they're related to financial performance although they appear to get paid whether targets are achieved or not. They're more likely to be offered to the upper echelons rather than as an incentive to all, as in the profit-sharing approach of the John Lewis Partnership. Too often they relate to short-term financial performance when, as we've seen, longer-term thinking makes for greater stability. Could they not, instead, be related to social, environmental or triple bottom-line performance – if they're necessary at all? Yes, they could, and in a small but growing number of mainstream businesses, such as Intel, they are.

How to decide which impacts to measure? What if a socially beneficial impact (heaven forbid) has a negative cost benefit? If we could motivate people to behave in socially and environmentally better ways without a fiscal incentive, wouldn't that be more sustainable? Profit sharing certainly incentivises, but so do doing good and protecting the environment.

Purpose, values and mission

There's always been a reluctance by governments to legislate on the broader responsibilities of business, prompted by a belief on the left that social policy is the bailiwick of government and on the right that business works best when external 'interference' is at a minimum. On a practical level, it's impossible to contemplate legislation that would cover every aspect of responsibility and there's a justifiable fear that setting legal minimum standards encourages an approach of 'compliance and no more'. Convinced and committed voluntary champions, people like Paul Polman who lead from the front through a passionate belief in responsible business, can demonstrate that it works in both social and financial terms and thus act as the best recruiting sergeants.

Indeed, the approach to non-fiduciary responsibility in business is changing. The International Chamber of Commerce believes that:

> While all businesses have an implicit set of inherent values, the number of businesses that have formally written values and principles is rapidly increasing. These principles have become more and more explicit and provide the framework for corporate behaviour beyond their legal obligations. At the same time, growing numbers of companies have been adding environmental and social indicators to their economic and financial results in reports . . . Indeed, sustained profits and principles are mutually supportive and an increasing number of companies view corporate responsibility as integral to their systems of governance. This is part of the requirements for doing business in today's global economy.[4]

The passage is significant as the ICC hasn't historically championed company citizenship. The phrase 'sustained profits and principles are mutually supportive' reflects the growing influence of voluntary initiatives such as the UN Global Compact, the Global Reporting Index and, in Britain, the reporting regulations embodied, for some, in the 2006 Companies Act. Indeed, codes of practice for business activity date from the ILO in the 1930s and the 1948 Universal Declaration of Human Rights through the United Nations, OECD, the Caux Principles on Moral Capitalism at Work,[5] the Sullivan Principles (aimed at opposing apartheid in South Africa)[6] and the European Parliament.

The Caux Principles were created in the 1980s to help reduce trade tensions between cultures and the associated threats to peace and stability. They've evolved into an international 'round table' endorsed by the UN and other bodies supporting business ethics and responsibility. The Principles are a 'moral compass' for business, governments, NGOs, wealth owners and the process of globalisation. They can be summarised as follows.

- Respect stakeholders beyond shareholders.
- Contribute to economic, social and environmental development of communities.

- Build trust by going beyond the letter of the law and exhibiting transparency.
- Respect local, national and international laws, rules and conventions.
- Support responsible globalisation, open and fair international trade.
- Respect and where possible improve the environment, minimise waste of resources.
- Avoid illicit activities, support their reduction and prevention.

The principles regard globalisation as an opportunity for global capital to invest wisely in developing economies, with a view to tackling poverty and creating new markets. However, Caux notes that conventional criteria for measuring returns on investment have not fundamentally altered: national and global politicians need to create an environment in which the risks associated with investment in 'bottom of the pyramid' economies can be minimised.

In practical terms, Tomorrow's Company concluded that in the politically and economically challenging post-Brexit period business has to get its house in order if it wants to rebuild trust with the British people and help lead the country into a new future. Nine actions, they say, would demonstrate their worth:

1 Reduce dividends and buybacks, not investment, wages or employment;
2 Commit to increase investment in the UK economy and in people's skills;
3 Make a bold and public commitment on executive pay;
4 Increase support for community initiatives;
5 Shorten supplier payment terms;
6 Build more overseas connections;
7 Don't wait for politicians to act, form industry collaborations to tackle joint problems;
8 Articulate a clear purpose, embedded throughout the culture of the organisation; and
9 Reform governance structures to provide a voice for stakeholders.

I couldn't have put it better myself, except: why save such measures for crisis mode? We'll return to some of these issues but let's dwell on 'purpose'.

It's difficult to argue against Stafford Beer's 2001 dictum that: 'The purpose of a system is what it does.'

In nine short words the management cybernetician dismisses the hypocrisy, faint-heartism and double standards that sometimes accompany good intent in the business world. He's saying that purpose should be backed by actions; if actions aren't consistent with words then either the purpose has been misstated or the system's not working: neither is acceptable.

The purpose of purpose is 'to allow a person to be their whole self, to be confident in that decision and in that wholeness'; to encourage aspiration 'to be the best that they can be' and 'to bring a collective together in a common venture', says Loughlin Hickey, formerly of KPMG and now an advocate for the Blueprint for Better Business.[7] Purpose provides a point of reference; as long as it's authentic and realistic it inspires employees and defines a business' role in society and not just the economy. The Blueprint approach, emanating from Catholic theology, is endorsed by respected economist John Kay, Unilever's Polman and a growing band of business leaders. As Kay says (with my emphasis below), just as breathing is essential to life but is not the purpose of life, so commerce is essential to business but is not the purpose of business:

> The purpose of a corporation is to produce goods and services to meet economic *and social* needs, to create satisfying and rewarding employment, to earn returns for its shareholders and other investors *and* to make a positive contribution to the social and physical environment in which it operates.[8]

Purpose is known to be a major motivator of staff. It's been suggested that whilst sales and marketing help us achieve basic and psychological needs, 'purpose' equates to 'self fulfilment' as a peak motivating factor in people's behaviour: 'purpose' plays to the summit of Maslow's Hierarchy of Needs.[9]

The 'culture' element is equally important because statements of purpose, values or mission are meaningless if they exist only on paper. They have to be lived, experienced, used to guide the company forwards.

Values make up the framework upon which purpose is built. Ed Mayo of Co-operatives UK argues that aligning values and purpose is essential in implementing the commercial and ethical imperatives of sustainability:

> Values are an essential component of the sustainability agenda. So much of the modern agenda on sustainable business is couched in language and framing that is common to business life – focusing on managerial process, for the 'how', or economic and commercial advantage, for the 'why'. Values . . . are different in that they are the only way in which people can move beyond their self-interest or group identifications to start to respond to more open calls on how to behave and act.[10]

Rather than focusing on how to respond to the world's social and environmental problems, would it not be better if business adopted the values and purposes that would prevent them? The Government's Office of Civil Society recently commissioned an advisory panel to report on 'mission-led business'. Writing in the foreword of his Panel's report Nigel Fisher, CEO of Legal & General, said:

> There's a new social contract developing between business and society, in which businesses engage with stakeholders beyond their current narrow remit to create benefits for employees, citizens and society at large.
>
> We have found evidence that businesses that embrace social priorities perform better, reflect people's ideals and ambitions and so are primed for success.[11]

Crucially important is that this report doesn't focus on social enterprise, B Corps or 'not-for-profit' members of the social economy. Rather it makes the case (as I urged in my contribution) for all businesses, in all circumstances, to 'embrace social priorities'. Nine of the panel's ten recommendations make very positive sense whilst the other addresses a problem that doesn't exist. The nine are straightforward and feasible, nudging, empowering, urging greater transparency, mainstreaming debate about mission-led business and acknowledging the powerful nature of 'investment for good' both for business and investors, not least pension funds. 'Mission' must never be a niche activity. The odd one out is recommendation 9: 'Government to explore the introduction of "benefit company" status in English law.'

The Benefit Company is an American concept (the 'Benefit Corporation') which allows a company to state that its first priority or purpose is social or environmental rather than focused solely on profit maximisation – which would otherwise be the default purpose of any American-registered business. I've studied several Benefit Corporations including the two largest in the world, Ben & Jerry's in Vermont and Natura in Brazil, plus an early pioneer, Greystone Bakery in New York; in *Welcome to GoodCo* I outlined the journey that the movement took over its first decade. That journey gained momentum in 2011 when Delaware, where 85 per cent of US corporations are registered, recognised the legal status of the Benefit Corporation, effectively making it an option available for any US company to adopt. As UK law makes no assumptions about the purpose of a registered company there's no bar to British companies having a primary social rather than profit purpose and therefore no need for a separate legal status here. The review's own 7th recommendation acknowledges the relaxed nature of UK law: 'Government to promote the flexibility offered under English law for companies to act with a social purpose and align shareholder and stakeholder interests' whilst making the important point that there's no conflict between doing good and making profit. The relative success of mission-led business shows a clear alignment of stakeholder and shareholder or owner interests.

In affording 'business for good' a specific legal status recommendation 9 is divisive: in effect it's saying 'those in the minority vanguard are good guys and the rest haven't yet obtained that level'. Having a social purpose through social, ethical and environmental responsibility, whether profit is the main priority or not, should be a default goal for all companies, irrespective of whether they have progressed far enough on that journey to be allowed to choose a particular legal status. Moving along the journey is what counts.

A related movement to Benefit Corporations, whose title suggests 'Benefit Corporation-lite', is B Corps.[12] This is an accreditation programme, not a legal status: it challenges any business to demonstrate its social and environmental credentials and priorities through regular objective measurements. The Mission-Led Business report says that B Corp status was launched in Britain in 2015 but in truth that was its re-launch; winning only eight UK adherents in its first decade, the re-launch did attract almost 100 in the following year. Such certification can be a useful progress measure or benchmarking tool.

The Mission-Led Business working group was informed by Deloitte that there were over 120,000 mission-led businesses in Britain, a very encouraging figure, mostly SMEs, of which a little over half were social enterprises.[13] Four of every five are companies limited by guarantee, a mainstream legal form which offers both flexibility and adaptability. Together Mission-Led Businesses account for over 4 per cent of private sector turnover, employ more than 1.4 million people and tend to exhibit certain features:

- diverse leadership (in terms of gender, ethnicity, etc.);
- less hierarchical structures;
- high employee engagement levels;
- strong integration of social purpose and business strategy;
- reporting on their social and environmental impacts; and
- many operate within sectors of the economy traditionally linked to the 'common good'.

Co-operatives and social enterprises are the most rapidly growing part of our economy and have a relatively high survival rate over their early years compared with 'mainstream' start-ups.

The Centre for Social Justice is a free-thinking and influential source of policy ideas. Originating on the centre right of British politics it's proved itself capable of incisive, inclusive and progressive thinking. Their publication, *Everybody's Business: Making Business Work for All*, was launched in the same week as the Mission-Led Business Review, and is a masterpiece. Its very first recommendation is: 'Government must make a purpose declaration a requirement of incorporation to signal its belief that the role of business extends beyond the maximisation of profit.'[14]

Indeed. Every business ought to have a public reason for being. This leaves it open for the entrepreneur to enter his purpose as 'making as much money as possible' – just – though the report implies that a company may be judged on its purpose as much as on its financial stability or its prospects. A statement of purpose, it asserts, tells us what values the company espouses.

If there's one group of companies where we really ought to be told how they perceive their purpose, it's investment fund managers. Simply, their purpose should be stewardship, the long-term management of our assets, including pension assets, for the common good. Of course purpose can and should be nuanced, but Will Hutton's Big Innovation Centre is right to call for fund managers – along with their assets under management – to be qualified with a stated, rational, long-term purpose.[15]

Short-term pressures (and quarterly reporting in particular) often stand in the way of long-term change and long termism is universally regarded as more compatible with ethical purpose. 'Focusing Capital on the Long Term' is a

2015 initiative supported by, amongst others, McKinsey, BlackRock, Tata Steel and Schroders.[16] There's polarisation in response to a changing market as 87 per cent of global executives report growing pressure to demonstrate results within two years, compared with 79 per cent just two years earlier, a trend that's even greater in immature markets than in Europe or USA. Before leaving the vice-presidential office Joe Biden called for changes to tax laws and reporting standards to boost long termism and FCLT agrees, calling also for long-term shareholders to be given increased voting rights or dividends compared with their more ephemeral colleagues. These are ideas worth considering.

Clearly not every company has a purpose other than that which it says on the tin. The values-driven purpose is an ethical statement, a declaration of where the company fits into society and not just the market place. Purists claim that the business with a social purpose and the one which is exclusively an economic entity are the twain that shall never meet, but it must be possible to transition from being a for-profit company with no stated values or purpose to one which has both, for this is the route to Company Citizenship.

Many mission-led businesses are literally purpose-built and, in the absence of a required constitution, certification procedure or legal status, it's not difficult for others to contemplate transition. Such a change will always be harder for larger organisations due to the difficulty in getting employees and operations distant from the core to commit to the essential 'buy in' to the proposed mission. Leopards in the business jungle can – and must be able to – change their spots although, like oil tankers, they can't do it in a hurry. A surprise announcement from the boardroom that 'from today we're a mission-led business' doesn't sound authentic and is unlikely to succeed. Whilst this sort of enthusiasm is essential, so are preparation, planning and patience.

The chosen purpose or mission must be relevant to the company and its stakeholders, not least to the employees who are both its productivity engine and its ambassadors. Employees at all levels of company hierarchy need to relate to that purpose and this can't be imposed; if the values behind it are too abstract, or employees feel no degree of ownership or empathy, transition will fail.

Tomorrow's Company has identified a number of potential barriers to a company successfully imbuing its activities with purpose and values but there are 'fixes' for all of them, the most universal of which is patience. They note that it's easier to create purpose and values in a start-up than in an established company; growth targets can blur the purpose by diverting attention away from the qualitative. Short-term pressures distract, as banks found when clumsily maximising sales of payment protection insurance rather than working with clients to assess what was best for them and how the bank could (profitably) help them attain it. Perhaps the biggest danger is lack of authenticity: if those driving values and purpose don't sound genuine then embedding is at risk. Complex messages amidst a forest of communication don't help and there's a chance that a boardroom initiative on purpose, aimed at employee foot soldiers, could inadvertently fail to engage middle management whose role it should be to deliver those goals.[17]

Unilever was voted the seventh best company to work for in Britain in 2017 in a poll of employees that was topped by Expedia.[18] Rising up from ninth, its strong sense of purpose must help – Unilever regards it as: 'The highest standards of corporate behaviour towards everyone we work with, the communities we touch, and the environment on which we have an impact.'

This is backed by four values: integrity, respect, responsibility and the pioneer spirit. In turn these are supported by 14 code principles which cover the 'how' of ethical business.[19] Then follows 42 pages of detail, though to anyone who understands their values and principles these contain few surprises. Very little of the content is focused on food and household products, Unilever's 'bread and butter', all are of general application; and the pursuit of profit is not even mentioned. Commitments to shareholders are cast in terms of good governance and transparency rather than on maximising returns. Unilever's CEO, Paul Polman, says of the pursuit of purpose: 'You need to . . . have an impact that aligns with your values. It will drive your passion.'

Purposefulness could boost company performance in the UK by up to 7 per cent in productivity and sales, reports the Big Innovation Centre, in a country where two thirds of companies underperform. Purposefulness brings stakeholders together in common cause, inspires customers, motivates employees and engages suppliers. By failing to create purposeful businesses, whether by neglect or design, UK companies are losing the equivalent of £130bn/year, they say.[20] Will Hutton goes on to describe the purposeful company as one where policies on reporting, capital investment and pay support each other in each cycle of purpose development.

Trust in business is falling at the same time as our expectation that business should be open and responsible is rising; delivering purpose on societal issues may help restore confidence.

London and Harvard Business Schools monitored the progress of 180 American companies whose ambitions were ranked as 'high' sustainability or 'low', over 18 years. The high sustainability companies had ESG policies not only on climate change but on work-life balance, human rights and more and a generally positive understanding of the relationship between business and society, says Professor Ioannis Ioannou. That sense of place and mission drove a commitment to purpose, a framework against which every kind of corporate behaviour could be judged.[21]

The research concluded that high sustainability companies were managed in a fundamentally different manner than others. Sustainability became a purpose around which the board could unite and engage, especially when executive and other pay levels were linked to sustainability outcomes (as at Intel). Thinking became more long term, attracting a more stable and patient investor, creating a better environment for innovation. Stakeholder engagement was deeper and more coherent than in low sustainability companies and non-financial issues played a bigger role in the company's deliberations. All this led to greater levels of transparency, putting much high-quality data into the public domain. From such outcomes they concluded that companies which fail to send out a consistent and credible message about who they are don't establish their purpose in the minds of stakeholders; such as when social responsibility is part of the media rhetoric but only financial performance is incentivised. Those that set broad, ambitious but achievable goals are more likely to inspire, enable and empower their teams at all levels.

Purpose-driven companies, the researchers went on, offer a more secure, vibrant work environment than others, one that promotes experimentation and tolerates failure. Stakeholder management is the job of all managers, they conclude, not just company leaders, and the social licence to operate depends upon it. Such companies invest their way out of difficulty, not cut, and they use sensible metrics to report on financial and non-financial issues with equal fervour.

Finally, after the 18-year study was over, they added one more conclusion: the high-sustainability companies had dramatically outperformed the low-sustainability ones in stock market and other measures of financial performance. Professor Alex Edmans of London Business School, in parallel work, showed that over a 26-year period companies with a clear purpose outperformed the market by 2–3 per cent every year[22] whilst Unilever reports that its 17 brands which have 'integrated sustainability' into them, including Lifebuoy and Knorr, are growing 30 per cent faster than others; those Sustainable Development Goals, says Paul Polman, are 'the economic opportunity of a lifetime' for business.[23]

Purpose, declare those who have embedded it into their business, works.

Zappos was established in 1999 to sell shoes online, becoming part of the Amazon empire ten years later. Despite amalgamation, the values of the company – couched in rather Californian terms – have survived: 'We seek to WOW our customers, our co-workers, our vendors, our partners, and in the long run, our investors.'[24]

Embracing change, creating fun, 'weirdness', creativity, family spirit, passion and humility are also Zappos' values. New employees are trained in both the nuts and bolts of the business and its philosophical approach, following which they're offered $5,000 to walk away. Those that refuse the payment are hired in the knowledge that their personal values are worth more to the employee than filthy lucre.

Novo Nordisk is more conventional. It's been fighting diabetes, obesity, haemophilia and growth disorders through medical and technological innovation for 90 years: 'Every day we must make difficult choices, always keeping in mind what is best for patients, our employees and our shareholders in the long run.'[25]

The 'Novo Nordisk Way' talks of ambitions, aspirations, ethics, values and passion. They practice investment in people, long-term, triple bottom-line accounting and integrated reporting. They're definitely a business and not a charity, though they're nominally owned by a Danish Foundation: 'Growing our business and delivering competitive financial results is what allows us to help patients live better lives, offer an attractive return to our shareholders and contribute to our communities.'

In 2016 they grew profits by 32 per cent, topping $5bn, paying more than $1bn in tax. Their 42,000 employees served 27 million diabetes patients (up 10 per cent in a year) while reducing their carbon footprint by a tenth; they aim for zero carbon by 2020. They meet up to half of global demand for insulin.[26] I've great respect for this model and approach, but is it really necessary to make a surplus profit of $5bn in a single year?

It's said that the aim of every charity should be to put itself out of business, to end the injustice against which it campaigns – such as disease or poverty. Novo Nordisk, which has considered and rejected diversification away from its key purpose, has that goal in sight too – as Lars Sørenson ('Global CEO of the Year', 2015) told *Harvard Business Review*:

> After I became CEO, in 2000, I predicted we would cure diabetes in 15 years. We're still 15 years away. But that's the big goal. I tell my employees, if we wind up curing diabetes and that destroys a big part of our business, we can be proud, and you can get a job anywhere.[27]

Another pharmaceutical company, GSK, has had its share of the spotlight in recent years but under Sir Andrew Whitty made great strides in re-energising the ethical basis of their work. GSK's mission – 'to help people do more, feel better, live longer' – is underpinned by core values: to be patient and consumer focused, act with integrity, demonstrate respect for people and operate with transparency. The values are actively promoted across the international workforce. Practices which were open to abuse in the past, such as paying healthcare professionals to promote products amongst those who could influence prescribing policy, have ended and the company's approach to transparency now goes well beyond industry standards. L'Oreal lists courage as a value: making the right call on difficult ethical decisions, speaking out, deploying its other values of respect, transparency and integrity. L'Oreal recently sold ethical pioneer The Body Shop to the world's largest B Corp, Natura; falling profits at Anita Roddick's creation for five of its ten years under L'Oreal might be linked to the claim that their ethical roots and sustainable purpose are no longer as distinctive as they once were. No doubt Natura will address that.[28] Insurance giant Aviva has an ethical code of four values, five principles and a toolkit, to which every employee is asked to commit on an annual basis.[29]

Throughout this debate there's considerable blurring of the concepts of purpose, mission, goals and values. Ultimately purpose is what drives a company forward and there's ample evidence that when the purpose and mission properly embody human values the company gains both reputation and profitability. Perhaps the key questions should be:

- *What* does your company do? The mission.
- *Why* does it do it? A statement of purpose and context.
- *How* does it do it? Its framework of values and principles.
- *Where* does it intend to go in the future? Mission, goals and progress in practice.

Blueprint's Loughlin Hickey sums it up:

> You could conclude that . . . financial and market value define what matters most, and that human value is just a means for achieving it. Such a conclusion misunderstands the relationship between the two; financial value is an outcome of creating human value in a business context, not the measure of it. Human value – understood as the value the business delivers to society – is what matters more.[30]

NewCo has no particular claim to the moral high ground but it does provide a platform for companies to share passion and purpose. The NewCo movement is neither a legal status nor a certification scheme but a coming together of for-profit companies, of all shapes and sizes, who want to do things differently. They're enablers, collaborators, innovators, they're transparent, open-minded and nimble, connected to communities, each other and the world through the internet. Starting in San Francisco five years ago like-minded companies are in 16 cities around the world, mostly in the US but including London; driven by ideas and stories they see business as an expression of identity and reject the old corporate model of 'command and control'. Most are small, all are ambitious and mission-driven but signatories include Google, whose goal is to make information accessible to all, P&G, Barclays and the BBC.[31]

On one day in May 2017, 44 London NewCos opened their doors and invited the world in. Many of the day's 300 visitors were London Business School MBA students and alumni, sharing hour-long seminars in up to five premises during the day. Of the three I visited, one celebrates good food and good cooking by serving up packs of ingredients for you to cook at home – with close to zero waste. The 300 UK employees 'serve' customers every day across nine countries, all coming with typical NewCo condiments of happy excitement, powerful enthusiasm and innovative flair. Another works with major charities to develop new forms of fundraising, motivated by the fact that new regulations look set to cost the sector dearly. The new era they anticipate is unwaveringly online where they seek to promote commerce, extend markets and develop business strategies. Using the tools of business, as it were, to create public good. A third is a vibrant incubator of new talent, with a good record of turning ideas into business reality. In recent years 35 of the 40 start-ups it's launched have failed – that's the way of the world. Having one in eight ideas succeed is a good rate, achieved by encouraging the positive attributes of innovation to go to scale.

This movement has an energy which is rare amongst businesses. NewCos are driven by purpose, integrating traditional business rules with a positive outlook on life. It would be wonderful to think that a movement measured in hundreds could become mainstream within a decade.

Phil Knight says that success is a matter of belief, that selling mutual funds and encyclopaedias early in his career wasn't successful because believing in 'selling' didn't create a common bond with the people to whom he was selling. Nor did a belief in shoes; but his belief in running – that it was healthy, pleasurable, positive – was something that customers, he found, did want to share. So he founded Nike.[32]

In February 2017 an attempted predatory takeover of Unilever by the American company Kraft Heinz, possibly prompted by the imbalance between UK and US currencies that followed the Brexit vote, was rebuffed in no uncertain terms. Kraft doesn't have the most sensitive and caring of reputations and British memories were raw with the disappointment that followed their acquisition of Cadbury a few years earlier. After a skirmish which lasted barely a weekend it was clear that neither the British business establishment nor public mood wanted the Unilever takeover to go ahead. Paul Polman summed up his feelings of the incompatibility of the two companies' values in an email to me at the time: 'One [was] seeking value for a few, the other seeking values for many.'

As Robert Philips of Jericho Chambers consultancy so rightly has it: 'Purpose means nothing unless you do something.'[33]

The circular economy

Companies such as Walmart and Unilever have managed to increase both their turnover and their profits whilst reducing their carbon footprint. Can we apply the same principle to physical things as they do to energy?

We know that shortage of commodities raises costs, forcing radical rethinking: many metals, for example, will cease to be commercially extractable within two or three decades. Those already extracted become lost to future generations because of our traditional approach of turning them into products and later discarding them irresponsibly. The Circular Economy addresses these issues.

Each year about 70 billion tonnes of raw materials enters the world's supply chains that are not replaced – the planet is literally being eaten up. In Scotland alone, where the government has already adopted circular economy principles, about £10m worth of gold enters the country each year inside manufactured goods such as televisions and mobile phones, gold that once hidden inside such products would never be seen nor accounted for again. The Scottish government has set out a comprehensive strategy of slashing energy usage, cutting food waste by a third and investing £70m in the processes of redesign that new approaches to manufacturing will need to meet. There's a political, as well as environmental and economic potential in the circular economy.[34]

Before 1996 the UK Government imposed no tax on the dumping of waste in licensed sites such as former quarries. Apart from restrictions on toxic waste almost anything could find its final resting place in a hole in the ground. In creating a tax of £7/tonne John Major's government introduced the first environmental levy to discourage the use of landfill except where there was no feasible alternative, thereby promoting other means of safe disposal such as recycling. In that first year revenue from the tax was almost half a billion pounds – we had a lot of holes needing filling – but the aim was always to steadily increase the rate. Today it's over £80/tonne, although inert or 'natural' waste is only taxed at £2.50/tonne (plus site fees).

Since 2004, despite population growth, annual household waste going to landfill has fallen slightly, to about 25m tonnes, but industrial waste other than construction has halved – to around 40m tonnes. Construction's inert waste remains steady at around 100m tonnes. Recycling rates have been close to target as a result, in part, of increasing Landfill Tax. Since 2009 electricity generated from waste has doubled.

But Landfill Tax is only a start. As an approach to waste management the old mantra of 'reduce, re-use, recycle' has had to become more sophisticated. In the 'Circular Economy' a business case is made not only for reducing waste to an absolute minimum, by regarding end-of-life products as a resource rather than something to be jettisoned, but also for product design to facilitate end-of-life processing. It rejects the old approach of planned obsolescence, even anticipating a reduced carbon footprint throughout the whole product lifecycle. Failing components can be readily substituted so, when one part fails, the whole creation doesn't have to be abandoned; ease of repair is enabled by design. Re-use is there again but it's global, assuming a market for second-hand goods, but then there's a new stage: refurbish, designing products so that when they die all of their components can be re-used as though they carried a universal donor card. The last resort is not refuse but our old friend recycle, to deconstruct the object to its materials and find new homes for them.

If 'rejoice' is the celebration of longevity then the mantra has become 'rethink, reduce, rejoice, repair, re-use, refurbish, recycle'.

The Circular Economy must be part of the way forward: we can't just wish resources into existence that can no longer be secured from the ground. First postulated in the 1970s, its prime advocate today is Dame Ellen MacArthur, who went from a champion solo sailor to high priestess of sustainability in barely ten years. Working with McKinsey and others, her Foundation brings together thinkers, business people, economists and environmentalists to develop ideas around this minimum impact approach to business. Their 2012 report, supported by 'founding partners' B&Q, BT, Cisco, National Grid and Renault, argued that between then and 2020 a circular-economy approach could generate $630bn each year across Europe by stimulating economic activity in product development, remanufacturing and refurbishment. The European Union agreed.[35]

The Foundation describes the Circular Economy's ability to increase the productivity of materials as being powered by four qualities.

1 The power of the inner circle: the tighter the circle, the less a product needs to change between use and re-use, the faster it does so, with consequent savings in labour, energy and materials, reducing negative externalities.
2 The power of circling longer: designing products to be re-used several times before repair and refurbishment are initiated.

3 The power of cascaded use: some products lose characteristics with constant re-use but their utility can still be maximised. (Cotton clothing can be repaired and re-used repeatedly but loses texture with use. Its fibres may become upholstery filling or insulation material before burial and decomposition.)
4 The power of pure circles: minimising contamination reduces reprocessing costs throughout the cycle.

Levi Strauss has the technology to turn five used cotton tee-shirts into a pair of 511 jeans indistinguishable from the original and H&M is doing something similar. Interface is well on the way to making new carpets out of . . . old carpets, using new technology to separate carpet fibre from its backing. Ninety-two per cent of Nike waste is reused and over 70 per cent of their products now include recovered materials. Dell's aim of a 'closed-loop supply chain' is more advanced than any other computer manufacturer and Patagonia not only sponsors America's largest garment repair service but sells used clothing too.[36] Within hiking distance of the Peak District is Made by Scavenger; they deconstruct worn-out climbing gear, tarpaulins and outdoor equipment to make attractive accessories for walkers and climbers. They have a dozen collection points and sell through 20 shops, though it's tough to compete with new, imported, Chinese goods.[37]

Within this approach, almost a philosophy, is the concept of the sharing economy. This argues that we have enough 'things' already: on a housing estate does every home really need its own electric drill? Gardening tools? Food processor? *Sound of Music* DVD? By sharing these and other resources – cooking together, perhaps – neighbours could cut costs and get more usage from the products they already own, collectively, by creating a sharing community using a local aggregator platform (see Chapter 8).[38] Leasing washing machines to a community, rather than selling to many individuals, can generate savings for both people and their environment and more profit per machine for the manufacturer.

No desperate measure, at a time of resource stress adversity the Circular Economy is an exciting opportunity for the Company Citizen to develop new skills, new products and new senses: of both achievement and of being at one with the world.

The inclusive economy

Inclusive growth, says the United Nations Development Programme, is at the heart of an inclusive economy:

> Growth is inclusive when it takes place in the sectors in which the poor work (e.g. agriculture); occurs in places where the poor live (undeveloped areas with few resources); uses the factors of production that the poor possess (unskilled labour); and reduces the prices of consumption of items that the poor consume (food, fuel and clothing).[39]

The UNDP were referring to countries where incomes are under $8 per day. Home to 4 billion people worldwide, this is where companies like Unilever and IKEA are developing a sustainable approach to the triple bottom line. Under the heading 'Inclusive business', Unilever writes:

> As a result of our scale, we have a unique opportunity to include millions of people in our business, for example: smallholder farmers who may lack access to skills or markets; small-scale retailers who can earn a living by starting or expanding a business selling our products; and young entrepreneurs who may need training.
>
> In this way, we can promote strong, healthy communities that work to respect rights. At the same time, this is an opportunity to expand the market for our products and make our business model more resilient in an uncertain world.[40]

It's easy to see how inclusive business practices might be more effective in a poorer country than in a rich one. Poor countries contain high numbers of potential new customers, people who're not only not buying your product yet but aren't buying that of your rivals either. As Unilever has found, packaging goods such as soap powder in smaller parcels makes them more affordable by poorer families – any added cost of production per kilo can be mitigated by reducing the packaging (an environmental benefit) and other technological innovations. Marketing is cheaper than in richer countries and there are new opportunities for low-cost marketing, such as through mobile phone technology in Africa. Britain's higher income base, despite its growing inequalities, means that the relative potential of pro-poor marketing here may not be as high and the temptation to say 'it's the state's role to look after them' higher, but our state is failing on many fronts; might inclusive business principles apply here too?

In 2016, at a summit where Australia's Malcolm Turnbull called upon global policymakers to 'civilise capitalism', the G20 group of nations acknowledged the need for 'more inclusive growth' within their own borders. 'Growth' has too often been seen, especially in red and green political camps, as the enemy, capitalism rampant, only interested in profit; a consumer of resources inconsistent with environmental sustainability and associated with the trickle-down theory of wealth sharing that has comprehensively failed to deliver. Much of this is true, yet growth itself is values-free. Criticisms of 'growth' are invariably criticisms of the means used to achieve it and despair at how its products have been distributed. Creating 50,000 jobs in recycling, environmental protection and renewable energy might sound like a green nirvana, but they would still show as 'growth' on the national balance sheet. 'Growth' has to be on our agenda because its opposites, recession and depression, are no one's friend.

The British Government recognised the dangers of divisiveness and the benefits of economic inclusion at home in 2016 with the launch of its Inclusive Economy Unit, aimed at building 'an economy and a Britain that works for everyone, not just the privileged few'.

For a Conservative government this was a first, perhaps bringing Mrs May's 'head' to the 'heart' behind the 'Big Society' of her immediate predecessor. David Cameron took social enterprise and impact investment seriously, but it's to Theresa May's credit that she aligned these values with mainstream domestic economic thinking. Unfortunately, the unit was based in the Office for Civil Society (aka the charity brief) within the Department of Digital, Culture, Media and Sport, a result of her 'shuffle for shuffle's sake' upon coming to office in 2016. Few take this juxtaposition seriously, and there's doubt that the unit will have the clout to make a difference across government.

Nevertheless, the goals are laudable. They include giving greater priority to (private) investments that generate social returns, improving commissioning within the public service and encouraging 'responsible business' through companies that deliver 'profit with purpose'.[41]

Such harmony between social and economic policy will be welcomed by many, not least as this was advocated by the RSA's Inclusive Growth Commission, which also called for an industrial strategy for Britain linking physical and human infrastructure, plus:

> We need to change the policy and measurement frameworks for major investments to tilt the balance towards more broadly defined growth benefits. The report proposes 'quality GVA' [Gross Value Added] as a wider measurement framework for growth, enabling us to measure not just aggregate growth, but also changes in inequality, the impact of investment on deprived populations and how far economic prosperity has spread.[42]

Inherent in this is what RSA and others call 'place-based' development alongside 'devo-max', the maximum devolution of decision-making power. This would allow communities – not least cities – to take more responsibility for what happens politically and economically in their regions on the basis of subsidiarity, taking decisions at the most appropriate level of government. During an extensive period of consultation the response of business was so mixed, with many larger companies said to be lacking any sense of 'place', that specific recommendations on their future role were not included in the final RSA report. Pity.

Stephanie Flanders, the economist who chaired the Commission, says that much of the angst associated with Britain's 'no' to the European Union might properly be seen as rejecting an economic system that fails to include, empower and reward those at the base of the economic pyramid, a system of which the EU is only a part. No Brexiteer, Flanders makes the point that creating an inclusive economy involves leaving behind old assumptions and juxtapositions and that Britain, unlike other countries facing similar quandaries, has perhaps declared that it's ready for radical change.[43] Perhaps.

One wouldn't expect an oil company like Exxon Mobil to announce something like: 'The concept that growth will "trickle down" to the poor and most disadvantaged among us has been proven to be fundamentally flawed.'[44] Yet this is the conclusion the Rockefeller Foundation has reached. Over 100 years ago, one of the world's largest charities (today's assets are over $4bn) was endowed by 'America's greatest philanthropist' John D. Rockefeller, from the wealth of Standard Oil, the precursor of Esso and Exxon Mobil. Economies, says the Foundation, should focus on investment from the bottom up and, whilst both growth and the development of equities are important, they shouldn't divert attention from the needs of the poor and vulnerable. Equal opportunities for all and guaranteed levels of security and economic predictability are at the heart of the inclusive economy, the output of which should be a more equitable distribution of property and wellbeing.

Even entrepreneurs, early in their career, are ordinary people. They live in communities. They have ideas and drive and they need access to investment. But if they come from a deprived community, with a dysfunctional micro-economy, and succeed against the odds they tend to leave that community behind. Bottom-of-the-pyramid communities have fewer businesses in them than others so that key link between entrepreneur, workforce and community is broken. Our most deprived communities, that most lack supportive social infrastructure, are also those which most lack opportunity through work. Businesses can both provide these qualities and benefit from doing so, which explains why far-sighted investors such as Bridges Ventures practice inclusive economics by prioritising investments in deprived communities – though it's an uphill job.

In most European countries between 2 and 3.5 per cent of adults are business owners. UK is at the top of that range and we do even better on younger entrepreneurs.[45] Access to capital is universally the biggest barrier to success by entrepreneurs across Europe, raising again the fundamental question of whether banks' limited appetite for risk can support the inclusive economy of the future; we need banks to return to the purposes for which they were created 200 years ago, of making partners of lenders and borrowers.

An inclusive economy is a framework within which the social responsibilities of business are recognised and promoted without removing companies' historic role in innovation and wealth creation. It promotes economic growth in which the benefits are shared more equitably than they are at present: Virgin Mobile Australia allows customers to donate unused data allowance to friends – and strangers – who can't afford their own data plan, thus broadening digital access.

Inclusive markets function better and give a higher priority to individual and community wellbeing, especially of the underprivileged. They better define income and wellbeing thresholds, below which people should not be allowed to fall. They encourage social mobility, with a greater emphasis on developing the skills that individuals, businesses and communities will need in the future; social and economic resilience, protection against shock. An inclusive economy sees all of these things in a longer-term perspective than most do today and performs them all in ways which are sustainable, in every sense of the word.

It's about doing all of these things in partnership, business, workforce, entrepreneurs and civil society, rich and poor, with a facilitating and empowering, but not overpowering, state using its economic levers to support the process.

Cemex 'got' inclusion back in 1998. About 40 per cent of Mexican users of their building products were self-builders, people too poor to buy or build a home in any other way, with whom the company had literally no relationship. They bought bricks by the dozen, not by the ton. Prior to that Cemex 'did' CSR where their employees worked, not where their poorest customers lived. Conventional marketing to these shanty-town communities didn't work. Recruiting and empowering women from those communities to take out their messages, by word of mouth, about buying bricks and cement was more effective – but only when combined with an innovative credit scheme designed for low-income households and access to affordable advice on how best to build your home. Today the Patrimonio Hoy scheme, never regarded as philanthropic, strictly commercial, operates across five Latin American countries, has a credit repayment rate of almost 100 per cent and has won several awards.

Cemex reports that staff, directly involved in Patrimonio Hoy or not, get huge job satisfaction and pride from watching customers break out of the poverty trap and that the scheme is a commercial success.[46] They don't call it 'inclusion'. They call it 'understanding our market'.

They ask: 'Why don't others follow?'

Getting away with it

Are companies' commitments to social and environmental responsibility as genuine as they would like us to think?

There's no doubt that a reputation based on company citizenship is beneficial when selling to the public. Transparency helps to protect that reputation – it's integral to the 'G' of ESG – the environmental, social and governance criteria by which responsible businesses are measured.

If your reputation for tackling climate change was good, way beyond that required in law, why might you want to oppose tighter regulations on carbon emissions? Here are two possible reasons for a company wanting to deter others from meeting the obligations endowed by its own statement of values.

1. Perhaps the good behaviour which separates you from the pack is such a commercial boon that you don't want to see competitors operate at the same standard. 'A rising tide floats all boats' and the munificence that distinguishes you would be devalued, even lost, if others were required to be as good as you.
2. Or maybe you consider your high level of achievement has come at a cost which you aren't prepared to pay in perpetuity; you may wish to relax your performance and can envisage a future in which a higher minimum regulatory standard may embarrass you.

So how do you stand out as an icon of good practice whilst encouraging the authorities to undermine the very standards which you champion? You get a trade association to do it for you.

Britain's 1,600 trade associations and their European partners provide advice and services to their members and are especially helpful to smaller businesses who lack resources such as in-house legal advice. They're advocates for their industry and often its public face, though some get accused of anticompetitive behaviour by arbitrarily limiting admission to a market. And they are lobbyists on behalf of their sector, attempting to influence public policy. To some, membership of an association is routine, what's expected; it provides access to support, reassurance on a rainy day, entry to networks that help generate future business. As with a roadside rescue service, you may join in the fervent hope that you'll never need to use it. Whilst trade associations will protest that they can do only what their members allow, in many cases it's unlikely that a majority of their members have ever spoken out on any subject, let alone done so in harmony. Some claim to follow their members rather than lead, an excuse for lacking innovation or originality, but in other cases it's puzzling to work out from where particular mandates – such as opposing climate change regulation – have come from.

ShareAction buys small numbers of shares in big companies in order to contribute an ethical voice to corporate annual meetings. My first experience as a volunteer in their 'AGM Army' was in 2015, at the chemical giant Johnson Matthey. Pioneers of catalytic converters, Johnson Matthey is sound on environmental issues.

The Chair invited representatives of 145 million shares to put questions to the board. I asked: 'How does this reputable and sustainable company, a sector leader on environmental matters, square this position with membership of two European trade associations which lobby against the EU taking a lead on tackling climate change?' The Chair welcomed my 'important question' but denied specific knowledge of such clashes. However, he clearly accepted that they could challenge the company's credibility and promised an investigation. In a brief conversation afterwards he conceded that the European chemical industry didn't speak with a common and progressive voice on climate issues and implied that the industry should be taking climate change more seriously.

Governments listen, of course, to business. They need to know what it needs, how they can help and how business perceives barriers to progress. How much easier it is to listen to trade associations than to canvass the views of every individual company. Government doesn't ask how representative an association is, that's a matter for the members. Access to politicians by proxy is another reason why companies join trade associations, though hundreds of members will rarely be unanimous in their priorities.

So who exactly does a trade association represent? A paper by Transparency International (TI) describes lobbying via a trade association as a 'blunt instrument': their views may represent either the lowest common denominator of opinion or the organisation's loudest voices, not necessarily the majority. Some companies' views are in direct contradiction to those expressed by their association; yet lobbyists prefer to prosecute causes with bold clarity rather than subtle nuance. Even though companies may champion accountability in their own governance, the way by which their trade association decides priorities is often obscure.[47] Transparency International report that three quarters of the world's largest 500 companies use trade associations to lobby on climate change, more than on any other policy, and those associations campaign almost exclusively against regulation. The US Chamber of Commerce, a giant amongst lobbyists, spent $35m on the 2014 Federal elections – over and above political advertising costs. Apple had already resigned from USCC, in 2009, over the association's climate scepticism and in 2014 Unilever quit Business Europe when the latter's call for deregulation on climate issues clashed with Unilever's own stance of improving standards.[48]

The UN Principles of Responsible Investment has commented on the dichotomy between what companies say and what trade associations claim on their behalf:

> While an increasing number of companies have robust climate change policies and position statements and play a constructive role in policy discussions, we are concerned that many are also members or supporters of trade associations, think tanks and other third-party organisations who lobby against policies to mitigate climate change in a way which is inconsistent with our goal of maximising long term portfolio value.

Transparency ought to be at the heart of any representative organisation but that's inconsistent with serving influential vested interests. Perhaps the time has come for ordinary members of trade associations to be heard – to make sure that these organisations really do speak in the long-term interests of Company Citizens.

Notes

1 www.bbc.co.uk/news/business-34989844.
2 www.home.barclays/content/dam/barclayspublic/docs/AboutUs/Purpose-Values/BAR_TheBarclaysWay%20cropped%2023_07_2015.pdf.
3 In May 2016 Antony Jenkins spoke with Mark Goyder of Tomorrow's Company on values and innovation: http://tomorrowscompany.com/publication/discussion-antony-jenkins/.
4 www.iccwbo.org/products-and-services/trade-facilitation/9-steps-to-responsible-business-conduct/.
5 www.cauxroundtable.org/index.cfm?menuid=8.
6 http://hrlibrary.umn.edu/links/sullivanprinciples.html. (See also *Welcome to GoodCo.*)
7 www.blueprintforbusiness.org/purpose/.
8 Ibid.
9 www.adweek.com/brand-marketing/brands-have-learned-the-value-of-purpose-now-they-must-actually-become-purpose-led/.

10 http://drcaroladams.net/understanding-the-importance-of-values-to-the-sustain ability-agenda/.
11 www.gov.uk/government/uploads/system/uploads/attachment_data/file/574694/Advisory_Panel_Report_-_Mission-led_Business.pdf.
12 http://bcorporation.uk.
13 www.bigsocietycapital.com/sites/default/files/attachments/In%20pursuit%20of%20impact.pdf.
14 www.centreforsocialjustice.org.uk/library/everyones-business-making-business-work.
15 http://biginnovationcentre.com/media/uploads/pdf/TPC_Policy%20Report.pdf.
16 www.fcltglobal.org.
17 http://tomorrowscompany.com/wp-content/uploads/2016/05/Embedding-purpose-roundtable-summary-17th-September-1.pdf. Following the general election of 2017 Grant Thornton published a call to arms on 'purpose': www.grantthornton.co.uk/en/insights/a-blueprint-for-the-uk-recommendations-on-trust/.
18 www.telegraph.co.uk/business/2016/12/07/revealed-top-10-ukcompanies-work-2017/.
19 www.unilever.co.uk/about/who-we-are/purpose-and-principles/.
20 www.biginnovationcentre.com/media/uploads/pdf/The%20Purposeful%20Company%20Interim%20Report.pdf.
21 www.london.edu/faculty-and-research/lbsr/li-four-principles-translating-purpose-into-practice#.WFLzoXecaRt.
22 Told to a Blueprint for Better Business event, September 2016. Professor Edmans' TED talk on social responsibility is also recommended: www.youtube.com/watch?v=Z5KZhm19EO0.
23 www.theguardian.com/sustainable-business/2016/sep/30/businesses-ignore-un-sustainable-development-goals-survey?CMP=ema-1706&CMP=.
24 www.zapposinsights.com/about/zappos/our-unique-culture.
25 www.novonordisk.co.uk/about-novo-nordisk-in-uk/novo-nordisk-way.html.
26 www.novonordisk.com/content/dam/Denmark/HQ/AnnualReport/2016/PDF/Novo-Nordisk-Annual-Report-2016.pdf.
27 https://hbr.org/2015/11/novo-nordisk-ceo-on-what-propelled-him-to-the-top.
28 www.ft.com/content/09bd4432-ef9f-11e6-930f-061b01e23655 and www.bbc.co.uk/news/business-40417961.
29 www.ibe.org.uk/default.aspx?upid=142&pname=30-Days-of-Ethics.
30 www.jerichochambers.com/relationships-of-value/.
31 https://newco.co.
32 https://medium.com/startupph-chronicles/a-sales-lesson-from-phil-knight-founder-of-nike-dd00a21c8d8#.ss64xrc27.
33 www.managementtoday.co.uk/purpose-means-nothing-unless-actually-some thing/reputation-matters/article/1434813#GtAvsQ3cOhdtfiVr.99.
34 www.gov.scot/Resource/0049/00494471.pdf.
35 www.ellenmacarthurfoundation.org/publications.
36 www.triplepundit.com/2016/09/3p-weekend-7-companies-making-circular-economy-reality/.
37 www.madebyscavenger.com.
38 http://thepeoplewhoshare.com/re.com/index.cfm/.
39 www.undp.org/content/undp/en/home/blog/2015/7/31/What-does-inclusive-economic-growth-actually-mean-in-practice-.html.
40 www.unilever.com/sustainable-living/the-sustainable-living-plan/enhancing-live lihoods/inclusive-business/.

41 www.gov.uk/government/news/government-announces-inclusive-economy-unit. The Inclusive Economy Partnership, an impressive collection of business and civil society leaders with ministers, met for the first time in September 2017. www.gov.uk/government/news/business-and-civil-society-leaders-form-partnership-to-tackle-challenges-in-society.

42 www.thersa.org/discover/publications-and-articles/reports/emerging-findings-of-the-inclusive-growth-commission.

43 'Growing Together', in 'The Inclusive Economy', *RSA Journal* 3, 2016; www.thersa.org/discover/publications-and-articles/reports/final-report-of-the-inclusive-growth-commission. See also www.jrf.org.uk/blog/what-inclusive-growth-and-why-does-it-matter.

44 www.rockefellerfoundation.org/blog/five-characteristics-inclusive-economy-getting-beyond-equity-growth-dichotomy/.

45 www.oecd-ilibrary.org/industry-and-services/inclusive-business-creation-good-practice-compendium_9789264251496-en.

46 www.linkedin.com/pulse/opportunity-new-age-uncertainty-javier-santoyo-mba?.

47 www.transparency.org.uk/publications/wise-counsel-or-dark-arts-principles-and-guidance-for-responsible-corporate-political-engagement/.

48 https://business-humanrights.org/en/unilever-quits-businesseurope-following-tensions-over-lobby-groups-stance-on-environment-climate-change.

5 Stakeholders are ready

Everything a business does must make sense, support its long-term plans and be in accord with whatever values, mission and purpose it has adopted to guide its work. No company operates in isolation; stakeholders are those whose lives are impacted by a business as it carries out its mission. Owners, shareholders, investors, customers, suppliers, neighbours and employees are 'the family' to whom a business owes loyalty, predictability, respect and a duty of care.

The shareholder

Few shareholders are dependent on massive blocks of shares in a single company; most invest in portfolios. Nevertheless, some shareholders believe they are *primus inter pares* of stakeholders, that companies exist solely for their benefit – and US law has always supported this idea. However, UK statute law has not, though case law has upheld shareholder rights in the face of unreasonable behaviour: in 1883 the directors of the West Cork Railway were deemed wrong to divide the residual assets amongst themselves, rather than the shareholders, when the company was wound up. Prior to 1850 shareholding was rare, shareholders had little influence on the running of companies and most ownership was by families, owner managers whose generational horizons gave them a paternalistic, inclusive view of their socially immobile workforce. Indeed, only since the 1980s has the language of corporate success used the vocabulary of share price growth. Before then the dividend was the driving force, reflecting loyal shareholders' longer-term interest in company fortunes. The rise of shareholder influence in the mid-twentieth century was, perhaps naively (given the consequent move towards short-termism), regarded by many as the democratisation of business, a development of the 'common good', epitomising Margaret Thatcher's vision of the 'shareholding democracy'.[1]

Whilst the 2006 Companies Act lays down in statute the responsibilities of directors to company owners (read: 'shareholders') it places that responsibility in a broad context, insisting that managers should 'have regard' to the impact of their actions upon employees, customers, suppliers and the wider community: the stakeholders. It's sometimes argued that Section 172 instils the primacy of the shareholder for the first time – but no company has ever invoked that clause as a reason to abandon progress towards meeting the broad responsibilities of Company Citizenship. Section 172 says that the duty of directors is to: 'Promote the success of the company for the benefit of its members as a whole.'

This allows for a narrow, profit-orientated definition of 'success' but doesn't insist upon it. 'Success' is a broad term and 'have regard' and 'as a whole' are even more vague.

Directors aren't moral arbiters: the Act obliges them to behave as balanced citizens, not as profit-hungry automata. A decade later it's time to review the Act, make it even more citizenship-orientated. At the very least it should toughen its influence beyond the 1,000 or so large companies currently obliged to report on the discharge of their social and environmental responsibilities. Private companies, owned by individuals, families or partnerships, aren't covered by this part of the legislation although France has shown that there's no good reason why not.

The primacy of the shareholder is a myth, at least in the UK. No matter that it's paradoxical, says the estimable commentator Professor John Kay, but: 'The era of shareholder value is coming to an end.'[2] At how many Annual General Meetings, where directors are held nominally accountable to the body of shareholders, does the Chairman sit with a pocket of proxy votes lined up to support whatever management proposes? We'll consider some of the issues which create friction between forward-looking shareholders and management, often backed by a supine conservative faction, later. Directors will often argue that maximum shareholder value is best created by delivering results as soon as possible – another myth. Short-termism is known to produce suboptimal returns: long-term markets, especially those defined as ethical, consistently produce better returns in terms of dividend, share price and Total Shareholder Value. When Unilever broke from the pack and ceased quarterly reporting in favour of annual, in 2009, the first shareholders to jump ship were those who relied on short-term changes to make big gains, hedge funds who bought and sold whatever suited them with rapid frequency, rather than putting the company's interest first. Upon their departure the company's share price became more stable and predictable, a better basis for long-term planning and investment than under quarterly reporting. A trend has started: 'Quarterly reporting risks diverting the attention of senior management teams away from long-term aims and objectives.' So said James Laing of Aberdeen Asset Management, when National Grid became the largest FTSE company to abandon the practice.[3] The regulatory requirement to issue quarterly reports ('interim management statements') was lifted in 2016 under the EU Transparency Directive.

The real beneficiary of 'maximising shareholder return' is often not the shareholder at all, but senior managers and fund managers. Short-term returns, especially in financial industries, are often tightly linked to bonuses. In the investment world even the long-term needs of pension fund members are moderated in deference to the interests of 'independent' investment managers, of whom the legendary Warren Buffet says: 'When trillions of dollars are managed by Wall Streeters charging high fees, it will usually be the [fund] managers who reap outsized profits, not the clients.'[4]

Vast payouts increase inequality, which has social consequences. Short termism also breeds a frame of mind which dismisses externalities, the negative impacts of business activity on society, as 'nothing to do with us'; it plunders resources, recklessly creating waste and pollution.[5]

Short termism is the single factor that most undermines Company Citizenship.

Some shares are owned by companies themselves. Through 'buybacks' managers effectively control the company that employs them. An ethical reason for doing this might be to grant shares to a wider group of employees, either by right or reward, creating an employee constituency within the company's shareholder community. Another might be to prevent a hostile takeover. Buyback can also be used to lure away 'troublesome' shareholders or boost the value of remaining shares. In the decade from 2004 Fortune 500 companies spent $3.4tn on buybacks, paying out more money in 2014 alone to shareholders ($885bn) than their total net income for that year, money which could otherwise have improved productivity, tackled climate change, reduced prices and increased wages (Jacobs and Mazzacuto, 2016).

Not all shareholders fall into the traditional mode, as Walmart discovered in 2006. The biggest company in the world, employing one in every 100 American workers, came under attack from a shareholder. Norway's massive national pension fund – Europe's biggest institutional investor, owning elements of over 7,000 companies – announced plans to disinvest from Walmart.[6] The reasons, they said, were 'serious breaches of human rights' and because it tolerated unacceptable environmental damage in its supply chain. Dozens of companies suffered Norwegian divestment in that purge, usually for manufacturing weapons or tobacco products in addition to the reasons given for Walmart; some had investments withdrawn for supporting illegal settlements in the West Bank. Five years later, Wikileaks disclosed a US Government cable which reported that Norway had alleged that the company's supply chain:

> consistently and systematically employs minors in contravention of international rules, that working conditions at many of its suppliers are dangerous or health-hazardous, that workers are pressured into working overtime without compensations, [and] that the company systematically discriminates against women in pay.[7]

Walmart's response was to embark upon a 'ten-year journey', a comprehensive realignment of its values to focus on justice, sustainability and engagement. They spent a year listening to customers, government and civil society. Hurricane Katrina was an even bigger wake-up call, according to then CEO Lee Scott, than the threat of divestment. It brought home to the company's leaders that companies and communities shared vulnerability to catastrophe and that the world's environmental challenges were, in effect, 'Katrina in slow motion'. In a speech full of the zeal of a religious convert Scott pledged the company to 100 per cent renewable energy, zero waste and to selling products that sustained resources and the environment – before admitting that he didn't, at that stage, know how to achieve these goals.[8]

Scott's approach was both ruthless and led by the bottom line. Supply chains from prawns to organic yoga outfits were re-imagined, landfill use reduced and greater fuel efficiency achieved to drive huge savings, whilst a revolutionary approach to transparency and reporting was announced. A million employees were offered affordable health care, a community disaster fund was established, helping 87 communities in the following decade, and the company lobbied the government to increase the legal minimum wage which had been frozen for ten years.

Prompted or not by divestment the changes were profound – and sustained. Scott concluded: 'For us there is virtually no distinction between being a responsible citizen and a successful business . . . they are one and the same for Walmart.'

In terms of turning around, there's no oil tanker quite like a $500bn retail store: the journey was slow and not easy. Ten years on, the *Guardian* compared the vision to the progress: a 20-million-ton reduction in supply-chain greenhouse gases had been exceeded by almost half and fertiliser use slashed. Vehicle efficiency had doubled and a million acres of wildlife habitat had been preserved on Walmart-owned land. Through the Alliance for Bangladesh Worker Safety and other groups the company was working to reduce human trafficking. Although carbon emissions from Walmart stores continued to rise until 2012 they then fell, despite the company continuing to grow. Its initial climate change targets had been criticised as unscientific (below COP22 standards) and renewable energy only accounted for a quarter of their energy use (Scott had pledged 100 per cent in ten years).[9]

In its 2017 CSR report Walmart moved up another gear: having reduced carbon emissions by 40 million tonnes in a decade the target for the next ten years was revealed as a billion across the global supply chain, the equivalent of Germany, whilst doubling their use of renewable energy by 2025.[10]

Shareholders have been flexing their muscles elsewhere too.

In 2016 the board of the satellite broadcaster, Sky, voted to reinstate James Murdoch as Chairman, a role he'd previously had before the UK phone hacking scandal had rocked the family empire. The move was expected but the appointment, supported by a majority of shareholders, disguised an ominous threat: 39 per cent of Sky is owned by 21st Century Fox, where James, son of Rupert, was already Chief Executive. Amongst the independent shareholders James Murdoch had actually lost the vote; their concern was that market rumours, the relative strength of dollar to pound and other factors suggested that a hostile takeover from Fox News was in the offing. As Fox was also Murdoch-owned they didn't trust their previous, now present, Chairman to put Sky's needs first were such a bid ever to be made.[11] It was.

In recent years Shell shareholders have approved a resolution obliging the energy company to report on its climate change risk; food companies have taken more progressive stances on palm oil and food growers have reduced the use of bee-harming pesticides following shareholder resolutions. In 2014 a record number of shareholder resolutions were filed in America, half of them concerning climate change or political donations.[12]

ShareAction sees shareholding as a force for good, believing that responsible shareholders interested in long-term prosperity must reject the idea that short-term profit is the paramount definition of value. In five years the group's been contacted by over 40,000 investors and has lobbied 500 pension funds, helping establish standing lobby groups of fund beneficiaries in 18. Over 100 companies have witnessed ShareAction activity, not least by members of their 'AGM Army', people like me who attend corporate AGMs to put boards on the spot through well-researched questions.

Recent ShareAction campaigns have focused on engaging with refugees, factory farming, antibiotics in food and the perennial issue of climate change. Over half of FTSE100 companies are now accredited Living Wage employers, often thanks to ShareAction's intervention. ShareAction was part of the coalition which tabled that Shell resolution on climate risk and a subsequent one at BP, which both passed with board support and the necessary 75 per cent of shareholder votes. The dominance of climate and energy issues in their portfolio is understandable – a quarter of all market capitalisation in Britain is associated with fossil fuels.[13]

Executive pay prompts growing interest from shareholder activists – plus Theresa May as Prime Minister and the Institute of Directors, who warned Britain's highest paid bosses that they were in the 'last chance saloon'. Excessive pay drives inequality and there's simply no reliable cost–benefit analysis to show that mega-salaries create value for companies.[14] In 2009 four-fifths of shareholders at the troubled bank RBS opposed a deal to raise top pay and in 2012, a short era dubbed 'shareholder spring', 59 per cent at the advertising giant WPP tried to block a £6.8m rise for founder CEO Martin Sorrell. Sorrell received £200m over the next four years and it was not until 2017 that his pay was severely restrained in the face of even stronger shareholder concerns.[15] Shell and Aviva had similar experiences. In 2016 more than 60 per cent of BP shareholders voted against a £14m pay package for chief executive Bob Dudley as the oil company reported record losses, cut thousands of jobs and froze employees' pay. On the same day, Smith & Nephew shareholders voted down a £2m award to their executives on the simple grounds that bonus criteria had not been achieved; meanwhile Centrica (British Gas) lost 250,000 customers in 2015–16 and still gave their CEO a 40 per cent rise, to over £4m.[16] Reckitt Benckiser, makers of Nurofen, slashed their CEO's 2016 pay by a third – to a mere £14.9m with no bonuses – apparently to head off a shareholder revolt.[17] In all of these cases shareholder votes are advisory, not binding, though at BP the remuneration committee responded to the vote by thoroughly revising their package. The new deal cut Dudley's basic pay by 40 per cent, installed more testing bonus criteria across senior management and included a greater proportion of bonuses to be paid in long-term share options.[18] Although shareholder unease on top pay is greater now than in 2012 fewer than 10 per cent of AGMs actually revolt.

Is shareholder power a paper tiger? Sometimes the thorn in the side is more powerful than outright confrontation. Cogent argument and a strong business case can be effective without a mathematical majority, though at too many AGMs the Chair's bundle of proxies, together with top brass lobbying of shareholders, can still ensure majorities whenever management is under threat. Shareholders are in a difficult position: whatever their consciences tell them, individually or collectively, a company with leadership that's perceived to be weak, disorganised or vulnerable may pose a threat to the very share price which attracted so many of them to become shareholders. Others might reply that companies regarded as irresponsible, unresponsive or arrogant pose a similar threat. They might add that, over any ten-year period, inclusive, collaborative and responsible Company Citizens, with their long-term thinking, can collectively boast bigger rises in share price than those that don't prioritise such principles.

The investor

Investors are motivated by any number of causes. Most investors are passive, some choose investment portfolios which are 'ethical', 'responsible' or simply aimed at maximising income and most are, in any case, trusted to others to invest on their behalf. How well aligned those intermediaries may be to the investor's values is a question. An 'active investor' is directly involved in managing their portfolio but an 'activist investor', as described in Oliver Walker's *Barbarians in the Boardroom*, is something else. Typically nimble, the activist's own company's wealth is deployed to buy influence on boards and thereby guide the major decisions of others, including board membership, mergers and takeovers, in the interests of . . . the activist investor. This is usually achieved without a majority shareholding but with a high degree of leverage; such engagement is relatively short term and frequently destabilising. In 2017 one of the more notorious activist investors, Jana, shook up Whole Foods, the domain of Conscious Capitalism guru John Mackey, by weaponising just an 8 per cent share and forcing the company's sale to Amazon.[19]

Let's focus instead on the responsible use of investment.

In *Welcome to GoodCo* we looked at ethical, social, responsible and impact investing; the latter, now 'officially' a decade old, has been deemed to work. As much as $112bn is invested in impact investment programmes, mostly in developing countries, bringing about both change for good and a medium-to-long-term return. Indeed, 98 per cent of such investors believe that their money has met or exceeded expectations of impact and 91 per cent have met or exceeded financial goals too, says their international network GIIN.

During 2016 the global value of investment funds committed to pulling out of fossil-fuel assets doubled to over $5tn.[20] As recently as 2010 there was little ethical momentum in the investment world but that's changing. In 2016, 688 investment institutions and 58,000 people in 78 countries divested themselves of oil assets which, in their view, had no long-term future. Only a year after Bill Gates had described fossil-fuel divestment as 'a diversion' his own £40bn foundation sold almost all of its carbon holdings. In 2014 Nobel Peace prize winner Archbishop Desmond Tutu called upon the Nobel Foundation itself to join the movement, saying: 'People of conscience need to break their ties with corporations financing the injustice of climate change.'

Fifteen hundred corporate investors have now committed to the United Nations' Principles of Responsible Investment, an independent agency formed in 2006 to champion Environmental, Society and Governance (ESG) issues within business, and since 2013 their combined assets have doubled to $60tn. Social and responsible investing programmes made up a fifth of all American assets under management in 2016.[21]

You have to be an investor before you can deploy divestment, the nuclear option, as a tool. Was American divestment in South Africa in the apartheid years done to end apartheid (if so, it failed) or to appease the growing demands of confident black Americans?

Research shows that in Britain 'ethical' investment generally out-performs the FTSE index over five years: in the period to September 2016 the FTSE4-Good basket of funds gave a 63.5 per cent return on investment compared with 58.8 per cent for the mainstream.[22] One explanation for this is purely practical: adopting an ESG approach obliges investors (and companies) to identify material risks affecting the success of the company early, thus enabling them to be managed better. Environmental, Society and Governance investments tend to commit longer term than mainstream ones and there's a definite trend towards 'investing for good' amongst both women and the millennial generation, two growing populations of investors.

The quality of investment depends on the quality of reporting. Investors can only target ESG funds effectively if companies are open about their operations, warts and all. London Stock Exchange Group has observed that the profile of ESG reporting has moved 'from niche to mainstream', ESG funds now account for a third of all investment money (perhaps two thirds of all pension fund holdings). The Group advises investees how to integrate ESG factors into investor reporting and communications, based on the Financial Stability Board's Task Force on Climate-Related Financial Disclosures and those ubiquitous Sustainable Development Goals.

Consistency is the weakness of both legislation and voluntary reporting codes, even though more companies are choosing to adopt the Global Reporting Index (GRI), which covers many bases.[23] The GRI has evolved into something widely regarded as useful and its future development will be around how reporting is undertaken rather than the content which, reflecting the SDGs, GRI believes is now settled. Our 2006 Companies Act legislated for environmental and social criteria to be considered by all and formally reported by some, but much has changed in a decade: the law now lags behind good practice. A culture of openness, rather than an annual sneaky peak, is essential in meeting the ever-increasing demands of long term ESG investors.[24]

Companies like Diageo, whose annual report is structured around the SDGs, lead the way.

The world's biggest asset manager is Larry Fink's BlackRock, with over $5tn of other people's funds under management. Fink was trusted by the US government to help 'clean up' after the 2008 crash. Today, BlackRock Impact fund's 'pitch' aims at conscientious millennials who seek both financial and non-financial goals, sustainable solutions where both 'purpose and performance' have 'a long term, positive impact on the world'. Their approach embodies all three elements of social investment, offering portfolios which are either ethical (screening out companies which don't deliver your values), positively ESG-orientated (working with those so aligned) or impactful, where longer term, measurable, positive non-financial outcomes are delivered alongside acceptable financial returns.

Impact is just one BlackRock fund, one of more than 20 sustainable funds launched in USA in 2015 compared with just three the previous year. In that year the money invested in sustainable US portfolios rose by half. 'Impact' was started because existing investors were already looking for social and environmental outcomes and were willing to walk away from BlackRock to find them.[25]

BlackRock has issued repeated warnings of the economic damage that climate change can wreak. Some of its own investors, however, have complained that it too often fails to support proposals to reduce or mitigate carbon emissions, as at the 2016 AGMs of four giant oil companies. BlackRock's response was to call for tighter reporting codes to hold companies to account on climate issues. It claims that engaging with investees at boardroom level is more effective than through AGM confrontations; such considerations don't stop others targeting their criticisms on climate responsibility more publicly. In May 2017 BlackRock finally lost patience, using its substantial vote to oblige both Occidental and Exxon to report on climate risk.[26]

Early in 2016 Fink wrote to 500 US CEOs to urge them to end quarterly financial reporting, the antithesis of a triple-bottom-line sustainable economy.[27] His letter anticipated the corporate reporting season although its timing wasn't a bad pitch for recognition in a future Clinton administration, as Hillary had professed sympathy with his views during her ill-fated Presidential campaign. Stop focusing on the odd pennies of earnings per share, Fink told his peers, rather pursue 'a strategic framework for long-term value creation'. Railing against the growing trend of inward-looking buybacks, he lamented that business treats investors badly, reporting on historic events rather than engaging them in future planning for the co-enterprise that is the company, acknowledging that similar criticism could be made of CEOs who don't even engage properly with their boards.

In short, his was a plea for Company Citizens to grow up, smell the Fairtrade coffee and plan for the future in an inclusive, positive, socially and environmentally responsible way.

Amen to that.

The customer

We get a warm glow when we do something good. In humans achievement, affection, philanthropy (including volunteering) and sensory stimulation all prompt the release of dopamine in the brain, creating a sense of happiness. People at work also strive for dopamine hits, which can come from being valued, teamwork, achieving a goal. Such things help a business be both happy and successful.

That's the theory. In practice, much work time is spent carrying out routines, avoiding unnecessary risks (even though risk-taking also prompts dopamine production) and planning for a dry, transactional and mundane future.

Chemical happiness can be generated naturally in other ways: why do people buy some brands and not others? Sometimes it's rational – better value for money, more convenient, 'it was just there' – but sometimes dopamine craving gets the better of the customer. The word 'luxury' distinguishes between two almost identical ice creams; ditto, toilet paper. 'Luxury' usually means 'price premium' but dopamine-hungry humans will pay it. Who prefers perfume from the 'convenience' shelf?

The Ecover brand has never appeared on the cheap shelf. Since its launch in Belgium in 1979 it's always sold at a premium but that's not stopped its inexorable rise in the responsible cleaning products market of 40 countries, generating a turnover of $200m. It's one of the larger European B Corps, a group of companies opting to be rated according to objective measures of environmental and social responsibility. Not without controversy – the spotlight of scrutiny falls even on the rights of water fleas – as it's grown it's maintained a regime of plant-based ingredients, using recycled and recyclable plastic, eschewing testing on vertebrates.

Part of the reason Ecover products sell well is because they appeal to the dopamine addict: buying this product helps me to save the planet. Irrespective of the unit cost of manufacture, which must have fallen as Ecover's scale has grown, this 'feel-good factor' is something for which the customer agrees to pay extra. The year 2016 was the UK's 14th consecutive year of growth in ethical consumer goods; at £38bn the market's now twice the size of tobacco. Over half of all British shoppers now say that ethics plays some part in informing them what to buy, compared with only a third of retail customers globally.[28]

The airline which invites you to plant trees to offset the carbon footprint of your flight is telling the passenger 'you share the responsibility for our burning fuel'. This common bond may lower carbon offset costs to the airline and it helps to assuage the customer's polluting guilt in a dopamine-inducing way. As you disembark they invite you to empty your pockets of shrapnel: that's a service worth paying for too.

The same feel-good factor applies to businesses that associate themselves with charities. The partnership between Boots retail pharmacies and Macmillan Cancer Care is a clear convergence between organisations whose common interest is health. Cancer patients are signposted to the charity's caring services earlier in their 'journey' than they otherwise might, the charity benefits both from cash and proximity to a trusted brand and the company can demonstrate that its commitment to health and wellbeing is genuine. Patients and their families feel cared for and involved over a distressing and stressful period. Everyone can think 'there but for the Grace of God . . .' and if the company gains a few extra customers from amongst the caring or the cared for, who begrudges that?

Marketing involves both gaining customers and retaining them. Once the former is achieved an 'invitation to bid' exists for the next opportunity, a never-ending journey, especially now social media targets the individual rather than the clan. A good name's a valuable asset; a strong relationship between customer and company, based on what's right and not just habit, can help protect against reputational damage.

Customer allegiance protects companies from that one thing they most dread: falling sales. Getting on the consumer's wrong side is never a good idea although examples of customers creating havoc in revenge for corporate misdemeanours are few: the boycott has a chequered history. As we've seen, Volkswagen falsified test results, suggesting that the emissions from their diesel cars were 40 times less polluting than they really were. But what price did they pay?

The offences came to light in 2015, were committed over at least seven years, and involved 15 VW models. A year later total UK car sales were up 2.8 per cent, with fleet purchases showing stronger growth than private sales, and petrol-driven vehicles were up too, with diesel engines down by 0.8 per cent. Over that year Volkswagen lost a quarter of its sales, to around 7 per cent of the market, where they stabilised, though two VW models, Golf (4th) and Polo (6th), were still top-selling brands.[29] It's likely that brand allegiance helped the company whilst it performed badly in attracting new customers; years of being known for good products had enabled the company to build the credibility needed to protect against 'reputational shock'. We shall see how long that sales dip persists.

Various consumer boycotts of South African companies and produce over 30 years are sometimes credited with helping bring down apartheid, but didn't South African companies just find markets elsewhere? Of course they did. Barclays ended its business investment in South Africa in 2016, only 45 years after some of us campaigned to 'Boycott Barclays'. Their departure tells us more about the dire South African economy than the efficacy of boycotts.

Student unions in Britain have been boycotting Nestlé products since the 1970s in protest against aggressive marketing of baby-milk substitutes, which has been independently and internationally regulated since 1981. Since then scores of complaints have continued to be made but proven significant breaches by any company have been rare. The world's second biggest food manufacturer supports the code of global good practice, claiming that the UK boycott (targeting all Nestlé products) has not affected their sales. The then-candidate Donald Trump's call for a boycott of Oreos after Nabisco 'pulled out of Chicago' to make their biscuits in Mexico was not only based on fake news (they only downsized in Chicago and US-consumed Oreos are still made in US) but was also ineffective. When Starbucks' unbelievably small contribution to UK corporation tax was revealed the coffee shop took an instant but brief hit on UK sales, which were restored long before it announced the regularisation of its tax affairs. New York Police Department's call for people to boycott Quentin Tarantino's films, after he described police officers as 'murderers', doesn't seem to have done him much harm.

Not all boycotts are progressive: American radical Christians arranged one against the Disney Corporation because the company's films were too tolerant of gay characters (and the company of gay employees). A boycott of a US restaurant chain, after its CEO spoke out against gay marriage, was countered by contrarians who supported his stance, staging a 'buy-cott', in which people preferentially bought the chain's products. The result appears to have been a draw. In 2001 Coca-Cola anonymously launched a campaign, H2No, to persuade people to shun tap water in restaurants and drink branded beverages instead. The trend appears to have been the reverse.

Honourable are companies who stand up to prejudice: at Starbucks' 2013 AGM a shareholder opined that the company had lost trade because of its support for same-sex marriage. Chief Executive Officer Howard Schulz responded: 'It's not an economic decision to me. The lens in which we're making that decision is through the lens of our people. We employ over 200,000 people . . . and we want to embrace diversity. Of all kinds.'[30]

An ongoing campaign urges a boycott of Israeli products in protest against the country's occupation of the Palestinian West Bank and, in particular, the illegal building of settlements there. At its most active in universities, dismissed as the actions of 'corduroy-jacketed academics' by Boris Johnson, the campaign has achieved a specific goal: the European Union now insists that products grown by settlers in the occupied West Bank and imported to the EU cannot be labelled as being of Israeli origin and must be labelled, for example, 'From the West Bank (Israeli settlement)'. Whilst not preventing their import this transparency does make it easier for consumers to decline to purchase products where they wish to do so.[31]

Possibly the most successful consumer boycott ever, producing radical outcomes which were unlikely without such action, was that led by Oxfam against Nike. The charity accused the world's biggest sports apparel brand of exploitation after a 2001 BBC report found child labourers working 16 hours a day, seven days a week in south east Asia for a Nike supplier.[32] Previously, suppliers had been found in breach of local minimum wage legislation and safety issues at work were a constant concern. The company was ripe for a consumer boycott – its lack of supply-chain stewardship was about as public as these things get.

Stung by the impact of the boycott in a highly competitive market, Nike turned itself around.[33] Independent sources now suggest that it's one of the most environmentally friendly corporates in the world, with reporting and transparency standards second to none. Those standards still reveal supply-chain audit violations, excessive overtime and other breaches, although 93 per cent of its supplier factories were deemed 'incident-free' in 2013, up from 87 per cent a year previously. The company has also been ruthless in ditching suppliers who don't improve conditions and, to protect local drinking water, they've almost eliminated water from their textile dyeing. In the words of the web site Triple Pundit, an advocate of triple-bottom-line accounting: 'It's hard to question the ultimate business benefits Nike gleaned by adopting a more stringent CSR policy. Here's to hoping others in the apparel industry . . . take notice.'[34]

Customers are a diverse lot. They are manipulable but predictable, loyal but fickle. Whilst we've considered retail customers here, 'the public', much of the same could be said of B2B customers and sales into the public sector and elsewhere. Relationships between Company Citizens and citizen citizens are complex but the values upon which they're based – trust and reliability – are not.

The workforce

It's a cliché to say that employees are a company's greatest asset yet UK productivity is poor, employee engagement is in free fall and the pay of most 'ordinary workers' hasn't risen for a decade in real terms. Unemployment is low which is unusual, given other economic indicators, and the number of people living in poverty whilst in work is at record levels. That doesn't reflect the respect that 'greatest assets' deserve.

At least workers aren't normally treated like this.

For thirty years Mike Ashley has been Mr Sports Direct. Leaving school at 16, foregoing a sports career through injury, he built Britain's biggest retail sportswear chain from nothing; today he's the 15th richest Briton, having proved himself nimble and agile in the world of acquisitions. He owns 60 per cent of Sports Direct, an empire which includes Lillywhites, Dunlop Slazenger, Lonsdale and familiar outdoor brands such as Kangol and Karrimor. Ashley also owns Newcastle United Football Club and significant shareholdings in rival retailers Black's, Milletts, French Connection and Debenhams.[35]

Some 3,000 of Sports Direct's 20,000 employees work in its warehouse and distribution centre in Shirebrook, Derbyshire, which opened in 2005. Most are agency workers on zero-hours contracts. Around half of the staff are employed through Transline which, following the Sports Direct 'affair', lost a lucrative contract with Amazon (and subsequently had to be rescued). Shirebrook staff work unpredictable hours, are paid only for time actually worked, have few employment rights and represent the ultimate 'flexible labour force'. Whilst such contracts are not illegal, many argue that they're open to abuse and the Sports Direct experience does nothing to counter that belief. It was claimed, and admitted, that security checks on employees leaving work were so prolonged that they effectively reduced employee hourly earnings to below the legal minimum wage. A former Sports Direct retail employee told the BBC: 'Sometimes, on my zero-hours contract, I'd end up working for 10 days in a row, for 10 hours a day. On other weeks I would get given only one three-hour shift the whole week. There was no routine.'[36]

It was further claimed that a climate of fear existed in the warehouse: workers could be sacked on a 'six strikes and you're out' basis for offences including using a mobile phone, spending too long in the toilet and 'chatting'. Shop staff who clocked in electronically a minute late had 15 minutes pay deducted, MPs heard. A Channel 4 documentary claimed that employees who talked in public about their working conditions were disciplined and ambulances frequently called on site, suggesting a poor safety regime. Sick employees, many of whom spoke little English, were too scared to ask to go home. On occasions women went into labour at work rather than request time off.

In 2015 Sports Direct was found in serious breach of National Minimum Wage regulations, fined £10m and made to pay £1m in back pay. Between 2013 and November 2015 the company's share price averaged 700p, the highest point in its history; eight weeks later it was under 260p, reducing the company's value by £400m. Ashley's appearance before a Parliamentary select committee turned into a pantomime in which he blamed the company's poor reputation on its trade unions, denying knowledge of many of the alleged breaches (though not denying that they happened).

In December 2016 the company reported half yearly profits down by a quarter. This was due to a poor currency exchange rate and an 'extreme political, union and media campaign' which had 'not only damaged [our] reputation and influenced our customers, it [had] impacted negatively on the morale of our people', said company chairman, former Chief Constable Keith Hellawell, as the company announced that it was buying a £40m private jet.[37] The following month two Polish men were jailed for six years for conspiracy to defraud after they'd taken £35,000 from the wages of 18 vulnerable men who'd been recruited in Poland and trafficked to Britain to work as bonded labour, effectively slaves, in that infamous Shirebrook warehouse.[38] Whilst the company can't be held directly responsible for that, it speaks volumes about the underlying culture and lack of awareness of what was really happening under their noses.

The Institute of Directors branded Sports Direct 'a scar on British business'[39] and a shareholder said the company's reputation was 'atrocious'. Business Select Committee chairman Iain Wright MP described working conditions as 'closer to that of a Victorian workhouse than that of a modern, reputable High Street retailer'. He went on: 'It seems incredible that Mike Ashley, who visits the warehouse at least once a week, was unaware of these appalling practices.'[40] Quite so. Not only does ignorance bring bliss but so, I guess, does a personal fortune of £3bn.

Fortunately it's not difficult to find the other side of the coin, the business which regards its employees as partners on a mission and treats them with appropriate levels of respect. Employee engagement is the emotional attachment that employees have to their work place, a personal investment in its success.

There are only three things that ultimately matter to people, three communities to which we all belong: our families, our localities and our workplaces.

We sleep for a third of our lives and then many of us work for more than a third of what's left – especially if you add 'work-based socialising' and 'worrying about work' to the time formally committed to employment and work-related travel. Every politician knows the dictum 'all politics is local': my vote is largely determined by what's happening to me, my loved ones, my neighbourhood and my workplace. Even the economy, that perennial influencer of voting intentions, is seen through the prism of work-related issues, my income and the demands made upon it.

Fascinating and thorough research by Weber Shandwick makes it clear that employee engagement in Britain is not what it could be. They boldly state the benefits of engagement: 'Engaged employees tend to be more aligned around common objectives, more productive, more likely to be ambassadors and promoters of their employers' brands and more likely to have long tenures.'[41]

Long tenure is important for cost reasons: whenever an employee is replaced there's the cost of recruitment itself, a frequent loss of productivity as notice is served, a lag period before a new employee reaches optimum productivity (maybe 20 to 30 weeks) and possibly significant training costs for the newcomer too. Such costs can amount to £30,000 per replacement.[42] More engaged companies tend to attract a higher calibre of recruit whilst some employment agencies specialise in recruiting people to ethical employers, such as those accredited by BITC's CR Index.

And yet, say Weber Shandwick, only half of the UK workforce could be described as 'engaged' and only half would recommend their job to others. Watch out, UK employers! Only a third of your employees feel valued and four out of ten would leave your firm if the opportunity arose.[43]

Every word of this report's worth reading: it shows that the most engaged employees are highly motivated whilst actions to motivate employees with low engagement tends to fail, however it's measured. Science and engineering score highly (powered by independence and discovery, a sense of purpose), followed by technology (ditto) and health care (appealing to the highly empathetic). A similar spectrum differentiated between artistic and creative roles (high engagement), down through technical, managerial, clerical and sales, with manual work exhibiting the lowest level of engagement. Some 19 values were seen to influence engagement levels and amongst these the starkest contrasts were with just two: the most engaged companies showed the highest respect for their workforce and the most integrity in their operations. In contrast, these two criteria scored very poorly amongst the least engaged workplaces. 'Empathy' and 'creating an atmosphere of shared values' were the criteria exhibited by fewest employers in total.

The report argues that any strategy for improving employee engagement should include:

- a culture of shared values, including empathy and mutual respect;
- a focus on purpose and meaning: 'our jobs matter, we make a difference';
- a more creative working environment: including bottom-up innovation;

- demonstrating conscience and ethics: involving staff in aspects of responsible business; and
- education and inspiration: personal and professional skills development.

This is the approach of the Company Citizen.

In Chapter 4 we considered the purpose of business; let's look now at how companies generate a sense of common purpose within their workforce. The British railway industry employs 100,000 people and since 2010 one in ten has received training in suicide prevention. The Rail Industry Suicide Prevention Programme involves Network Rail, the Samaritans, British Transport Police, train operating companies, unions and the NHS. Public-facing staff are equipped to identify and support potential suicide victims at risk of jumping off a bridge or stepping in front of a train. This empowers staff, creating a real sense of purpose: what could be more meaningful than having the skills to save a life? One participant, whose new skills were tested, successfully, just weeks after his training, says:

> Without my training, I may have approached her, but would have felt scared in case I wouldn't have been able to handle the situation. Since the training . . . I have more of an understanding of how they feel and the best way to interact with them. If this incident had happened before I took the Samaritans' course the outcome could have been very different.[44]

No doubt many lives have been saved through the awareness and intervention of Network Rail staff, sometimes at an emotional cost to themselves, especially when, sadly, their intervention is unsuccessful. Passengers won't be aware of the bond between employer and employee created by the trust and empowerment that such training creates; nor will they even know when their train is only running on time because massive disruption of the network, caused by a strategically unfortunate suicide, has been avoided. Avoided, too, are potentially millions of pounds in costs to and fines upon Network Rail each time a significant timetable disruption happens, and the costs to the train companies themselves each time a stressed driver needs time off to recover from witnessing a violent death. The scheme has won at least one national award every year since its inception, including at the 2017 Third Sector Business Charity Awards.

The word 'community' on the Willmott Dixon web site is no mere window dressing. For the conscientious person looking for a company citizen to work for they tick many boxes. They don't just build the homes that people need, whilst pursuing carbon neutrality, but values and purpose are written through the company as though through seaside rock. Both Willmott Dixon and its associated Foundation have a positive impact on the community, both home and abroad, so what's it like as a place to work?

It's a family company with a 160-year pedigree and a fifth-generation Willmott at the helm, so longer-term thinking comes naturally. It has 3,000 employees and a billion-pound turnover but a clear value statement too: 'As a privately run company we put shared value before share price' and '[we] answer to householders, not shareholders.' It claims to be not a construction company but a 'people' company which constructs buildings, where the fostering of career development, the 'sharing of success' and long-term loyalty are explicit goals. Key Performance Indicators include employee engagement, outperforming industry norms on diversity, apprenticeships, training and length of tenure: 'We provide a working environment that makes people want to stay and give of their best', for which they've won several awards. Staff are actively canvassed on ways of improving the company which are reported at board level and acted upon where feasible. The presence of non-executive director Jonathon Porritt, formerly of Friends of the Earth and creator of the Forum for the Future, is a reassuring sign that the company's heart is genuinely in sustainable growth.

The company has reported on progress on sustainability since 2009 and is moving towards fully integrated reporting. Posts with sustainable development responsibilities exist throughout the company, including at board level, and Willmott Dixon was Edie's 2015 Sustainable Business of the Year: no surprise to anyone who's read their excellent Sustainable Development Review.[45]

Like Willmott Dixon, Alium Partners is a 'for profit' company. This London recruitment agency, founded in 2003, specialises in the appointment of senior interim managers. They, too, are a 'people company' though on a much smaller scale. Through a project called Fastlaners, coordinated by the charity UpRising, Alium contributes to a programme to help young graduates in the deprived parts of Tower Hamlets reduce their barriers to employment. The professional recruiters help young people through practice job interviews, writing CVs, advice and mentoring, as they might with paying clients, but with the aim of helping those less fortunate than their regular service users.

Seven out of ten of Alium's staff took part in the programme in its first 18 months as the company donated 600 hours of staff time to the cause. Half of the young people involved moved into employment within three months of the 'treatment' and three quarters within nine months. Although the principal beneficiaries are, of course, the graduates seeking work the company itself has, they claim, become more effective as a result and a better place to work. Involvement has helped them to both embed a culture of professional development within their staff and identify new entry-level team members. Some successful applicants for employment within Alium were initially attracted by the positive reputation they had generated. In 2015 their work was recognised by a Dragon Award from the Lord Mayor of London. Such schemes, part of a growing trend in community engagement to replace fence painting with up-skilling, can typically create an 11:1 Social Return on Investment.

Another way for an employer to earn the engagement of employees is to show them that they care. This ranges from recognising and working with their trade union to providing a caring service to support them – ideas which are not mutually exclusive. Neyber exists to enable employers to promote employee wellbeing through financial security at (literally) no cost to the employer. Recognising that financial stress can cripple an employee Neyber helps the caring employer provide a solution. Two thirds of employees suffer financial problems at some point each year, often leading to stress, anxiety, loss of focus and productivity – one in 12 will take time off for debt-related reasons. Neyber provides UK employees with low interest (single digit APR) cash loans through the workplace, repaid through their salary – and even pays participating employers for the privilege.[46] Two early major clients were the police service and the NHS, not a bad start, though the service is available to companies with as few as 20 employees.

Awareness of employees' needs, helping where you can: how better to boost employee engagement and, with it, productivity?

Employee ownership

Employee-owned businesses create £1 in every £25 of Britain's Gross Domestic Product. The definition of 'employee-owned' is that employees own anything up to 100 per cent of the business, controlling its direction and values. Best known is the John Lewis Partnership, a company owned by a trust accountable to its 91,000 employees or 'members', created in the 1920s as a way of heading off any possible communist insurgency in Britain. John Lewis Partnership is a founder member of what's now the Employee Ownership Association.[47] Other notables amongst its 250 members are the Arup Partnership, Unipart and Capita along with several prominent law and other partnerships; many more, smaller, employee-owned ventures might not be members.

Governance structures of employee-owned firms vary significantly. They include co-operatives, social enterprises, for-profit companies and legal partnerships; some are spin-outs, some became employee-owned, others were born so. Some are regular shareholder-owned companies in which employees have a significant holding. Some were created by a management buy-out, perhaps the rescue of a closing enterprise, others become employee-owned in order to change the nature of the company. In some cases ownership was gifted to the employees when the private owner had no other succession plan, as with the chemical company Scott Bader. They can be directly owned by employees as shareholders, indirectly through a trust or a combination of the two. More significant than their structures is their performance.

Employee engagement levels are usually very high in employee-owned businesses because the employee has a clear long-term vested interest in the company's performance: as a result productivity, innovation and resilience to economic shock are all higher than in comparable companies elsewhere. Stress levels are lower and employment standards are generally better too. Employee engagement is linked to high levels of community engagement and a more joined-up approach to triple-bottom-line sustainability.

A 2012 Government report concluded that employee-owned businesses thrive because of their long-term focus, both in planning and in management of capital, which avoids them becoming 'preoccupied' with ephemera. They are less dependent on external capital (conveniently, as banks tend to be wary of them, especially smaller ones) and they benefit from a positive image. A typical employee-owned business actively encourages employees to be engaged in training and development, with half of them involved at any time compared with only 5 per cent elsewhere. Levels of employee ownership of up to 30 per cent were found to have a modest impact on performance and levels of over 60 conferred no greater advantage than those achieved by the best performing '30–60 per cent' bracket. Staff are clearly, unsurprisingly, afforded a high priority in employee-owned business both as a community and as a resource: such companies offer more flexible working conditions and gain more benefit from employee-inspired innovation than do mainstream businesses.[48]

The report also detected a concern that policy makers didn't recognise or overtly support the case for extending employee ownership.

Two million workers in Britain hold shares in their companies through Employee Share Ownership Plans involving eight out of ten FTSE companies. Employee Share Ownership Plans (ESOPs) are mostly minority holdings which can't be described as the employees owning the company, and in only about 70 FTSE-listed companies is the holding more than 3 per cent. Employee Share Ownership Plan companies nevertheless also claim that even low levels of share engagement can enhance productivity and staff retention.

Not everything runs smoothly in the world of ESOPs: ask Roadchef. Following a 1983 management buy-out, a fifth of Roadchef's shares were gifted to the restaurant chain's 500 employees across the country, one of the UK's first ever ESOPs. Over the years further transfers grew employee interests to a third of all shares but the tide got reversed. By 1998 the Managing Director held a majority of shares and members of the first ESOP owned just 4.4 per cent. A second ESOP was in play, open only to senior staff. The transfer of shares away from the first ESOP to the second was ruled invalid by the High Court in 2014 but compensation, believed to be of the order of £27,000 per employee, has yet to be paid; as of mid-2017 more court cases are pending, the tax status of back payments is unclear and no settlement is in sight. Meanwhile the CEO has sold his 60 per cent share to Japanese investors.[49] The case clearly illustrates the need for professional standards and guidelines amongst ESOP trustees.

Upon privatisation of Royal Mail a tenth of shares were gifted to employees in a controversial move which lacked many of the safeguards that good ESOPs should have, so there's little evidence of benefit amid widespread cynicism of management. Share values rose by half on their first day of trading, representing a huge missed opportunity for the taxpayer, in whose interests the then Chancellor was supposed to be acting. Some employees, unsurprisingly, cashed in and the breadth of employee share ownership collapsed, which wouldn't have happened had safeguards been created – such as holding the shares in a trust representing employee shareholder interests or restricting sales to fellow employees only. In 2017 employees remaining in the scheme owned assets averaging £3,700 each.

There's good news about ESOPs for investors. The UK Employee Ownership Index is a basket of shares in companies where employee shareholding is over 3 per cent. Although the Index has been published since 1995, and has only existed as an investment plan in recent years, it takes 2003 as a baseline where both the basket and the FTSE All-Share Index were set at 100. At the end of the first quarter of 2016 the ESOP Index of Total Shareholder Return stood at 894 compared with the All-Share equivalent, 283: a degree of employee share ownership had delivered three times the benefit to shareholders than had the market as a whole.

Not only does employee ownership, in whole or in part, deliver more on values and engagement but if shareholder return really is the prime concern of business, as the dinosaurs claim, then there ought to be an awful lot more employee share ownership.

'Corporate Social Responsibility'

In 1955 'Corporate Social Responsibility' first appeared in academic literature and the 1970s saw the first despairing claim that the acronym 'CSR' had lost authenticity. Essentially CSR describes how the company engages with society and this ranges from the superficial – a box-ticking, fun-loving, disengaged culture wrapped in the warm glow of team days out – to the profound, in which aspects of responsibility imbue every action undertaken both by and within the company. Chapter 7 explores the Company Citizen's approach to community engagement.

Perhaps in order to distinguish that 'optional' approach from one of ingrained 'responsible' activity, such practices also go by the name of CR (corporate responsibility), CRS (corporate responsibility and sustainability) and investors' preferred term, ESG. The subtle differences between these themes need not worry us but one distinction is worth observing: if community engagement is the responsibility of the public affairs department or an *ad hoc* grouping it's likely to be traditional CSR, but if it's of operational significance, in the purview of human resources or procurement, or reporting directly into the board, it's more likely to be CR or CRS. One of the reasons why these acronyms proliferate is because it's true, as the CEO of Dollar UK wrote for the CBI's 'Great Business Debate' blog in 2016, that: 'Some cynics still insist that CSR is at best an act of empty corporate philanthropy, and at worst a smokescreen used to hide a multitude of corporate sins.'[50] Mr Howard says that at Dollar they 'see CSR as a central function that underpins the ethos of the whole company'.

Wonderful. But he goes on to describe his employees undertaking 'bake sales and sponsored runs' and allowing them half a day per year of paid volunteering time. Which 'ethos' is being underpinned here? Such activity might be corporate, though not in a very positive sense; it might be social, as people are certainly socialising; but is it the action of a responsible company? Responsibility is about so much more than raising charity money, it's about trading responsibly too. Dollar's a finance company whose major subsidiary, Money Shop, was ordered in 2015 to return to low-income customers £15m which it hadn't been entitled to take from them.[51] That's neither responsible lending nor responsible business, so perhaps the cynics are right: I know a 'smokescreen' when I see one.

Roast is an upmarket restaurant in the bijou surroundings of London's Borough Market, but 'bijou' isn't how Iqbal Wahhab started life. Before this award-winning restaurateur created Roast (and a Westminster icon, The Cinnamon Club), he'd grown up with the gangs of South London. Starting at the bottom and having his contemporaries die too young was a wake-up call so, after university, he committed himself to doing good and helping to address society's problems, both in Britain and the developing world. This he's done, not by working in public service or donating to charity but by direct intervention, using the tools of business.

Wahhab spends many thousands of his company's pounds on coaching prison inmates for careers in hospitality, working to improve the nutrition of school meals and empowering entrepreneurs in deprived communities because business, he says, is the best way to deliver 'good'. Taxation, he argues, is inefficient at generating benefit and charities range from the ineffective to the downright corrupt.[52] Furthermore, on discovering that 80 of his 100 employees came to him because they were inspired by the social impact of his work, and that such causes help him attract customers, he's concluded that *Charity Sucks* (Wahhab, 2016).

It's an interesting proposition. I can understand why someone with his experience of public and voluntary sector services, perhaps judging that they failed his contemporaries as children, and now empowered by the wealth and conscience of the philanthropist, might reach this conclusion. He's undoubtedly correct to say that the tools of business, used in this way, can produce sustainable and long term positive social change; his experience does demonstrate how dynamic processes based on skills acquisition can empower the voiceless and that the 'haves' can benefit from being systematically generous towards the have-nots. But he's wrong to claim that business can do this alone, implying that other sectors have no role to play.

No sector has a monopoly on good works but the public sector has the scale, diversity, ubiquity and purpose to provide both 'the hand out and the hand up'. The charity sector is a huge resource of values and experience, concentrated around the principles of voluntary action and the process of mass giving, which other sectors aren't. Don't be misled by Iqbal's stories of charity leaders living the life of Riley at the expense of beneficiaries; such tales stand out simply because they're so far from the norm. And do wonder at what power could be unleashed if public, private and voluntary sectors were to work together strategically, systematically, purposefully, better than they do today.

Because volunteerism relates to the private sector too. One reason Iqbal does such a great job with the people he works with is precisely because he's not obliged to do it. He doesn't have to be dragged towards minimum standards of philanthropic conformity, he's had the freedom to discover for himself that business doing good is doing good business. He's right to say that business could have a profound positive impact on society, dwarfing the sometimes questionable benefits of superficial CSR. My past research suggests that some 60 per cent of small businesses believe it's right for them to engage actively in the community. They have many ways of expressing this, whilst most think that they can – and should – be doing more than they presently are.

Someone has to make sure that there are enough Roasts to go round; that no child in the gutter is abandoned because there's no entrepreneur available to partner with him. That's what the tax-funded public sector is for, at the very least: a framework for focus and prioritisation to which others can contribute, to make sure, in theory, that no one gets missed. The voluntary sector is people like Iqbal, doing exactly what he's doing, but whose available toolbox of resources – intellectual, temporal, financial, skill-based – is as individuals rather than as businesses. They need to achieve scale and impact together.

The problem with high net worth philanthropy, which is essentially what Iqbal is doing, is that individuals with access to resources, usually money, are deciding on their charitable priorities, their means of helping, at a time and place to suit them. At its worst this can undermine the strategically focused approach of others (I'm certainly *not* asserting that this happens in his case). Philanthropic intervention can raise expectations whilst lacking the infrastructure needed to fulfil them. In other instances it duplicates what others are doing and in yet more it's so off target that a philanthropic endeavour can prove irrelevant to the communities it claims to serve. That's why Bill Gates is a successful business-based philanthropist: he doesn't deliver anything. He uses his funds to enable others to do more, bringing others together to work in partnership and focusing on goals and proven strategies agreed by people who understand. That way he and his collaborators bring scale to their impact.

I've seen business people give money to good causes in ways which border on the irresponsible: indulgent, short sighted, short term. I call the recipients of such bountifulness 'philanthro-pets', the pampered lap dogs of the charity world.

What Iqbal is doing is great, it's proportionate and business-focused, its logic is simple and he operates at a scale and intensity allowed by his own resources, comfort zone and skill set. I wish there were more like him, not to take over from the charity world but to work with it – as he does, through the Prince's Trust – and to empower it; to use their resources to enable charities to move up a gear, to spread their influence and make good better.

At the end of the day, business can't do this alone. Thank goodness he doesn't call it 'CSR'.

I've been using the term 'CSR' although I don't like it. As the Director of Responsible Business at Lloyds Banking Group has said:

> Traditional Corporate Responsibility, the 'Ministry of Good Works' in the corner, the one that issues the oversized cheques for chairmen to sign, is no longer fit for purpose. Like the fax machine, it quietly passed away some time ago without many organisations noticing or even caring. We shouldn't mourn its passing.[53]

'Corporate Social Responsibility' is an over-used, under-valued idea which alienates some ('we're not a corporate') and means little to others. However, it's the language on Responsibility Street even if 'Company Citizen' is, I believe, a more meaningful and inclusive term. So my references to 'CSR' generally relate to existing practices and terminology rather than how things might be.

In 2014 India introduced a raft of 'CSR' legislation, positive in spirit but highly bureaucratic and with several 'catch-all' clauses in it. Three years on, has that helped? Priya Naik, founder and CEO of CSR consultancy Samhita, says:

> Even though we're seeing a steady increase in the amount of money being allocated by firms under CSR, there appears to be a disconnect in what the requirements on the ground are and what the companies are allocating money towards.[54]

In the absence of a major push on cultural change, perhaps this could have been predicted.

The Institute for Corporate Responsibility and Sustainability (ICRS) evolved from a small gathering of companies called the Corporate Responsibility Group.[55] Created in 2015 this forum for companies and individual practitioners provides a framework for CRS, CSR, ESG and related professionals to share good practice, develop their careers, authenticate their experiences and provide learning opportunities with the aim of eventually accrediting professional qualifications in CRS. Most of its 300+ individual members are graduates who live in London and the South East of England.

I applaud ICRS for its diligence, purpose and commitment to making 'a positive difference to society and our planet' through business and I enjoy working with its enthusiastic and purpose-driven members and officers. I welcome the idea that there should be professional recognition of people who pull together sustainability issues, proselytise responsibility within companies and seek to influence mainstream corporate thinking – rather than leaving traditional 'CSR' activity to groups of volunteers on a take it or leave it basis (as too many companies still do, if at all).

But speaking at an ICRS event at the Royal Society for the Arts (RSA) I questioned the cosy London-centric graduate demographic of the profession, a demographic which suggests that more CRS professionals are employed in corporate headquarters than on the shop floor, and I called for a more radical approach. This approach is not an alternative to increasing the professionalism of CRS but goes alongside it. Just as working against discrimination and observing health & safety rules are the duties of everyone at work then so should be promoting responsible business practices.

Every manager, every employee, should be aware of the company's impact on society and the environment and their own contribution to it; everyone should seek to accentuate the positive, the ethical, and eliminate the negative both through their own actions at work and in influencing corporate policies.

The chain of Company Citizenship may only be as strong as its weakest link.

Notes

1 www.bankofengland.co.uk/publications/Pages/speeches/2015/833.aspx.
2 ESG Magazine 6, 2016.
3 www.ft.com/content/3f4a6fd8-a5fc-11e4-abe9-00144feab7de.
4 https://nonprofitchronicles.com/2017/03/14/warren-buffett-has-some-excellent-advice-for-foundations-that-they-probably-wont-take/.
5 www.purposeofcorporation.org/en#how-this-affects-companies.
6 http://usatoday30.usatoday.com/money/industries/retail/2006-06-06-norway-walmart_x.htm.
7 www.worldpolicy.org/blog/2011/01/24/norwegian-wouldnt.
8 http://news.walmart.com/executive-viewpoints/twenty-first-century-leadership.
9 www.theguardian.com/sustainable-business/2015/nov/18/walmart-climate-change-carbon-emissions-renewabe-energy-environment.
10 www.edie.net/news/6/Walmart-launches-plan-to-cut-one-billion-tonnes-of-supply-chain-emissions-by-2030.
11 www.ft.com/content/8ad34584-911d-11e6-a72e-b428cb934b78.
12 www.triplepundit.com/2014/03/record-number-social-environmental-share holder-resolutions-filed-2014/.
13 http://shareaction.org/wp-content/uploads/2016/02/CaseStudy-Shareholder-Resolutions.pdf.
14 www.parliament.uk/business/committees/committees-a-z/commons-select/business-energy-industrial-strategy/news-parliament-2015/corporate-governance-report-published-16-17/.
15 www.theguardian.com/business/2017/apr/27/wpp-to-cut-martin-sorrells-pay-in-bid-to-calm-investors.
16 www.ft.com/content/44f00452-0f1d-11e7-b030-768954394623.
17 www.standard.co.uk/business/reckitt-benckiser-bows-to-city-pressure-as-it-cuts-chief-s-pay-a3503991.html.
18 www.bbc.co.uk/news/business-39512035.
19 https://amp.theguardian.com/commentisfree/2017/may/29/whole-foods-failures-conscious-capitalism? and https://finance.yahoo.com/news/hedge-fund-jana-partners-discloses-blue-apron-position-164051766.html.
20 www.theguardian.com/environment/2016/dec/12/fossil-fuel-divestment-funds-double-5tn-in-a-year.
21 http://ga-institute.com/Sustainability-Update/tag/blackrock/.
22 http://home.bt.com/lifestyle/money/investing-pensions/can-you-make-good-returns-from-ethical-investing-11364109964325. Please note: nothing in this chapter constitutes financial advice. The value of investments . . . , etc.
23 www.globalreporting.org/.
24 www.mondovisione.com/media-and-resources/news/london-stock-exchange-group-launches-guidance-for-esg-reporting/.
25 www.bloomberg.com/news/articles/2015-10-12/blackrock-tries-do-good-investing-after-millenials-convince-fink.
26 https://medium.com/impactalpha/blackrock-tips-shareholder-vote-to-press-oil-giant-on-climate-risk-f0fc5831bca3.
27 www.nytimes.com/2016/02/02/business/dealbook/some-heresy-on-wall-street-look-past-the-quarter.html.
28 www.positive.news/2017/economics/24827/uk-ethical-markets-doubles-tobacco/ and www.businessgreen.com/bg/news/3001828/unilever-a-third-of-consumers-now-buy-from-good-brands.

29 www.autocar.co.uk/car-news/industry/uk-car-registrations-regain-traction-vw-sales-falter.
30 www.london.edu/faculty-and-research/lbsr/li-four-principles-translating-purpose-into-practice#.WFLzoXecaRt. Many of these examples are from http://freakonomics.com/podcast/do-boycotts-work-a-new-freakonomics-radio-podcast/.
31 www.al-monitor.com/pulse/originals/2015/11/israel-palestine-european-labeling-guidelines-settlements.html.
32 http://oxfamblogs.org/fp2p/supporting-labour-rights-in-indonesias-sportswear-factories-draft-case-study-for-your-comments/ and http://news.bbc.co.uk/1/hi/world/asia-pacific/1859232.stm.
33 www.theguardian.com/vital-signs/2015/jan/06/boycotts-shopping-protests-activists-consumers.
34 www.triplepundit.com/special/roi-of-sustainability/how-nike-embraced-csr-and-went-from-villain-to-hero/.
35 http://uk.businessinsider.com/sports-direct-billionaire-mike-ashley-increases-stake-in-debenhams-to-1609-2017-3.
36 www.bbc.co.uk/news/uk-36864345.
37 www.bbc.co.uk/news/business-38247155.
38 http://metro.co.uk/2017/01/23/brothers-jailed-for-slavery-over-workers-they-recruited-for-sports-direct-6400444/.
39 www.theguardian.com/business/2015/dec/10/sports-direct-share-price-falls-following-guardian-working-practices-revelations.
40 www.bbc.co.uk/news/uk-england-derbyshire-36855374.
41 http://webershandwick.co.uk/wp-content/uploads/2014/07/17639-WS-SOI-24pp_14JUL2014_FINAL.pdf.
42 www.hrreview.co.uk/hr-news/recruitment/it-costs-over-30k-to-replace-a-staff-member/50677.
43 Weber Shandwick, ibid.
44 www.samaritans.org/for-business/rail-suicide-prevention/saving-lives.
45 www.willmottdixon.co.uk.
46 www.neyber.co.uk/employers.
47 I explored John Lewis Partnership in *Welcome to GoodCo*.
48 www.gov.uk/government/uploads/system/uploads/attachment_data/file/31668/12-929-employee-ownership-advantage-benefits-and-consequences.pdf.
49 www.esopcentre.com/2017/02/roadchef-employee-shareholders-still-await-compensation/.
50 www.greatbusinessdebate.co.uk/case_study/to-have-a-true-csr-impact-you-must-involve-the-whole-company/.
51 www.bbc.co.uk/news/business-34639178.
52 www.irishtimes.com/culture/books/look-to-business-not-the-state-or-charities-to-fix-our-problems-1.2850596?platform=hootsuite.
53 www.ibe.org.uk/30days/30dayitem.aspx?pname=Responsible-Business-Lloyds-Banking-Group&itemid=24312.
54 http://thecsrjournal.in/three-years-of-csr-spending-on-the-rise-yet-hurdles-remain/. There's more about the Indian CSR Act in *Welcome to GoodCo*.
55 https://icrs.info.

6 The supply chain is ready

The supply chain has gained increasing prominence and scrutiny over recent years in a world that's ever more interconnected, where no business is an island. Attitudes to purchasing what a company needs once included 'we've always used them' and 'we buy the cheapest' but those simple days are gone. As the profile of the supply issues have risen so have transparency and accountability, even through new laws. The supply chain has emerged as a major source of potential risk, whether in terms of convenience ('delivery might be late'), reputation ('your shirts are made by children'), politics ('no supplies since last week's coup') or resources ('keep going at this rate and there'll be nothing left').

It's never been more important to know and build relationships between purchaser and supply chain. Within relationships conversation can avoid surprises, create solutions, make allowances and reward common success. Increasingly, the head of the supply chain doesn't want to see their values undermined by their suppliers: the reputational risk of a child sewing your shirts is that they're sewing your shirts, not that you get found out. The exploitation of abject poverty is something from which neither supplied nor supplier would want to profit, we'd like to think.

Two issues affecting supply chains have been the subjects of recent UK legislation: slavery and corruption. It's in the interests of business to eliminate both. The word 'exploit' will never cross the Company Citizen's lips, though 'partners' will, and the word will be matched by actions. Not every circumstance is covered here, but the following issues are topical, pertinent – and high priority for the Company Citizen.

Modern slavery

'Modern slavery' is a chilling neologism, since slavery's been illegal in Britain since 1833. Theresa May, when Home Secretary, said in her White Paper that preceded the Modern Slavery Bill:

> Young girls are raped, beaten, passed from abuser to abuser and sexually exploited for profit. Vulnerable men are tricked into long hours of

> hard labour before being locked away in cold sheds or rundown caravans. People are made to work in fields, in factories, and on fishing vessels. Women are forced into prostitution and children systematically exploited. Domestic workers are imprisoned and made to work all hours of the day and night for little or no pay.[1]

She acknowledged that there could be 13,000 people subjected to slavery in Britain, not all of them trafficked into the country, and that UK is the world's third most popular trafficking destination. These figures pale, though not into insignificance, when compared with a global market for forced labour worth about $150bn/year. Slave labour is a haven for organised crime and, relatively speaking, a bigger market today than was historical slavery at its peak. Its impact is highest in the third tier of supply-chain hierarchy and below, where scrutiny from the company at the top is often weak. Children as young as four work in Congolese mines for 8p a day;[2] even in EU-applicant Turkey 94,000 under 18s (excluding apprentices) were working, largely in agriculture, with no legal rights or protection in 2016.[3]

The 2015 legislation applies to 12,000 companies operating in UK, each turning over more than £36m. Although the clauses relating to supply chains weren't included in early drafts of the Bill, lobbying from NGOs, Unilever, IKEA and investors Hermes and Alliance Trust ensured that the opportunity to make a difference wasn't missed.[4] Companies must now make an annual statement explaining their supply chain structure, its vulnerability to modern slavery issues such as child or forced labour, its relevant performance indicators and the process of due diligence it uses to expunge it. It should also describe steps it's taking to ensure that relevant staff – within both company and suppliers – are aware of their obligations to ensure a chain free from slavery.

The Act refers to company 'operations' so isn't restricted to supply chains. Companies should know that they are recruiting from amongst free agents, not bonded labour, and the level of fees, if any, recruits have paid (sometimes continue to pay) to agencies in UK or abroad. Companies whose CSR operations carry out social audits are rarely skilled in detecting or acknowledging employment abuse. Brazil, uniquely, publishes a black list of companies banned from receiving state funding because of questionable activities in this field.[5] A high-profile name on this 600-strong list is fashion company Zara, whose 2014 court attempt to be taken off the list was denied after one of their suppliers was found to be using slave labour. In banking, the supply chain may be low risk for slavery but their customers may not be. So some UK banks try to identify spending patterns linked to small-time prostitution in order to identify and avoid being linked to clients who profit from trafficking. More lucrative clients, one suspects, may be too big for such scrutiny.

Eliminating slavery is not mere 'political correctness'. Most leading companies believe their supply chains could be vulnerable and 97 per cent say slavery is a reputational risk. 'Reputation' doesn't mean 'window dressing': a company can be brought down by reputational damage and, even in less serious cases, lawyers could have a field day.[6] Research by Triodos Bank suggests that 74 per cent of investors won't invest in companies associated with human rights abuses like slavery – more than would avoid pornography (56), the arms trade (46), animal testing (40) or tobacco (27).[7]

Know the Chain was formed in 2013 to promote company engagement with Californian legislation against modern slavery in supply chains. They produce data on companies, assessing them on their capacity to root out the illegal exploitation of workers, and contributed to the development of Britain's Modern Slavery Act. Within the global food and beverage industry Know the Chain concluded that Unilever, Coca-Cola and Nestlé, all scoring over 50 per cent, stood head and shoulders above other companies. Of the 20 major global food companies surveyed the household name Kraft Heinz is near the bottom, scoring just 9: they're aware of the issues and have clauses to prevent modern slavery in their supply chain contracts but do next to nothing, said Know the Chain, to monitor standards or correct breaches.[8] Most household names in technology score at least as well as the best food and beverage companies – except Canon, with a disappointing 12/100. Even at the top of these leagues there's room for improvement.

Hot spots for modern slavery include the south-east-Asian prawn industry, where Thai-based CP Foods is a £20bn business serving, amongst others, most UK supermarkets. Whilst it doesn't employ people directly under slave conditions, the fact that it has hundreds of suppliers makes detailed monitoring very difficult. Three hundred thousand people work in the Thai prawn supply chain and many are migrants, largely from Myanmar and Cambodia, working illegally in international waters to harvest food for the prawn farms.

There could be 45 million slaves in the world. Construction Management web site advises companies on how to spot exploitation and where to report it, noting that during the building of New York University's Abu Dhabi campus 10,000 'unregistered workers' were employed without the University's knowledge.[9] Two thirds of the $400bn market in packaging is associated with food and the industry is considered relatively free of modern slavery: for now. However, EY have singled out packaging as a future 'high risk' area as demand rises, especially in BRIC countries, due to growing affluence.[10] Whilst child labour is banned in Uzbekistan the government stifles opposition to the high levels of adult forced labour in the world's fifth largest cotton exporter.[11]

In April 2013 shockwaves rippled across the fashion industry as 1,134 people were killed and over 2,500 injured when an eight-storey building collapsed in Rana Plaza in Dhaka, Bangladesh. Major brands were initially unable or unwilling to say whether any of their suppliers were amongst the companies that employed 5,000 garment factory workers there, though labels from Benetton, Monsoon, Primark, Walmart, Matalan and others were found amongst the rubble. Cracks had been found the day before the collapse and retail workers on lower floors evacuated; whether or not the garment companies were warned, no evacuation from upper floors was attempted.

Those who died that day may or may not technically have been slaves or forced labour, but their welfare was certainly of little concern to the brands at the head of several supply chains – at the time. Since then 100 brands, working together, have made a difference in Bangladesh – not least through an accord on Fire and Building Safety between brands, unions and suppliers. Twenty leading brands including C&A, Gap, H&M, Next and Primark, backed by their investors, have called upon the Bangladeshi Government to conduct a sector wage review and stop targeting trade union leaders, after pay protests led to 1,600 workers being suspended and 35 union leaders and others arrested. In April 2017, following legal action, the main tannery in Dhaka was shut down on safety grounds, leaving 30,000 leather workers seeking alternative work.[12]

The response of the fashion industry to Rana Plaza was rapid as the hashtag #fashionrevolution invaded Twitter. Seventy thousand people asked manufacturers 'Who made my clothes?', establishing networks of concerned individuals around the world during Fashion Revolution Week 2016, the anniversary of Rana Plaza, double the number for the previous year.

The call for transparency and care in fashion was backed by a 2016 survey of leading companies using available data. Only three scored 75/100 (Levi Strauss was top with 77) for a basket of criteria whilst 28 of the 40 scored less than 50. The very reasonable criteria included 'policy commitments to ethical supply', 'traceability', 'social/environmental audit', 'engagement/collaboration' and 'governance'. Only six companies published targets for improving supply-chain conditions (Gap, Primark, Levi Strauss, H&M, Inditex and Nike). Most had codes of conduct but 16 of the 40 didn't monitor compliance with labour standards covering their supply chains and only 11 worked with trade unions on working conditions: a code of conduct alone improves nothing. A third had no system to support whistleblowers.[13]

The survey was repeated in 2017 with 100 companies (many volunteering to take part) and broader but more stringent criteria. None passed 50 per cent overall though Adidas, Reebok, M&S and H&M all came close. A third scored under 10 and three scored zero as they disclosed nothing. Although this time nearly 30 topics were assessed they were dominated by labour issues. Only a third made their information on tier 1 traceability public, the most comprehensive being M&S.[14]

Clothing is a huge global industry, labour intensive and price sensitive, touching every household. Clearly legislation alone is insufficient to bring about change and transparency is essential – some companies hide behind 'commercial confidence' whilst others readily reveal information. Legitimate consumer interest must have access to good data.[15] Policies are not enough: there's no excuse for non-disclosure.

Myanmar (Burma) exported almost $1bn worth of clothing in 2014, trebling the output of three years earlier when it was under military control and subject to trade sanctions. Exports to the EU had doubled in just one year. Almost all of Myanmar's clothing industry fails the decency test, with child labour rife, casual labour (with no employment contracts) widespread and trade unions almost absent, despite improvements in the country's laws. The legal minimum wage is widely ignored.

At the height of international sanctions Myanmar had only 130 clothing factories, almost exclusively supporting far-eastern supply chains. Today there are over 400, mostly Taiwanese, Chinese and Korean-owned. A recent independent report alerted companies to problems caused when suppliers moved to source from Myanmar without consulting the top of their chains. Diligent companies like C&A, New Look and H&M investigated concerns. M&S trialled sourcing from Myanmar but didn't proceed on ethical grounds whilst a dozen others, including Sports Direct, didn't respond to questions about conditions in their suppliers' factories. An alliance of 18 brands has been working with trade unions and others (including BSR and ETI) since 2015 to improve wages and sourcing practices.[16]

Modern slavery is not just a third-world issue. In 2017 Channel 4's 'Dispatches' revealed that Fashion Square, a clothing factory in Leicestershire, UK, blatantly paid workers less than half the National Minimum Wage, didn't check on illegal working, locked its fire doors and committed other health and safety breaches. New Look, which has reduced its UK supply base significantly in a move to clean up its supply chain, immediately cancelled its relationship with its supplier, TS Knitwear, who'd previously been instructed not to sub-contract to Fashion Square.[17] Taking functions back internally from outsourcing partners is a not uncommon risk management response to the Modern Slavery Act.

Some businesses have complained that the law doesn't punish offenders as harshly for slavery as for comparable misdemeanours; bigger penalties would help businesses feel more supported when they take action against their own suppliers. Some suppliers will, no doubt, drop out of supply chains rather than meet the costs of compliance. Until similar legislation is adopted by more countries it will be easy for them, often working on small margins, to find less ethical customers elsewhere. In terms of enforcement, it's important that businesses 'sell' changes to their suppliers not as compliance but as business improvement, bowing to the demands of a more conscientious market; and that where instances of slavery are found they don't just put their own houses in order but they report offenders to the authorities.

Norman Pickavance of Grant Thornton has called for companies to campaign against slavery, as Josiah Wedgwood and his colleagues did in an earlier generation; to work together as an alliance of businesses, NGOs and others, and to share data, with the aim of putting slave traders out of business. Back in 1830 a slave would have been 'worth' about $40,000 in today's money – the equivalent price today is just $90. It's clear that such market forces need to be opposed.[18]

In 2015 the Thomson Reuter Foundation instigated an annual award to highlight companies leading the fight against slavery.[19]

Although there is much to be proud of in the Modern Slavery Act, of the first £3m of compensation extracted from slavers less than 5 per cent reached their victims.[20] Sixteen hundred cases are expected through the British courts in 2017 compared with under 300 just two years earlier.[21] The Californian Act preceded the UK one and the Netherlands followed; France, Australia and Switzerland are in the queue. The G20 has endorsed the Act and 28,000 companies worldwide now produce annual statements on slavery, many regarding the process as a route to innovation and smoother trade.[22] No true Company Citizen wants to profit from the unreasonable exploitation of vulnerable people, wherever in the world they are.

Bribery and corruption

Also welcomed by business was the Bribery & Corruption Act of 2010, which I helped scrutinise in the dying days of the Labour government – though the Act was implemented under the Coalition. It requires all companies to have 'adequate procedures' to prevent their agents being parties to corrupt acts by obliging them to make employees aware of their responsibilities and carry out appropriate risk assessments. If a procurer of goods for the company in a foreign country acquires goods or services in good faith, confident that bribery and corruption are not involved, then they're unlikely to face prosecution even if the supplier turns out not to have acted in good faith themselves. Many companies welcomed the clarity that the Act brought to sometimes dodgy practices whilst some worried that 'facilitation payments', typically cash transfers intended to get a product supplied on time, or perhaps released from a warehouse, were cultural norms in some countries and not therefore regarded as corrupt in those cultures. Lawyers responded that facilitation payments by British companies were already illegal under previous legislation.[23]

Transparency International (TI) estimate that two thirds of nations, including half the G20, have 'serious' corruption in their public services, whilst in many poorer and eastern countries trade is frequently dependent on the permission of public 'servants' who too often regard themselves as 'masters'. Transparency International claims that $1tn each year is spent other than as intended by public authorities, development agencies and private business because it is siphoned off to illicit destinations. If '100' means 'corruption-free' on the Corruption Perception Index then in 2016 only Denmark and New Zealand scored 90+. Thirteen European countries are in the cleanest top 20 (UK was joint 10th). Outside these countries few don't have a major corruption problem; even within Europe, Greece, Italy and Bulgaria each score under 50.

Some at the bottom of the list of 168 countries suffer from lack of data; if you want to know where your money's going, don't trade with Somalia, North Korea or either of the Sudans. Of the 20 most corrupt countries most have dysfunctional governments, several have oil and others are at war. Only 52 countries score 50 or more and there are few significant changes in rank order from one year to the next; both Brazil and Guatemala dropped points recently due to the Petrobas and La Linea scandals respectively.[24] In the former the state oil company allegedly made corrupt payments to the Workers' Party, costing the President her job, whilst in the latter corrupt importers paid only a third of their import taxes in return for passing money illegally to the state's Customs service.[25]

In 2017 Rolls Royce made a voluntary payment of £500m to the UK Serious Fraud Office (with lesser sums to the US and Brazil), plus costs, in lieu of prosecution under 2013 legislation which allows for this when companies refer themselves for investigation. The 'fine' relates to the activity of independent agents hired by the company to promote jet engine sales in a dozen African and Asian countries where illegal payments were made. Campaigners argue that payment in lieu of prosecution should not have been allowed as referral to the authorities was by a whistleblower, not by the company; prosecution should (and could) still apply.[26] Undoubtedly a court case would take years, cost the public purse millions and possibly result in lost jobs and exports. Is Rolls Royce, like our banks, 'too big to fail'? The bigger they come, apparently, the easier it is to mitigate the consequences of unfair play.

Corruption costs 5 per cent of global GDP and increases companies' costs by 10 per cent. There's an argument that companies whose beneficial owners are hidden, perhaps in tax havens, constitute a disproportionate source of corrupt business practice in a sphere where, by definition, little is known. Shell companies, like Russian dolls, rarely expose their innermost secrets and 77 countries are trying to regulate them into the open. Britain and Ukraine are leading the way, both establishing compulsory registers of beneficial ownership for anonymously-owned businesses. The two countries were stung by a revelation that much of Ukraine's Presidential estate was owned by a UK shell company, whilst other UK shells had acted as go-betweens for British arms deals with Ukraine and Libya.[27] France and South Africa are preparing to create such a register and others will follow. The USA, much of Africa and several Middle Eastern countries have no intention of doing so, choosing to defend the right to anonymity.[28] The US is the 'easiest place in the world to create a company where the real identity of the people who own or control them can be kept secret', says TI, in the wake of the Panama Papers' disclosures, which revealed so much about the lengths to which individuals and organisations will go to minimise their tax liabilities.[29]

That UK register of People with Significant Control of companies (owning more than 25 per cent) is a world first. Britain has banned the issuing of 'bearer shares' which are owned by the person who possesses them; shares must now have a name attached. Companies may not normally now be directors of other companies, either – only individuals can be.[30] However, Britain's Dependent Territories were not included in the UK legislation. The Panama Papers spotlighted the British Virgin Islands, exposing tax avoidance, tax evasion and money laundering. Its 30,000 people share their home with 600,000 registered companies, many of which are shells.

Globally, the number of corporate CEOs who are forced out of their job is low and falling – but within that figure the number departing for 'ethical lapses' is growing alarmingly, up from under 4 per cent of 'successions' (2007–11) to over 5 per cent (2012–16).[31]

Under Trump's deregulation crusade it's no longer necessary for US companies working with fossil fuels to report on payments made to foreign governments, a move which many say will promote corruption in places like Angola and Kazakhstan. The immediate reaction of 13 such companies, in harmony, was 'No'. The group, which includes Anglo American, BHP Billiton and Glencore, argue that: 'Consistency of financial disclosure makes good business sense . . . We will continue to disclose our payments of taxes and royalties.'[32]

These are the acts of Company Citizens who believe not just in doing the right thing but in doing so in public.

Human rights

In July 2000 the United Nations launched the Global Compact (UNGC), inviting companies to support ten principles governing private-sector engagement in ethical, social and environmental issues. Nine thousand companies, in over 160 countries, have signed the Compact and many of them operate in low-risk countries – but their supply chains source from nations where human rights abuse is commonplace. A quarter of the signatories are amongst the world's biggest companies; Nestlé has action plans on 11 human rights fronts across its supply chain under the UN Guiding Principles on Business and Human Rights, having trained 75,000 of its employees to identify and address such issues.[33] A handful of companies have been removed from Compact membership over the years, usually for turning a blind eye to supply-chain problems. The 'Ruggie Framework', adopted by the UN Human Rights Council in 2008, described respect for human rights – the use of due diligence to avoid infringing the rights of others and addressing adverse impacts – as a 'corporate responsibility' for the first time.

Neither consumers nor, increasingly, shareholders wish to be associated with practices that exploit workers in ways that are unethical or breach their human rights. Child labour, which 'deprives children of their childhood, potential or dignity' in ILO terminology, is increasingly frowned upon in supply chains even though in some countries it's apparently culturally acceptable. Child labour has fallen by a third since 2000, due to pressure from business combined with political progress in the poorest countries, though it's still thought to number 168 million, half of whom work in hazardous jobs. In some African countries a fifth of children work.

In the 1990s Manchester United, the world's fourth largest football business, commissioned branded footballs from a developing country. When they discovered that child labour was involved in their production they addressed the clear reputational risk by deciding to cease using that source. However, the reason that very young children were working was because their mothers, the bulk of the workforce, had nowhere else to send them: ending child labour would have cost many women their jobs. Working with Unicef, the club instead created a factory with an associated crèche, the first of its kind in that country, enabling the women to keep working and the children to be safe. Although Unicef's work with FC Barcelona is possibly the world's best-known charity/football partnership, this one between Unicef and United pre-dates it by some years.

Many business leaders argue that where civil society is stable, open, democratic and engaged risks to long-term investments are reduced. Not all have quite yet understood that these qualities ought to include an acceptance of workers' free collective bargaining, which is part of the UNGC approach. Improving working conditions is increasingly the subject of collaboration between businesses, as different companies often share the same ultimate sources of the goods that they sell. Recent global research by Business for Social Responsibility (BSR) suggests that although only one company in eight does nothing on this front there are inconsistencies in the approach to human rights adopted by businesses.[34]

Many of the world's champions of human rights are charities or other non-governmental organisations. Such NGOs are active in around 100 countries and in 2014 alone over 130 campaigners were killed. This number is growing as governments, including China, India and Russia, clamp down on NGOs operating in their countries.

The international Charities Aid Foundation asked the London School of Economics to look at co-operation between businesses and NGOs on human rights issues. Their 2016 report 'Beyond Integrity' described companies intervening to protect individuals whose freedom of expression was threatened, in their company's interest.[35]

- Angola: Rafael Marques' book on blood diamonds documented allegations of 500 crimes committed by military officers and mine owners. When he tried to have charges brought against seven generals they countersued for defamation, which could have put Marques in prison for nine years. In 2015 a judge ruled that his trial should happen behind closed doors, prompting international outrage. The Business and Human Rights Resource Centre (BHRRC) mobilised diamond companies and retail jewellers, including Tiffany's and Brilliant Earth, to protest against the manner of the trial and in support of supply chains free of human rights abuse. This threat clearly had influence. Although eventually Marques was allowed to continue his work he was subsequently deemed to have admitted guilt and received a six-month suspended sentence.
- Cambodia: garment workers supplying global brands would regularly work 100 hours a week for a legal minimum wage of under \$100. Demonstrations in support of a higher rate were violently suppressed, with deaths and detentions. The ILO backed the workers' call for \$170 but the Government was intransigent. In January 2014, 30 international brands and three labour unions, co-ordinated by the Ethical Trading Initiative, co-signed a letter to the government urging compromise and settlement. The Government agreed to meet Puma, Gap, H&M and the

alliance of manufacturing trade unions, IndustriALL; the minimum wage was subsequently raised to $140/week.

- Thailand: 80 per cent of Thailand's 2.5 million migrant workers are Burmese and many are illegals, vulnerable to severe exploitation. Many global supply chains start in Thailand, one of the world's labour and human rights black spots. In 2013 Finnwatch, a Finnish NGO, reported on poor migrant labour conditions in a major pineapple producer and two companies in the tuna industry. Within weeks Natural Fruit brought legal action against Andy Hall, a contributor to the report. The Thai Tuna Industry Association and the Thai Frozen Food Association together paid Hall's bail in line, they explained, with their own ethical codes on workers' rights.

In July 2016 Hall was tried, fined and given a suspended sentence, leaving Thailand for his own safety that November after his corporate allies paid the fine.[36] S Group, a Finnish supermarket chain, spoke in Hall's defence after ceasing trading with Natural Fruit because of their refusal to adopt independent human rights audits.[37] The Business and Human Rights Resource Centre tracks the human rights records of over 6,000 companies in 180 countries and helps to eradicate abuse. They report that mining is the most dangerous area for campaigners on corporate accountability: as many informants are attacked there as in the next three, agribusiness, hydrocarbons and dam building, combined.

In 2017 the Corporate Human Rights Benchmark was launched. It ranks 100 large corporates for their pro-human-rights stance in the key fields of extraction, apparel and food. Two mining companies, BHP Billiton (1st) and Rio Tinto (3rd), were amongst the top performers and M&S was second. Only three other companies scored over 50 per cent: Nestlé, Adidas and Unilever.[38] Adidas has said:

> We will . . . petition governments, alone or in concert with other actors, where we feel the rights and freedoms of human rights defenders with whom we are engaged have been impinged by the activities of the State.[39]

Human rights abuse is not going to end overnight even if every company sourcing from at-risk countries is actively involved. The UN itself, threatened with big cuts in American funding, can't guarantee to maintain its levels of vigilance. Or can it? In May 2017 Microsoft donated $5m towards a 'landmark' five-year technology partnership with the UN Commission on Human Rights to process and publish data on human rights abuses. Microsoft's President, Brad Smith, said: 'We have an untapped opportunity to use the power of technology to collect data, analyse that data, and equip the United Nations to advance human rights around the world.'[40]

A further study by BSR observed that human rights issues don't always occur where you most expect them, after a member noted that the worst breaches in their supply chain were found in their most trusted partner.[41]

Whose responsibility is it to address such issues: the supply chain head, the company concerned or the state? It's all of them, otherwise it's too easy for each to expect another to act whilst looking the other way. Within business there's an increasing amount of advice, learning and guidance from Company Citizens who are willing to share; some sectors' futures depend on it.

Employment rights

The 1990s saw several global campaigns to persuade corporates to insist on basic standards of dignity within their supply chains, such as that against Nike, as we've seen. Companies were developing codes of conduct at that time but they varied immensely; sometimes several inconsistent codes could apply to a single workplace. Some were weak, falling short even of established ILO conventions on workers' rights. A cross-sector group of concerned activists, supported by the UK's Department for International Development, decided to work towards the implementation of a common code of conduct across international supply chains and in 1998 the Ethical Trading Initiative (ETI) was born.[42] The founding companies were Asda (part of Walmart), Premier Brands, The Body Shop, Littlewoods and Sainsbury's and amongst its most effective champions today is Tesco – Europe's largest private-sector employer of unionised labour.

The Ethical Trading Initiative campaigns for the dignity of workers in the global supply chains of (mostly) British companies. It has more than 100 members: over 90 companies alongside NGOs, trade unions and their international umbrella groups. Together those companies have a turnover of £166bn and ten million people work in supply chains linked to them.

Their goals are to end forced, bonded and child labour, promote freedom of association and legitimate trade union activity and create safe, dignified workplaces in those supply chains. They support local minimum wage legislation and living wage conventions, reasonable working hours and, wherever possible, regular employment. They oppose abuse, intimidation and arbitrary discrimination, including against trade union members. Whilst all signatories to the ETI charter are asked to 'commit' to these values there are no strict rules as to how, or over what timescale, they should be attained. Whilst many companies do acknowledge that commitment is a precursor to action, several have been asked to leave ETI for laggardly or non-existent progress in delivering ethical trade themselves, let alone in their supply chains. Seven companies left membership in 2016, for a variety of reasons, but it's heartening to see some non-members adopt the ETI code – notably the delivery body for the London Olympics.

An early success for ETI was the introduction of gangmaster legislation in UK, which protects those in casual or temporary work in agriculture, shellfish gathering, food processing and packaging.[43] The Gangmaster Licensing Authority, established following the deaths of Chinese cockle-pickers in Morecambe Bay, can prosecute unlicensed operators. Besides regulating gangmasters, it's an advice and support centre for such workers to access their rights. In recent years both prosecutions and investigations have dwindled because, we're told, they now focus on more complex cases of organised crime. Following the 2016 Immigration Act the scope of what is now GLAA, the Gangmaster and Labour Abuse Authority, now includes modern slavery, the regulation of employment agencies and the ability to prosecute under Minimum Wage legislation. Some of the cases they prosecute are horrendous.[44]

In the stone industry, especially in India and China, standards are low, safety equipment is in short supply and life-limiting diseases such as silicosis, caused by breathing in stone dust, common. It's perhaps a sign of ETI's influence that some of these companies are not members but claim to be, misrepresenting their standards and undermining them.[45]

None of these negative issues and impacts would arise were it not for unscrupulous elements within business engaging in high risk and illegal acts or turning a blind eye to them. Countless vulnerable people suffer when supply chain prices in poorer countries are forced down without any guarantee that, if they were raised, the additional funds would be distributed fairly. We need radically better monitoring and conditionality from higher up the supply chain. Countries with dysfunctional governments tend to have a civil society that's disorganised and powerless and too many top companies still avert their gaze, keep their distance and contrive to benefit from poor practices.

Ultimately many companies with household names that provide us with goods must be availing themselves of the services of ruthless and brutal people who engage in inhuman and degrading treatment of their workforce, in order to supply markets at the cheapest possible price. If they didn't rely on them such practices wouldn't exist. Globalisation may itself be inevitable and values-free but the consequences we allow it to have are neither. Those companies that stand between us and potential abuse should not only be guardians of good practice, ethical stewards, but also the guarantors that we, the consumers, are not associated with inhumanity; that's what Company Citizens do.

Twenty-first-century supply chains are long, complex and interwoven; the interests and responsibilities of others crisscross and there are ever more laws, regulations and codes of practice about every aspect of corporate behaviour. Within the company responsibility is clear: the Company Citizen says 'these are my premises, my employees, my goods – I take responsibility for their safety, welfare and dignity'. Outside the company walls those responsibilities are no different for those upon whom they rely, influence and otherwise impact. They're part of the family – distant cousins perhaps, but blood's thicker than water.

What happens in the supply chain is the ultimate purchaser's responsibility and someone will tell the world if their agent, supplier or brand gets it wrong. Relying on others is always risky; minimising that risk is best done through co-operation and persuasion rather than shallow edict. Making sure the worst doesn't happen isn't a matter of going through checklists and ticking boxes, nor even about compliance and observation of law. It's about understanding your connections, an attitude of mind that values sustainability, human dignity and what's right.

When that thought prevails, all of the challenges supply chains face are easier to cope with: what do your values tell you to do? Can you live with your decision?

Prompt payment

If you ask Britain's Federation of Small Businesses (FSB) 'What's the one issue upon which the business community needs to get a grip?' they'll tell you: 'prompt payment'. This is a measure of the time it takes for a supply chain purchaser (usually a bigger company) to pay their bills. There's evidence, say lawyers, that small businesses aren't using available legal remedies to tame recalcitrant debtors for fear of upsetting their large customers and losing future business. They're allowed to charge interest at 8 per cent above base rate on payments that are contractually overdue, but very rarely do. Big companies exploit this reticence to challenge their late payment to their own financial advantage: 'If there's an error or a query with an invoice, they won't inform you until the 89th day. Then your invoice is put at the bottom of the pile and you can wait another 90 days.'[46]

The Prompt Payment Code was established in 2008 by the Chartered Institute of Credit Management, with government backing, as a voluntary agreement to promote good practice. Code signatories, including several FTSE100 businesses, undertake to pay suppliers within 30 days under the 'good practice' terms of the Code or within any term agreed in a contract (under European law a maximum of 60 days is obligatory). Almost 2,000 businesses and public authorities have committed to the 30-day code.[47] The government itself, a huge procurer of goods and services, has pledged to pay undisputed bills within just five days and all others within 30; legislation now requires all companies to declare their payment policies and practices.

Nevertheless, larger companies continue to prefer their '30 days from the end of the month in which the claim is made' (i.e. up to 60 days) practice, or 60, 90, even 120 days – because it suits them. According to the FSB tardy payers include some code signatories. The average debt payment time across the private sector is a massive 72 days, way longer than allowed, and the amount officially overdue at any time is a staggering £30bn.[48] This has been the case every year since 2008, a doubling of pre-recession levels. Failure of customers to pay promptly affects a million small businesses a year, say FSB, pointing out that late payment can trigger further late payments, force traders to borrow money and even put companies out of business.[49] Ministers have promised to give the code more teeth and to be 'rigorous' at removing erring corporates from the list of signatories.[50]

Companies suffering from late payment are scathing about their recalcitrant customers, 'usually the PLCs', whilst measures available to pursue them (once that inflated interest charge has been ruled out) are few and unreliable: 'we won't sell to you again' shoots yourself in the foot. The winding up order, having a PLC declared bankrupt in respect of debts over £750, is no way to win friends either. Small businesses are calling for a late payment Ombudsman, an idea which ministers are 'considering'.

There's nothing magical about 30 days but a balance must exist between the interests of purchaser and vendor. We've all made a significant purchase on that magical day five weeks before the credit card payment is taken from our account, but don't try walking your trolley out of a supermarket and promising them payment within 30 days. Reliability and reason are what matters. Fujitsu is a rare commercial beast that not only writes '30 days' into all of its contracts but makes automated payments to its 1,000 suppliers within 14 days if they opt to allow a 3 per cent discount.[51] For some small businesses that's a price worth paying.

Resource issues

Any industry that runs out of raw materials is soon out of business.

One of the problems of using human sewage as fertiliser is that it could be poisonous. A significant reason for this is the presence of toxic heavy metals which could, it turns out, be poo's saving grace. Every time you brush your teeth microscopic fragments of your gold cap are washed into the sewers or down your alimentary canal, to the extent that the concentration of gold in sewage, albeit tiny, could be as high as in some natural ores, sufficient to justify 'mining' it.

A ton of sewage sludge could contain hundreds of dollars of gold, but in sewers poo is diluted by industrial waste containing a cocktail of other metals. It's been calculated that a million-person city could recover $13m worth of metals each year, more than just gold and silver; in Arizona they 'mined' such sludge for 13 different elements and recovered metals worth $280/ton of sludge (that's $8m per million people, not far from that theoretical figure). A Japanese treatment plant, conveniently close to companies ready to purchase very small amounts of rare metals, wants to commercialise the process by recovering 2kg of gold from every ton of sewage ash left from burning sludge, though the extraction process is expensive and hasn't yet gone to scale.

Some companies are investigating making plastic from sewage, others extracting phosphorus and nitrogen compounds for the commercial production of fertiliser. Such approaches – at the innovative heart of the circular economy-oriented Company Citizen – may yet generate commercial opportunities.[52]

The food and drink industry is concerned about a looming shortage of materials for packaging. Whilst glass, aluminium and steel don't degrade from repeated recycling, paper and cardboard do. Seventy per cent of paper-based food packaging contains recycled materials, in corrugated cardboard it's 86. Yet because the world looks to replace oil and coal in energy production, there's growing demand for paper waste as a biofuel. Although biofuel is a possible substitute for fossil fuels it isn't carbon-free and it frequently competes for fertile land, unfairly, with food. Hold back on the biofuel: if packaging has to pay more for virgin wood pulp that will increase costs to the consumer and be environmentally retrograde.

The Thai-owned fish company John West made a commitment in 2011 to catch half of the tuna it sells in Britain by 2014 by 'pole and line'. This reduces the risk of netting members of the wrong species, especially dolphins. On this basis major UK supermarkets, having publicly committed to selling fish only from sustainable sources, agreed to retain them as suppliers. Unfortunately for John West ambition dwarfed reality: at the end of 2015 just 2 per cent of their catch was caught ethically. The Co-op, Waitrose and Sainsbury's have insisted they will only accept sustainably sourced fish after the end of 2017 whereas Tesco has already removed some John West products from its shelves. The fish company has promised UK supermarkets that their supplies will be ethical, which can only be achieved if John West relies even more on unsustainable sources for its less demanding customers – which rather misses the point.[53]

Some metals enjoying a new lease of commercial life in the mobile-phone industry are already running short. Unlike other metallic elements the 17 'rare earths' tend not to aggregate into mineable seams. Very few of their names would be recognised by the public unless they'd recently studied inorganic chemistry or smiled at Tom Lehrer's song *The Elements*.

Seventy of the planet's 83 stable, non-radioactive atomic elements are used in mobile phones. A single smartphone typically contains 60 of them including up to 16 of those rare earths.[54] There are 9kg of rare earths in the hybrid battery of my Toyota Prius . . . and two million such cars. Rare earths are used in switches, magnets, lasers, X-ray equipment, solar cells and, ubiquitously, mobile phones. There they make the glass screens tougher, enable speaker magnets to be smaller and allow the phone to vibrate.

Colour television kickstarted rare-earth extraction as europium was found to be ideal for creating screen 'red'. In the 1990s a major US producer suffered pollution breaches involving radioactive thorium, a side-product of the extraction process, and by 2002 the last US source had closed. China dominates rare-earth mining today. Their output, built on low labour rates and questionable pollution controls, increased five-fold whilst that of the rest of the world collapsed, even before mobile phones 'took off'.

Today demand is so high that several companies are looking to mine rare earths from sea water, the ocean floor or even the moon, which is particularly rich in them. Only 1 per cent of phones are properly recycled (though many more are re-used) yet they contain rare earths, gold, palladium, copper, silver, tungsten and platinum too. And 500 million phones are currently not being used.

That 1 per cent figure is not unusual; many metals in short supply are rarely recycled. The EU intends to follow up its 2008 raw materials initiative with tighter policies on the conservation of at least 13 metals, including some rare earths, where Europe almost wholly depends on imports.[55] By contrast, about half of all scrap steel is recycled.

Scientists believe that there's no substitute for most rare earths in mobile phones. Known reserves of several will run out by 2050 or, in the worst case scenario, by 2020; but native gold and copper might be gone too by 2050 – unless recycling and reclamation really take off. Discovering a new mineable copper seam today might not produce its first output for ten years but at current low prices who wants to invest in copper? Back to the idea of the Circular Economy. Or the sewage . . .

Notes

1 www.gov.uk/government/uploads/system/uploads/attachment_data/file/383764/Modern_Slavery_Strategy_FINAL_DEC2015.pdf.
2 https://news.sky.com/story/meet-dorsen-8-who-mines-cobalt-to-make-your-smartphone-work-10784120?.
3 www.hurriyetdailynews.com/around-100000-children-in-registered-labor-force-in-turkey-ministry.aspx?PageID=238&NID=109962&NewsCatID=338.
4 http://corporate-responsibility.org/issues/modern-slavery-bill/.
5 www.unodc.org/documents/human-trafficking/2015/Recruitment_Fees_Report-Final-22_June_2015_AG_Final.pdf.
6 http://community.businessfightspoverty.org/profiles/blogs/what-does-good-look-like-for-companies-trying-to-address-modern-s.
7 www.theguardian.com/money/2013/oct/12/what-best-ethical-funds.
8 https://knowthechain.org/benchmarks/2/. Know the Chain issued a subsequent, deeper diving report in April 2017: https://knowthechain.org/wp-content/uploads/KTC_CrossSectoralFindings_Final.pdf.
9 www.modernslaveryhelpline.org or 0800 0121 700 – http://tinyurl.com/m656ysr.
10 www.edie.net/blog/Tackling-modern-slavery-in-the-food--beverage-packaging-industry/6098166.
11 https://innovation-forum.co.uk/analysis.php?s=forced-labour-still-picks-uzbeks-cotton.
12 www.iccr.org/bangladesh-accord-illustrates-power-multi-stakeholder-collabora tion-address-supply-chain-issues.
13 http://fashionrevolution.org/wp-content/uploads/2016/04/FR_FashionTrans parencyIndex.pdf.
14 https://issuu.com/fashionrevolution/docs/fr_fashiontransparencyindex2017?e=25766662/47726047.
15 www.antislavery.org/reports-and-resources/research-reports/slavery-supply-chain-reports/.
16 www.somo.nl/the-myanmar-dilemma/.
17 www.huffingtonpost.co.uk/entry/channel-4-dispatches-britains-cheap-clothes-investigation-national-living-wage_uk_5885e797e4b0b8867de86378?ir=UK%3Fn cid%3Dnewsletter-uk.
18 http://vibranteconomy.grantthornton.co.uk/why-businesses-need-to-act-to-stop-modern-slavery/.
19 www.stopslaveryaward.com.
20 www.thetimes.co.uk/edition/news/slaves-miss-out-on-3m-compensation-fcz-5w9r7g.
21 *The Times*, 11 May 2017.
22 https://innovation-forum.co.uk/analysis.php?s=three-things-the-modern-slavery-act-has-achieved.
23 www.justice.gov.uk/downloads/legislation/bribery-act-2010-quick-start-guide.pdf.
24 www.transparency.org/news/feature/corruption_perceptions_index_2016#table.
25 www.insightcrime.org/news-analysis/guatemala-la-linea-customs-scandal-explained.
26 www.theguardian.com/business/2017/jan/16/rolls-royce-to-pay-671m-over-bribery-claims. I discussed this issue with Anne-Christine Wegener (see Cockcroft and Wegener, 2017).
27 www.globalwitness.org/sv/blog/transparent-company-ownership-how-does-uk-governments-proposed-action-live-its-rhetoric/.

28 http://ownershiptransparency.com.
29 http://blog.transparency.org/2016/09/22/a-growing-call-from-business-for-company-ownership-transparency/.
30 www.gov.uk/government/uploads/system/uploads/attachment_data/file/417328/bis_15_266_SBEE__Act_companies-transparency-fact-sheet.pdf.
31 www.strategy-business.com/feature/Are-CEOs-Less-Ethical-Than-in-the-Past?gko=50774.
32 https://innovation-forum.co.uk/analysis.php?s=why-companies-reject-pro-business-trump.
33 www.nestle.com/csv/human-rights-compliance/human-rights.
34 www.bsr.org/reports/BSR_GlobeScan_State_of_Sustainable_Business_Survey_2016.pdf.
35 www.cafonline.org/about-us/publications/2016-publications/beyond-integrity-report.
36 https://business-humanrights.org/en/andy-hall-2?.
37 www.finnwatch.org/en/news/391-finnwatch-and-retail-chain-s-group-to-testify-at-andy-hall%27s-trial.
38 www.corporatebenchmark.org/?token=1R5Z1T0FsVAGsQmF7iw6eP_JFEJ9cNHEqSOc-fp3wW8&webform_id=welcome.
39 Quoted by a Dutch Government minister: www.government.nl/documents/speeches/2017/04/19/speech-minister-ploumen-on-international-business-and-human-rights.
40 https://venturebeat.com/2017/05/16/microsoft-commits-5-million-to-landmark-united-nations-technology-partnership/.
41 www.bsr.org/en/collaboration/groups/human-rights-working-group.
42 www.ethicaltrade.org/about-eti/why-we-exist/etis-origins.
43 www.gla.gov.uk.
44 www.theguardian.com/uk-news/2014/nov/14/gangmaster-prosecutions-decline-home-office-hanson-may.
45 www.ethicaltrade.org/blog/eti-clamps-down-false-claims-in-uk-stone-industry.
46 www.theguardian.com/small-business-network/2013/sep/18/late-payment-pain-small-business.
47 www.promptpaymentcode.org.uk.
48 www.cityam.com/252127/theresa-may-failing-treat-small-businesses-partners.
49 www.bbc.co.uk/news/24497762.
50 www.out-law.com/en/articles/2015/march/compliance-with-uk-prompt-payment-code-to-be-rigorously-enforced-says-minister/.
51 www.fujitsu.com/uk/Images/fseu-general-purchasing-conditions.pdf.
52 www.sciencemag.org/news/2015/01/sewage-sludge-could-contain-millions-dollars-worth-gold.
53 www.thetimes.co.uk/article/co-op-threatens-to-ban-john-west-tuna-over-use-of-harmful-nets-78ldczc68.
54 www.techradar.com/news/phone-and-communications/mobile-phones/our-smartphone-addiction-is-costing-the-earth-1299378.
55 www.bgs.ac.uk/mineralsuk/statistics/criticalRawMaterials.html.

7 Communities are ready

A 'credo' is a statement of religious belief, but it's how Johnson & Johnson described their company mission statement in 1943. It includes the following:

> We are responsible to the communities in which we live and work and to the world community as well. We must be good citizens – support good works and charities and bear our fair share of taxes. We must encourage civic improvements and better health and education. We must maintain in good order the property we are privileged to use, protecting the environment and natural resources.[1]

The Company Citizen lives in a community. British people, who share their communities with businesses, regard profitable companies as important but don't trust their fellow (corporate) citizens, with fewer than a quarter agreeing that 'I trust businesses to do the right thing in the community'. Three fifths say that business is more interested in making money than in investing in their communities, 38 per cent don't trust business to pay their fair share of taxes and 41 per cent don't trust them with employees' pensions.[2]

People tend to judge what's 'fair' according to what they've heard or read. What's usually reported is the poor behaviour of a few headline-grabbing corporates, not so much 'fake news' as a lazy inclination to tar all with the same brush. We recognise that businesses create jobs, often regarded as their greatest contribution to society; communities, let alone families, can be devastated by significant job losses.

In most people's eyes anything positive that a company brings to a community, over and above employment, is an unexpected bonus. There's barely a football stadium not named after a corporate today, often foreign owned, reflecting the commercialisation of the modern game. I grew up allied to Stoke City, who played at the Victoria Ground with its imperial connotations. They moved to the Britannia stadium: I'd a sense of pride as building societies were a 'good thing' and the eponymous sponsor was headquartered locally. Nowadays the edifice is the Bet365 and I can find no positive emotional connection.

Businesses create traffic, noise, pollution, even smells; as an MP I recall Blue Circle announcing its intention to trial the burning of rubber tyres in their cement kilns in the village of Hope. Tyres often marred the Peak District landscape, weighing down tarpaulins over silage clamps and, being difficult to recycle, were an eyesore. To make it worse, the European Union banned their dumping in landfill sites: there's a limit to the demand for soft playground landing areas. Everyone knows that when you burn tyres they stink, create soot and pollute the air; Blue Circle knew that none of this happens in a cement kiln, twice as hot as a garden bonfire, where soot and other pollutants are reduced to gases which are 'scrubbed' from the plant's emissions.

The company conducted a PR exercise to win locals round and won hesitant approval. Then the complaints started – washing was speckled, visitors were deterred by the smell, the tyre burning must stop. Except: it hadn't started. There was no evidence to link concerns to the tyres; neighbours' fears were expressing themselves as fact. When the burning did actually start, nobody noticed. Not quite: Blue Circle's chemists found that the shredded tyres burned at a more reliable temperature than coal, producing a higher quality of cement, enhanced by the iron in the steel wires within the tyres – which was in exactly the right proportion for the mix. Blue Circle had found a cheap available replacement for almost half of the fossil fuels they used, removed an eyesore from the landscape and produced no environmental downside. And they'd won an important battle against prejudice through being open and transparent with their neighbours.

The Royal Society for the Encouragement of Arts, Manufactures and Commerce (RSA to its friends), with academic and other partners, investigated 'Connected Communities', a study of the connections between people in communities, how we move from vague political gestures to a society that values and promotes those connections:

> The vision of "Connected Communities" is one in which people are embedded within local networks of social support; in which social isolation is reduced and people experience greater wellbeing and other benefits from the better understanding, mobilisation and growth of "community capital" in their neighbourhoods.[3]

How right they were to place a high value on such connections and to explore ways to build and strengthen community capital; and to conclude that such connections bring benefit in terms of building personal and community wellbeing, supporting functioning and inclusive citizenship, developing social capacity and, of course, economic benefits. Given that 'Manufacture' and 'Commerce' are in the RSA name, the role and potential role of business in developing those connections was largely missing from the report. I don't blame the RSA: businesses are micro-communities in their own right and if their presence as players in the broader community is so easy to overlook then perhaps it should make itself more significant. We'll explore the business case for doing so, backed by economic and other benefits, later.

Respondents to the same ICM survey (above) were asked what businesses could do to 'give back' to society (a misleading but common phrase). The most popular ideas were jobs and training for young people (77 per cent), sourcing supplies locally (64) and working with schools (60).

Jobs and skills

Once upon a time companies queued up to grab the best school leavers before their rivals, but not today. Over centuries the rules and practices relating to apprenticeships have changed with alarming frequency.

From 1563 guilds prevented a master from leading more than three apprentices and an apprenticeship lasted seven years. Little changed until the industrial revolution. Apprenticeships waned in the 19th century but grew from the early 1900s: in the 1960s a third of all male school leavers became apprentices, though their quality was in decline. Numbers fell too and by 1995, when 'Modern Apprenticeships' were introduced, the figure was half that of 1979. A 2009 Act established the right to an apprenticeship for every qualifying 16–19-year-old – but the right wasn't implemented and was removed in 2011. Since then apprenticeship policy has been devolved, numbers have grown, school leavers now occupy a minority of places and females take up over half. About 500,000 new places have been created each year since 2011.[4] Since 2017 the largest companies (one in every 50) pay a payroll levy of 0.5 per cent to help fund a further 3 million.

Apprenticeships used to create specific skills to a high standard, giving the company what it needed and the employee the means to establish a career. Companies often delivered apprenticeships in higher numbers than they could employ. Today, employers claim, new recruits have to be re-taught basics before learning those skills that apprenticeships are supposed to address. Such claims may be subjective, reflecting unrealistic expectations, though school leavers' computing skills are generally acknowledged as not up to speed.

In 2015 the Scottish Government funded Business In The Community (BITC) to develop a pilot programme of sustainable relationships between businesses and early years centres in the poorest communities.[5] Extra help was needed because 5-year-old children in the lowest-income families were already a year behind in their development of vocabulary and problem-solving compared with the highest. Corporate activity was wide and varied, not restricted to the BITC Toolkit, often representing a rare contact between the institution and the world of business. It included everything from exploring a gritter lorry and designing road signs to reading workshops, make-overs for mums, nutrition and workplace visits linked to the curriculum.

Teachers reported high levels of engagement especially from more disadvantaged children, developing self-confidence and independence through interaction with adults, however brief. Equivalent traits were reported amongst volunteers, some of whom were engaging with deprived communities for the first time. Levels of employee satisfaction and achievement were high, leading to greater employee engagement, productivity and a community atmosphere at work.

In a letter to *The Times* (December 2016) three prominent businesses declared that over a third of employers were dissatisfied with the reading and literacy skills of school and college leavers and two in five were providing remedial literacy training to employees. This could hold back the British economy by £32bn, they said. Four in every five large companies now have school links, mostly with secondary schools and colleges, and half of them are increasing that commitment. Businesses are critical of the decline in careers education in schools and the poor preparation of young people for the world of work.[6] KPMG encourages employees to support literacy projects, some supermarkets provide reading areas for children and Boots Opticians are helping to reduce the impact of poor eyesight on reading standards (see page 161), though this is only a start.

Samsung's 'Solve for Tomorrow' programme is a remarkable annual challenge to American schools with $2m in prizes. Winners receive funding to make their ideas reality and take them to scale – the opportunity of a lifetime. Five teams per state, nominated by their teachers, present a lesson plan to show how technology, science and engineering can be used for social good to address a hitherto unresolved problem. After several rounds of elimination three national winners emerge. The results are stunning. In recent years finalists have included Alaskan village children developing early identification of beetles that could kill fir trees, before selective felling of infected trees for construction and fuel. Vegetable gardens arranged on vertical walls to save space were trialled and students developed a rapid recycling technique, utilising organic waste for growing mushrooms. Another group, concerned that schoolmates with physical disabilities struggled with classroom furniture, redesigned it in a low-cost manner to make it more disabled-friendly.

I'm sure Samsung plans to recoup its investment.[7] Perhaps one day 'Solve for Tomorrow' will come to Britain.

As with charities, a proportion of those who work in the education system are sceptical, even cynical, about business engagement and not all businesses are as sensitive as they could be. Though good practice does exist, opportunities to learn from it aren't being taken. A good engagement experience, valued on all sides, is an investment for the future. Hospitals and, to a lesser extent, care institutions also reach out to the community for volunteers to engage with them. Business is less involved here and perhaps ought to consider how it can become more so, to mutual benefit: such involvement will become increasingly valuable.

If 'jobs and training' is the most appreciated aspect of Company Citizenship then perhaps people are saying what they think they ought to say. It's the obvious answer. Part of the reason that we now require young people to remain in education until 18, rather than 16, is because that historic link between the school leaver and local employers no longer exists.

Local sourcing

It would be nice if companies sourced all their procurement needs locally but that's not possible. Money spent on locally produced products and services circulates up to three times faster than money spent on external goods and services, as Adam Smith would have recognised. This creates income for local people and increases the value of the local economy, an idea which sustains several 'local currency' projects in Britain. Yet supply chains of major manufacturers are international, almost by default, taking money out of reach of local economies. Cost considerations are fundamental to many companies' survival and, although cost usually trumps loyalty, 'local' sells – with Brexit obliging retailers to seek supplies nearer home as the uncertain prospect of tariffs looms.

Some businesses regard procurement as a tool for community engagement. Deloitte's Sustainable Procurement Policy recognises the benefits of lower transport costs through 'reducing the impact of deliveries and maximising local sourcing', whilst supermarkets are always quick to commit to generous levels of local recruitment when seeking planning permission for their stores.[8]

Local sourcing of goods, employees and services has other benefits:

- shorter supply chains mean lower delivery cost and smaller carbon footprint, greater reliability of supply;
- building relationships with suppliers is easier when they're local, creating flexibility; and
- being seen to procure locally is good for engagement with customers and employees.

Waitrose claims that by stocking larger quantities and more varieties of local produce it grew food sales during the recession of the early 2010s when other supermarkets saw them fall. Shoppers have long recognised that local produce ought to be fresher than comparable foods from elsewhere and the proportion who deliberately try to buy local doubled, to 54 per cent, between 2006 and 2010.[9] There's no standard definition of what 'local' means, though Waitrose define it as sourced within 30 miles of the store, whilst a third of Asda's 500 'local' suppliers deliver produce to their nine distribution hubs which have autonomous sourcing policies. The Red Tractor logo, a food quality assurance scheme for British farm produce – if that counts as local – is widely respected, commanding a massive 65 per cent brand recognition and involving 87,000 producers, processors and retailers.[10]

Companies ought to at least know what impact, positive and negative, they're having on the local economy. A firm which exploits low land prices by building in a deprived area but doesn't employ local people or source supplies locally has zero impact, other than through Business Rates.

Preston, Lancashire, is Britain's second most improved city since 2010, in social deprivation terms. The local authority, realising that alone they had limited impact, recruited police, housing associations and further education colleges to their 'buy local' campaign. The council doubled its local procurement (from 14 per cent of their budget to 28) and their pension fund invested in local student housing. Companies looking to move away were assisted to remain, businesses grew from winning local construction projects and local energy production is on the cards. 'The days of getting huge inward investments are over, so the sensible way is looking at how you can [utilise] your local area to make something new', says the councillor who led the drive, Matthew Brown.[11] 'Local' doesn't necessarily maximise 'social value' but the two approaches are clearly not incompatible.

In practice, local sourcing may not be an end in itself but a means to achieving other desirable goals; and sometimes it can run counter to them, as with fair trade procurement. 'Local' is no guarantee of quality, however, and no purchaser would accept a second-class service just because it is local.

'Buy Social' is a variation on this theme, in which companies involve social enterprises in their supply chains. Social enterprises, by their nature, have a positive impact on the community or environment so trade with them will create a positive social impact by proxy. Supporters argue that working with them allows mainstream companies to build diversity into their supply chain, reducing risk, whilst bringing them into contact with innovative organisations and sharing that positive impact. In the 'Buy Social Corporate Challenge', launched in 2016, companies are challenged by SEUK, BITC and the Government to spend £1bn between them on sourcing from social enterprises within four years, though SEUK Chair Lord Adebowale has declared that a billion is not enough. First off the blocks were Amey, Interserve, Johnson & Johnson, PwC, RBS Group, Robertson Group, Santander, Wates and Zurich, engaging 125 social enterprises to the tune of £20m of new business in the first year.

The Social Value Act

'Social value' is the securing of economic, social or environmental benefit when buying services, over and above the monetary value of a tender. In *Welcome to GoodCo* I celebrated the gestation and birth of the Public Services (Social Value) Act 2012, a measure which allows public sector bodies to stipulate social value criteria in their procurement practices. Technically it covers tenders for the delivery of services exceeding a threshold below which tendering is not required. The Act doesn't cover the provision of goods, nor smaller service contracts, nor construction 'works', nor business-to-business transactions although there is no reason why public bodies shouldn't apply it in all circumstances.

The Act obliges all local authorities to 'consider' the social impact of their spending and allows (but doesn't oblige) them to act on that consideration. Local authority procurement, principally from the private sector, may favour smaller and local providers in a way that central government's doesn't. Clearly social enterprises are well placed to deliver social-value outcomes, as such is their raison d'être, but the Act creates opportunities for 'for profit' Company Citizens to win contracts too. Say two companies bid for a tender to provide a service: company A prices their bid slightly higher than B. Different councils may give different priorities to different social-value criteria in different contracts, so let's say that A is reducing its carbon footprint faster than B, provides more apprenticeships and promotes more employee volunteering than B does. Under legislation prior to the Act these factors would be ignored and B would win the contract as its tender had been lower. Today, if the council has chosen to implement the Act, it could justify giving the contract to A if it assesses that the net social value generated by doing so was worth more than the difference in price, up to a limit of 10 per cent of the contract value.

In 2016 SEUK reviewed progress.[12] Unsurprisingly, larger local authorities had taken the measure to heart as cash-strapped councils need to eke out social value wherever they can find it. Three years on, a third of all councils were 'embracers' or 'adopters', applying the Act's criteria broadly to their procurement, which is welcome. Some had developed a social value policy, often exceeding the Act's scope, and 45 per cent 'considered' social value, as the Act requires, without exploiting it to the full; these were 'compliers'. The final fifth, mostly smaller authorities with few service contracts likely to exceed the threshold, were 'bystanders'. Typically 'embracers' allowed a strong social value score to make a bid up to ten per cent more competitive, in line with guidance, with some ranking social value even more highly on some contracts.

Enthusiasm for the Act is cross-party: amongst the 43 'embracers' 21 were then Labour authorities and 15 Conservative. An embracer typically uses the Act in all procurement activity, weights social value highly and assumes responsibility for the policy at a senior level. The online 'Social Value Portal' is where 'business comes to learn' about creating and measuring social value; it contains a beginner's guide and advice on submitting tenders and consultancy support.[13] Councils claim that using the Act brings improvements to cost efficiency, staff motivation, community wellbeing, image, service delivery and the local economy, though 'defining social benefit', says Croydon Council, wisely, 'is less important than securing it'.[14] However, a complementary report on NHS Clinical Commissioning Groups revealed that half had no social value policy and only one in eight an active one – a missed opportunity.[15]

So being a good Company Citizen can help a business to win local government contracts; but expect scrutiny. Greenwashing, using questionable claims to conscientious practices, will not be tolerated; providing evidence of positive social impact could become as routine as that for financial security.

The Social Value Act literally enables councils to create something from nothing – to achieve levels of social value which wouldn't otherwise have been realised. The community benefits from local businesses creating a more positive social and environmental impact and compliant businesses gain all the benefits that have already been claimed for Company Citizenship: employee engagement, purpose, innovation, sustainability and more. Interserve and Veolia, significant providers of services to councils, are certainly 'social value conscious'.

Lord (David) Young reviewed the Act's operation after just two years, in 2015, resulting in an important change: the European tendering threshold,

€209,000 when the Act was brought in, had been dramatically raised – more than tripled – taking most local government transactions outside the Act's scope and rendering it virtually impotent. Parliament agreed to freeze the original threshold, so now there's no formal process of reviewing it. Young was concerned about low levels of awareness, which may have improved. Although he recommended no increase in the Act's scope he called for a further review which, in February 2017, the responsible minister announced would be conducted by his department.

SEUK's modest and sensible recommendations were to provide more awareness and training around the Act within councils, make it more difficult for them to opt out, and for further research on the use of official guidance, especially on social value weighting. Councils have already shown that the threshold can be ignored and social value applied to all sizes of procurement, also that the Act can work when applied to tendering for goods and works as well as services.

But something much more exciting is going on.

In 2012–13 Fujitsu spent £751m with 1,000 UK suppliers, of which £150m went to the three quarters which were SMEs. In its SME Charter Fujitsu, ranked as 'Platinum' for its CSR activity by BITC, commits itself to fostering the company's values through its supply chain. In particular, they say:

> We are 100 per cent committed to being a responsible business. Responsible supply chain management in turn supports small businesses. Our procurement policy ensures that we source ethically and responsibly, and we actively aim to ensure that our supply chain shares our environmental and social values.[16]

They go on: 'We are supporters of the Public Services (Social Value) Act 2012 and what it stands for, and we seek to work with suppliers that share this view.'

Is this the first example of a major private-sector company adopting the Act for its own procurement? Has Fujitsu demonstrated that responsible business grasps and champions engagement with communities through social value channels? Should private businesses follow suit? Yes.

So, whilst I endorse SEUK's calls for the Act to be reviewed, I'd add three more elements:

- to promote the voluntary adoption of social-value procurement within the private sector;
- to remove the arbitrary distinction between goods, works and services; and
- to reconsider whether there needs to be a national threshold at all and, if so, how to define it.

Much of this could be achieved by adopting the radical Procurement Reform (Scotland) Act 2014 into UK law. What a political masterstroke that would be, post-Brexit, to say: 'We stand together as the United Kingdom, and we will (for the first time) take a piece of Scottish legislation and adopt it UK-wide.' Clause 9(1) of that Act is clear:

> 9. Sustainable procurement duty
>
> (1) For the purposes of this Act, the sustainable procurement duty is the duty of a contracting authority –
>
> (a) before carrying out a regulated procurement, to consider how in conducting the procurement process it can –
>
> (i) improve the economic, social, and environmental wellbeing of the authority's area,
>
> (ii) facilitate the involvement of small and medium enterprises, third sector bodies and supported businesses in the process, and
>
> (iii) promote innovation, and
>
> (b) in carrying out the procurement, to act with a view to securing such improvements identified as a result of paragraph (a)(i).

As well as that innovative reference to SMEs and innovation, sub-clause 4 invades new territory:

> (4) In this section, references to the wellbeing of the authority's area include, in particular, reducing inequality in the area.

Hooray! No thresholds, no arbitrary distinctions, no limit to scope.

In the meantime, our Government has already extended the Social Value Act's remit by quietly changing its guidance on the public procurement of materials involved in 'major' projects procured by public authorities involving the purchase of steel.[17] Without overtly saying so, guidance PPN11/16 brings goods into the social value arena by saying that procurement should 'ensure the best value for money by recognising relevant wider social and environment benefits where appropriate'. Clearly, the intention is to support the ailing British steel industry, deemed to have intrinsic 'social value'; the guidance even allows each public body to define 'major'.

There's much here that business can take on board, goals shared by Company Citizens and opportunities for cross-sector working, involving the private sector in a suite of very worthy causes.

The people

In Western Australia someone had a bright idea: why not employ trained people as helpful friends to infirm, elderly and vulnerable people in communities?

Why not help them access the support and advice they need, instead of expecting them to know where to go for assistance? Why not then help them avoid unnecessary contact with those same services by building supportive communities around those vulnerable people?

The City of Derby adopted the idea in 2012 for a trial – and it's worked. Consortia in the Isle of Wight and Thurrock then took it up. In two Derby wards over three years Local Area Coordinators (LACs) saved public services £4 for every £1 invested, produced positive outcomes for individuals and communities and took pressure off services. By 2015 Derby operated LACs in ten wards, discharging their duty to promote health and wellbeing whilst reducing or delaying the use of services. The ten coordinators had helped over 3,000 vulnerable people, average age 60, a third with mental health needs, mostly living in social housing. Health services reported that early intervention by LACs had helped to reduce patients' stress and the need for subsequent expensive treatment; joined-up working had improved and demand for the overworked Community Mental Health team was down. Social Care and the Children and Young People service reported similar outcomes and wards even reported reduced callouts for police, Community Support Officers and fire services. Community groups, councillors and the voluntary sector spoke about LACs 'making a positive difference and acting as a catalyst to help support the community'.[18]

To date none of the pilots is on record as engaging with their business communities. No deliberate snub, but if you want something done you don't first think of asking a local business; combine that with the perennial issue of businesses generally being physically absent from deprived areas, where social housing predominates. But there can be a role for business in aspects of social care, as the charity Turning Point asserted when they attempted to launch 'Connected Care' ten years ago. This programme would have engaged businesses in programmes to support young people leaving care to join the world of work. Their model had a clear positive Social Return on Investment but neither major local authorities nor private care providers could summon up the courage to adopt it. Maybe things will be different next time.

Local Area Coordinators are not volunteers but they tap into local voluntary infrastructure; they may discover new opportunities for employee volunteering. The LACs may identify community events which would benefit from sponsorship, facilities for which company fundraising might be appropriate. In short, plenty for business to talk about, issues which might engage their staff, skills and facilities with demonstrable value, allowing them to discharge the care element of their Company Citizenship.

An obvious way to do this, where they exist, is through a Business Connector. The BITC Business Connector service was launched in 2011 and has blossomed since.[19] Over 250 Connectors have been seconded from around 50 major companies, typically for a year at a time. They've built links between businesses and civil society, helping make over 120 local economies and communities, often the most deprived, more sustainable, successful, engaged and vibrant. Different areas have different needs so each Connector has a slightly different role. Around 60 Business Connectors are in post at any time, building up and learning from each other's experience and networks. In the first five years community contributions leveraged by Connectors were valued at over £17m of cash, kind, time and talent. Community organisations so assisted, frequently those focused on young adults' needs, report increased confidence, capacity and reach.

Queen's Park is one of London's most deprived wards, the most north-westerly in Westminster. Its unemployment level is the highest in the borough, so too its proportion of people on disability benefits. A third of households have dependent children and a fifth are overcrowded; a third are amongst the 10 per cent most deprived households in England.[20] Ethnically diverse Queen's Park is served not only by Westminster City Council but by London's only Parish Council, created as a community initiative in 2012, and since 1998 by the Paddington Development Trust (PDT), serving a slightly wider area. The PDT is a social enterprise dedicated to regenerating the local economy in an environmentally sustainable way, through the promotion of skills, employment, enterprise and community health initiatives. Each year they help 400 people into work and provide business consultancy, partly funded by RBS. A recent winner of the City Corporation's Sustainable Communities Award, PDT has an annual budget of over £2m from grants and trading and employs over 30 staff, mostly in premises literally beneath the elevated A40 road.

Part of PDT's function, with others, is to prepare the ground for inward investment and help address market failure. It provides an incubator for new business and micro-enterprises, especially in the creative sector. Promoting enterprise is key to local economic sustainability, but 'moving spirits', says CEO Neil Johnston, echoing my own experience, 'are hard to find in deprived areas'. In Paddington elected, active and inclusive Neighbourhood Forums have emerged after a struggle against the odds. Their Parish Council initiative was approved by 70 per cent of the electorate on a 35 per cent turnout, healthy by parish council standards; it has wide discretion over how to spend its £150,000 precept. In a locality where education standards are relatively low, and some prejudice exists, democratic engagement is a learning process. The PDT has public-sector partners but such relationships are frustrated by bureaucracy.

One of the functions of One Westminster, the local Council for Voluntary Services, is to link local businesses to volunteering opportunities with 'good causes'. Each year companies across Westminster donate about 6,000 hours, of which half take the form of skilled volunteering opportunities. Proportionally, Queen's Park should get 300 hours but there are few significant companies there, typical of a highly deprived area, so formal employee volunteering input is probably significantly lower.

Paddington Basin is an impressive new development which enhances our canal heritage, creates public open spaces, sprouts artisan coffee bars and ethnic lunch stalls and is home to several corporate headquarters, including

Vodaphone and M&S. The PDT is a few minutes' walk away: 'As far as they're concerned, Queen's Park doesn't exist', I'm told. Half of Westminster's Sure Start Children's Centres have shut and half of what's left are under threat. Created to support vulnerable families in deprived communities, Sure Starts are closing as a result of massive reductions in government grants to local authorities, with more to come.

A similar story exists in all of our most deprived cities. The Index of Multiple Deprivation (2015) confirms that, of 3,284 'neighbourhoods' in Britain, 70 per cent of the most highly deprived are in just 12 local authorities.[21] Eighty per cent of wards in the bottom decile in 2010 are still there today. In many, deprivation is getting worse.

The Local Government Association estimates that by 2019–20 councils will face a funding gap of almost £11bn although certain statutory services must grow – not least elderly care, due to demographic change.[22] As a rule of thumb, councils with higher levels of deprivation have, historically, received more funding. Since 2015 Government policy is to fund councils more 'equally', with a smaller proportion going to where needs are greatest, combined with a general need for 'austerity'.

Thus some services must be provided by other means or not at all. 'Other means' might include charging, though those in most need are least able to pay, or having a charity provide them. We know that charities' resources haven't increased since 2010 and, anyway, a significant amount of funding for their services comes through councils: between 2009 and 2013 public spending going through smaller charities (under £1m turnover) fell by almost half.[23] As with businesses, fewer charities are based in deprived areas than near middle-class neighbourhoods. (When charities claim that 80 per cent of people 'use charity services' they're including National Trust visitors, Royal Opera House patrons, RSPB members and some private health patients. Few such users live in Queen's Park.)

In many deprived areas the Social Economy, of charities and social enterprises, does valuable work: looking after people in old age, coping with mental health problems or supporting people near to death; helping those distant from the jobs market get closer to it; providing nursery care, allowing mothers the dignity of earning to help bring up their children. Such organisations might be small but they still need the books to balance.

If not taxation, public or third sectors, the only other source of wherewithal is business; and that's not going to happen, either – at least, not directly. Businesses aren't charities; their expertise lies elsewhere. However, in an earlier chapter we saw an extraordinary equation: focusing just 1 per cent of UK business assets on 'doing good' would match the value of the work of the entire UK charity sector; if that 1 per cent could leverage the output of the charity sector then multiples of its value of could be generated.

That second bit relies on business not replicating what charities do but putting resources into their strategic planning, skills and capacity-building in a way which also benefits the business. In practice this often means fundraising and low-skill activities that utilise time (rather than imagination, intellect or dexterity) but, planned properly, it all helps. Around a third of charities in northern England received at least some practical support from businesses in 2016, with larger charities generally receiving more than smaller, local ones.[24] We need more of this, more strategically targeted.

All citizens, individual and collective, in all sectors can and must play their role in building a values-led, local, collaborative social infrastructure fit for the 21st century. We can no longer assume that someone else will pick up the tab; we need sustainable community solutions to social challenges which break down silo barriers and utilise the available skills and muscle of business.

Such a place-based approach is implicit in our discussion of 'communities' but it needs to be made more explicit that Company Citizens, alongside others, will play their part.[25]

Engaging with the community

Employees, managers and shareholders are all citizens. They understand the bonds of community that unite and support our fellow humans. They've probably all contributed to a community in some way recently – from sharing the school run to endowing a cats' home in their will.

Occasionally acts of 'giving' or 'volunteering' arise spontaneously amongst employees, perhaps following an external prompt like a disaster appeal or a family tragedy such as childhood cancer. The secret is to harness that goodwill and organise it to create a positive impact on both community and business – without deflating the sense of spontaneity. The smallest companies usually have no structure or manager responsible for engagement so (unless an external local network exists) such activity is likely to be *ad hoc*. In bigger companies, with greater role diversification and more management strata than smaller ones, opportunities exist to allocate professional responsibility for community engagement at one or more levels.

Employees want their company to be actively engaged with the community: 42 per cent want to work for a company that has 'a positive impact on the world' whilst 36 per cent would work harder if they thought that society would benefit from it. Both figures rise to over half amongst millennials, the next generation of company leaders.[26]

Engagement is the emotional connection between an employee and their company, a prize worth nurturing; yet, as we saw in Chapter 5, as many as half of all UK employees today do not feel that connection. Half of all employees, especially younger ones, don't understand their employer's CSR strategy; millennials actively seek purpose, community involvement and employers who demonstrably 'care'.[27] Engagement improves productivity: disengaged employees take 3.5 sick days off per year more than those who are engaged. It promotes longevity, saving recruitment costs, and employees think more highly of their employer where such a strategy exists. Companies with a highly engaged workforce are 6 per cent more profitable than those without.[28]

Employees are more motivated by collective giving through the workplace than through individual efforts. Where the cause appears relevant and the impact of the activity profound, effective and worthwhile, the employee engagement generated is deep and widely shared amongst the body collective (staff) and the body corporate (company).[29]

Even some larger companies, oddly, appear to see virtue in keeping their 'CSR' operation essentially amateur. In doing so they'll fail to achieve the best community engagement levels or maximise employee engagement and social impact, missing out on significant benefits for the company itself. Companies that fail to optimise these factors are likely to be those which:

- give 'responsibility' for choosing a short-term charitable cause to volunteer employees with little power or influence, rather than building a professional relationship with charity partners whose missions or values complement those of the company;
- locate the responsibility for delivering community engagement in public relations or a stand-alone CSR operation accountable to no one, rather than to core departments like Human Resources or Procurement;
- fail to allocate responsibility for Company Citizenship at board level, with clear lines of accountability; and
- decline to deploy the same qualities of imagination, risk management, responsibility and investment to this part of the company's life as to any other part.

Noting that business–charity co-working in a common cause has diversified in recent years, nfpSynergy rightly warns against a creeping 'blandness', in which engagement comes to be routine and misses out on qualitative common gains by sticking to quantitative rituals (Saxton, 2015). No particular structure for delivering good community engagement is inherently best, but structure there should be. That structure needs to acknowledge just two basic rules:

- community engagement won't work without employee buy-in; and
- won't deliver maximum benefit without board and CEO leadership and accountability.

There are essentially three ways in which companies engage with communities: Cash & Kind, Time & Talent, Head & Heart. The first two represent transfers of value from the company to a 'good cause', whether within the local community (charity, community group or public service), a distant community (international charity or appeal), a virtual community (with dispersed beneficiaries, such as 'people with dementia') or an equivalent non-human cause (environmental, animal, cultural). The Head & Heart category is, we'll see, less straightforward.

Engagement activity usually involves a value transfer from a business to a charity acting as agent for the beneficiaries. Often the value received is higher than that given: half-an-hour's access to a photocopier, a minimal cost to the donor, may create a disproportionate benefit. An important element of the transaction is education: charities should want supporters to know about their cause whilst knowledge helps donors understand the world better and be more effective in their future giving.

There's no shame in calculating the benefit to the company of allowing, encouraging or creating a transfer of value. Giving is good for the soul (philosophers and psychologists agree) and 'making something good happen' is another dopamine prompt. The benefit to the company is maximised when supported by internal communications around the company's mission and purpose – as long as the company isn't seen to be 'piggybacking' on employee generosity or making unsubstantiated or exaggerated claims.

In each example that follows the benefit to the recipient of the transfer should be obvious even where highly context-dependent. The tables explore different modes of community engagement by companies and comment on the benefit to the company that they can bring. Each list includes both low-level, low-impact commitments and some that are more profound and, some might say, more convincing.

Cash & Kind

The least complex aspect of practical community engagement is Cash & Kind, sometimes originating as 'bottom up' ideas or initiatives within the workforce.

Table 7.1 Cash & Kind

Cash & Kind activity	*Comment / benefit to company*
Donating raffle prizes.	Very common, especially amongst SMEs. Little benefit.
Allowing charities to collect money on premises.	Popular with supermarkets. Limited employee engagement, effective marketing.
Raising money by employees, spontaneously or facilitated by company.	More effort – more engagement. Some team-building effect. Fundraising itself is an 'output', not an 'impact'.
Employees **collecting goods** to donate to appropriate good causes.	Limited, other than respect for allowing or facilitating collection. Some learning about beneficiary's cause.
Donation of money by company and/or its charitable foundation.	Limited employee pride by association. Image. Tax efficient. Relative impact higher if charity is smaller, local.
Allowing or promoting **payroll giving** and/or company **matching** employee donations.	Regular commitments help beneficiary more; enhanced where cause is supported by company mission/values.

(continued)

Table 7.1 (continued)

Cash & Kind activity	*Comment/benefit to company*
Sponsorship of event or publication.	Greater publicity, authenticity helps build image.
Charity of the Year: close relationship with particular charity over specified time, usually focused on fundraising.	Level of mutual benefit varies. A year's often insufficient to build proper relationship or learn. Experienced charities 'play the circuit'; mission convergence rarely a priority.
Donation of **unwanted goods**: second-hand equipment or furniture, unsaleable product (goods in wrongly printed packaging).	Reduced landfill costs. Impact on staff small. Image. Best to coordinate donation with need. Can be high profile (disaster relief, In Kind Direct, Fareshare).
Donation of **saleable goods** (surplus or otherwise) regularly or in response to crisis.	Ditto. Image and impact benefit higher?
Intangible gift in kind: loan of service: printing, conference room, crowd-research.	Limited employee engagement. Build and deepen company relationship with cause/enhance reputation.

Time & Talent

Unless your company is in construction, decorating or facilities management please avoid painting walls as part of your CSR operation. It may be fun, may help team building, but it's ultimately of limited benefit to recipients. If it's unavoidable, did employees insist it had to be in your charitable portfolio or did the charity ask for it? If they asked, was that because they couldn't think of another way to respond to your offer (or demand)? Or would they have preferred a professional job, almost certainly better than your enthusiastic marketing department could muster? In some community centres walls reserved for corporate volunteering days get painted four times a year. A corporate facilities manager once lamented: 'A charity asked us to donate paint for a corporate volunteering day. If they'd asked us to paint the room instead of that law firm we'd have done it for free, and done a better job!'

Time & Talent is volunteering. Remember that people who carry out planned charitable work outside their normal job description, in paid company time, may offer to do so but they aren't volunteering. It's the Company Citizen that's volunteering – making its time, skills and labour available for the community of which the workplace is part.

Managing employee volunteering is an art which might be shared with other Company Citizens, a service provided in different ways by Thirdbridge, Benefacto, local engagement networks and others.[30] Making a spectrum of opportunities available, rather than dictating what volunteers must do, allows choice and flexibility, affording employees responsibility, a degree of control. By encouraging them to employ different skills, interests and inclinations, greater overall fulfilment is possible. From that follows engagement. Such activity spreads the name and reputation of the company; every volunteer is an ambassador and some of those with whom they come into contact are potential customers or employees.

In America the Dell Foundation has identified a significant shift in corporate philanthropy, as they call it, away from Cash & Kind and towards Time & Talent, exactly as C&E Advisory found (Chapter 1). They insightfully describe the shift as from capital to competence, pure passion to pragmatic passion, intervention to innovation, coordination to collaboration and short-term fix to long-term involvement. Given a choice between a $100,000 gift and an equivalent value in counselling, skilled volunteering or access to decision-makers only four in ten of the 700 NGOs they work with, worldwide, would today choose the cash.[31]

Table 7.2 Time & Talent

Time & Talent activity	*Comment/benefit to company*
Employees coming together for voluntary work in their own time.	Little benefit. Acting wholly independently of company may reinforce lack of engagement.
Company brings employees together for voluntary work in their own time.	Without an existing relationship of trust this too may be neutral, even counterproductive unless cause is strong.
Coordinating low-skill **team volunteering in working hours**: gardening, litter-picking, fundraising.	Risk that team building goal overrides beneficiary support. Greater sense of purpose from more appropriate activity.
Individual **desk-based volunteering** for set period in company time: telephone befriending, online crowd-sourcing, crowd-coding.	Giving individual employees control over their volunteering empowers, builds trust and engagement (Age UK's 'A Call in Time').
Soft-skill volunteering, e.g. listening to children read (in company time). Individuals or team.	In customer-facing operations, help employees develop 'soft' interpersonal skills.
Professional skilled volunteering in company time, individuals or team.	Generates engagement, individual sense of responsibility and purpose.
Mentoring – professional skills: working with disadvantaged people (Alium Partners, Chapter 5).	Pro bono practice interviews, CV and work preparation services. Embeds culture of professional development in company, recruitment of like-minded employees.
Sustained period of skilled volunteering leave (VSO, secondment).	Significant cost (less if leave is unpaid); high benefit from employees learning leadership, professional responsibility.

Case study: Dementia Friends

Britain has over a million Dementia Friends, trained by the Alzheimer's Society to be aware of the needs of the growing number of fellow citizens who suffer from dementia. The programme aims to boost tolerance, understanding and support for people with a condition that's widely misunderstood but with which ever more families will have to cope as society grows older. Ten thousand volunteers are 'Champions', tasked with promoting and delivering training, face to face or online.

Several retail (and other) companies have realised the value of such training for staff dealing with older people who are confused about their needs, money or location; training can help them cope with frustrated customers when someone demands disproportionate attention at the checkout. A reputation for caring about vulnerable customers is worth having and enhances employee pride in their work. John Lewis, M&S, Boots Opticians and Lloyds Bank all support the cause as did David Cameron as Prime Minister, now the charity's patron. In 2016 Specsavers included dementia-awareness training in its online learning materials for staff and created over 1,200 Dementia Friends in just a few weeks.

Case study: Herbert Smith Freehills

Many City law firms support community activities in London's East End, where social problems are evident and professionals are routinely engaged in *pro bono* and voluntary work. The East End is accessible, on foot, from HSF's offices but Sierra Leone is not. In 2010 the company broke from their previous community engagement policy to send staff to the developing African country to work with local lawyers and others to help grow social capacity. They didn't anticipate the 2014 ebola outbreak.

The work didn't stop: the Sierra Leone authorities have paid tribute to the lawyers for their commitment, helping them at a time of need. Over three years they provided £1.2m worth of free legal advice which has been invaluable in managing the commercial impact of the crisis which, thankfully, has now passed.

What's the business case for this engagement? Apart from the professional and life-enhancing experiences of staff, Sierra Leone is a growing economy which could become a significant player in 21st-century Africa. Then the country will, no doubt, seek to engage international lawyers to help with developing trade. Who do you think they will turn to?[32]

Head & Heart

'One per cent is not a lot: but it means the world' is the delightful catchphrase ending a short video on the Salesforce web site.[33] The film spells out Marc Benioff's philosophy of 'integrated philanthropy': in 1999 the company used 1 per cent of its equity to create a foundation to fund charitable grants and overheads. In 2009 this was re-branded salesforce.org, to support non-profit and educational institutions by donating or discounting Salesforce software licence subscriptions. Profits from all sales to education and non-profits are retained by the foundation. In addition, salesforce.org organises each employee to use up to seven working days per year to help 'improve communities' globally. The reasoning, the film explains, is that there was a time when business was fully part of society – but it became hungry for profit, began to resent 'giving back' and became part of the world's problems when it should have been driving solutions. 'The business of business is to improve the state of the world', says Benioff, neatly rephrasing Milton Friedman. The 1:1:1 model has delivered two million employee-volunteer hours and $160m in grants to over 31,000 organisations and education institutions worldwide, making it possibly the world's biggest corporate community engagement programme. The company encourages customers and others to follow their example.

One per cent of working time is less than five minutes each day for most people, 1 per cent of resource is a penny per pound. Little, many times repeated, soon becomes a potent force for change when organised and focused.

Head & Heart engagement can be difficult to categorise but if it isn't Cash & Kind or Time & Talent, it's Head & Heart. In the Salesforce example the giving is clearly cash, kind, time and talent but the integrated all-pervading strategy is Head & Heart. Giving cash may be a substitute for action and giving time an extension of what happens at work, but the giving of the heart and the head of the Company Citizen requires three things to happen: there must be a strategic direction to follow, authority to implement and leadership to deliver. Such 'buy in' has to come from the top and will reflect the company's values and ethos – which can't be switched on and off.

As with the previous tables, the positive impacts of Head & Heart activity are readily envisaged. The reward to the company may be even higher here because the practices are often strategic and capable of being integrated into work routines; they represent a philosophy in practice.

Marc Benioff calls it 'integrated philanthropy'; I call it 'Company Citizenship'.[34]

Table 7.3 Head & Heart

Head & Heart activity	*Comment/benefit to company*
Procurement: **ethical** and **sustainable** (socially/environmentally friendly products).	Fairtrade products can enhance understanding of supply chain. Accredited, sustainable sources of timber, minerals, palm oil, fish, etc.
Procurement: buying **local**, buying **social** (see above).	Local procurement reduces supply risks, supports local economy. Sourcing from social enterprises supports social-value creation.

(continued)

Table 7.3 (continued)

Head & Heart activity	*Comment/benefit to company*
Promote quality **apprenticeships**, offer **work experience**.	Companies respected for numbers and quality of experience.
Charity **trustees**, **school governors**, **carers**: encourage self-help networks.	Your community ambassadors need time to carry out role and to feel supported. (Getting on Board, Trustees Unlimited.)
Dragon's Den events identify, encourage, promote, support worthy causes: start-ups, social enterprises, charities.	Judging, wise counsel and investment raise company profile, assist networking. Traditionally one-off, some (like Dragon's Apprentice, Hertfordshire) operate over time, command high local profile.
Reduce **waste** to landfill/**carbon footprint**.	Lower landfill tax/energy costs by tapping into employee insight and goodwill; sense of purpose/impact.
Reducing negative impacts, hazardous waste, harmful cleaning products, transport policy.	Awareness of business externalities, reducing/mitigating harm, enhance reputation.
Promote employee **health**.	Many positive returns (see below).
The **Living Wage** (Chapter 3).	Supported by employers who don't want to exploit people on poverty pay. Improved productivity, sense of fair play.
Use **professional networks** to raise Company Citizen profile.	Chambers of Commerce, CBI, IoD, FSB, trade associations could all do more. Spread good practice.
Open **training** to charities, start-ups and social enterprises.	Offer free training places in-house in retail skills, health and safety. Good practice for employees, enhanced reputation.
Support local **business engagement networks** (Heart of the City, Involve Swindon, Tameside 4 Good, Dutch Beursvloer).	Companies pool volunteering opportunities. Sometimes supported by corporates, ideal for SMEs lacking resources/expertise to manage volunteering programme. Saves cost, increases opportunities.
Multi-disciplinary projects (employees from a company ran sports day for a special needs school so staff could concentrate on supporting pupils).	Properly planned, give good cause holistic makeover (paint building, redesign web site, refresh marketing, create sensory garden). Good opportunity for cross-departmental working, for individuals to contribute and hone skills.
Inclusive product design (Inclusive Economy, Chapter 4).	Redesign standard unit of product for low income market: more people use it, company sells more. (Cemex, Chapter 4.)
Innovation challenge (see Samsung above).	Ford employees work with technology students in schools to harness and reward ideas, leading to innovation in design.

Supply chain discipline (UK):	
a) Social Value Act (see above).	a) Fujitsu encourages suppliers to comply with the Act.
b) Tackling repeat offending.	b) BITC supports 'Ban the Box', encouraging employment of ex-offenders (see the case study below).
c) Shared environmental targets.	c) See Chapter 2.
d) Prompt Payment Code.	d) See Chapter 6.
Supply chain discipline (international).	See Chapter 6. Engage with workforce on child labour, human rights, bribery, corruption issues. Reduces reputational risk.
Positive re **discrimination and identity** (pink pound, employing older/disabled staff, support for carers' needs).	Welcome diversity in workforce and customer base, such as LGBT-friendly. Enhance company reputation with customers, bonding with employees from disadvantaged groups.
Trade union engagement.	Successful companies work with unions as partners on common concerns – safety, productivity, etc.
Cause-related marketing: sharing advertising campaign with charity (Red Cross/Land Rover, Guide Dogs/Andrex).	Consumers buy products identified with good causes. Most CRM generates income/profile for charity, exposure/sales for company. Most convincing have clear shared mission.
Adopting/mentoring start-up business/social enterprise/charity.	Develop variety of high level skills, including leadership.
Charity partner – mission driven. Boots Chemists/Macmillan, supporting cancer patients. (Also Boots Opticians, see below.)	Patients access charity's services through shops, Boots attracts families of cancer patients as customers; charity trained Boots staff, Boots donated funds.
Campaigning, e.g. Unilever championing SDGs, Apple challenging US travel ban.	Handled carefully (not normally Party political), can enhance reputation for responsibility (IQ Business Case Study below).
Employee services: awareness campaigns, dealing with debt, physical fitness, loans for bicycles, healthy eating, services delivered by charities/social enterprises, on-site repairs.	Partners deliver workplace services to employees: Neyber (Chapter 5) provides low-cost loans to employees with domestic financial challenges. Relieves stress, reduces absenteeism. Company Shop sells low cost food to employees (Chapter 3).
Employee education: provide learning on combatting fraud, protecting your child on the internet, exploring the countryside.	Employee engagement enhanced through creating bonds of trust between employees (plus families) and company.

(continued)

Table 7.3 (continued)

Head & Heart activity	*Comment/benefit to company*
Mental Health problems cause massive loss of employee productivity.	Reduce cost of stress and anxiety at work, help sufferers return (see below).
Engaging comprehensively with schools (Education and Employers Taskforce).	Work experience, technology links, event sponsorship, governor support, seconding staff, contributing to curriculum development, helping run academies.
Compliance.	Legal and ISO compliance is easier when business learns from working with contrasting companies and across sectors.
Gender equality.	Gender-balanced boards make better decisions; equal pay without equal opportunities isn't worth having.
Recruitment: design discrimination out of recruitment and promotion practices.	Traditional practices may exclude talent. Millennials seek evidence of purpose. HR benefits from recruiting from non-traditional sources (ex-offenders, migrants, young/old/disabled people).
Capacity-building: Pilotlight or BeyondMe.	Teams of skilled volunteers increase impact of small, ambitious charities. (See case study below.)
Engaging charities to train employees on work-related issues, awareness of issues around suicide, disability, diversity.	Samaritans' training at Network Rail (Chapter 5). Cost-effective, makes employees feel valued. Greater engagement, customer satisfaction, sales.
Business Connectors (BITC).	A year's secondment to help businesses engage better with local community (see above).
Mixed purpose or **bifunctional** company.	For-profit company tied by constitution to a charitable/social purpose operation for funding and other purposes (Luta, see below).
Integrated philanthropy/ Salesforce model (see above).	Business philosophy not distinguishing 'CSR' from daily operation is pinnacle of Company Citizenship. Maximises triple-bottom-line sustainability with employee engagement, risk mitigation, enhanced reputation.

Case study: IQ Business

IQ Business is a true Company Citizen. It's South Africa's largest home grown business consultancy, focusing on consumer and financial services. In CEO Adam Craker's words, it's 'a balanced enterprise – with business profit and social impact goals'.

Whilst the company, multiracial and engaged at all levels, clearly walks and talks its values, much of its community engagement is through its partner charity, the IQ Foundation. The foundation's run by representatives of the company's 600 employees, overseeing much of the company's integrated community engagement work, currently with eight causes and civil society partners.[35] These include support for charities which help the homeless, inspire teenagers, educate orphans, protect vulnerable children, support children with cancer and protect wildlife. It also oversees the company's internal work on environmental sustainability. Such a range of causes is both focused, to ensure impact, and broad, to encourage participation through choice. Like Salesforce, the company encourages its clients to follow its citizenship lead.

The IQ Foundation benefits from a heightened level of employee engagement which inspires the workforce: 'The more we grow, the more we profit, the more help we can give', says Adam, who regularly leads his IQ team in the annual Johannesburg mass sleep-out campaign to highlight homelessness. In 2017 the company's political stance became more overt, actively supporting calls for President Zuma to step down made by one of their non-executive directors, Cheryl Carolus, formerly an ANC National Executive member and her country's Ambassador to Britain.[36]

Professionally, IQ has helped charities remodel to increase effectiveness and brought businesses together to forge a common approach to government on how best to implement their own National Development Plan (NDP). The NDP is a broad programme, part of Vision 2030 which the governing ANC has pursued since 2011, which has frequently lacked energy, impact, credibility and outcomes. Bureaucratic and other barriers have stifled delivery but when Craker and his colleagues proposed a concerted plan by business – not to change, dilute or delay the programme, but to make it more effective – they inexplicably received short shrift. Undeterred, IQ Business remains committed to the goal of a genuinely multiracial democratic South Africa, a properly functioning economy with caring, sustainable communities powered by partnerships.

IQ Business is on course to become one of South Africa's first B Corps and Deloitte ranks it as one of the 'Best Companies to Work For'. It's not quite a 'bifunctional company', an independent for-profit company which is constitutionally bound to a specific good cause. In *Welcome to GoodCo* we met the Brazilian online sportswear company Luta, a private company created in 2009 to donate half of its profits to the charity Fight for Peace, which helps young people escape the clutches of gang culture in the deprived communities of Rio de Janeiro (where it was founded in 2000), Jamaica and London.[37] In 2014 Reebok acquired Luta in 'a perfect marriage' to take both the business and the charity's operations to scale.[38]

Bifunctionality represents a stronger tie than the relationship between a company and its charitable foundation, on a potentially greater scale.

Case study: Boots Opticians

Boots Opticians has an impressive synergy with the purpose and values of the National Literacy Trust. On the face of it, they've philanthropically donated thousands of copies of *Zookeeper Zoe*, a book aimed at the youngest readers, supported by a network of employees who listen to children read. But the tale doesn't end there: Zoe's story contains special pictures, with instructions to parents and others on how to interpret children's comments. Zoe's Community Challenge is so much more than stories: the book contains eye tests.

In much of Britain there's no consistent programme to identify children with defective eyesight; this became Zoe's job. An estimated 1.5 million school-aged children in UK have an undiagnosed eye problem which can severely affect their ability to read. Zoe's quest is to identify them, provide access to free professional eye tests and work with the charity to address literacy problems before they start. Lifetime earning capacity is limited by poor reading and children in more deprived communities are most likely to miss routine eye tests.

Boots Opticians' staff are volunteering company time and expertise in identifying treatment needs locally, working with teachers in schools and playgroups, libraries, festivals, Beavers and Brownies, supporting anxious parents who've discovered that their child's eyesight is poor. Over 350,000 copies of the book have been given out, either by staff in this way or through Boots stores. Boots Opticians report that Zoe generates very high levels of job satisfaction amongst colleagues and an acute sense of purpose. They've gone further than planned in some cases, creating reading areas within their shops.

The programme won an award in the 2017 Third Sector Business Charity Awards.

Case study: Pilotlight and BeyondMe[39]

Pilotlight has supported 500 small local but aspirational charities since 2003. A small charity itself, it uses 'Pilotlighters', teams of three business executives from a mix of large corporates, to work with the charity CEO and others to create and implement a business plan. Over a year they come together for a few hours each month and two years after the process ends the impact is assessed. Charities typically increase their income by 25 per cent and their reach or impact by half. Other benefits gained by the charity are greater strategic vision, stronger financial management and more effective boards. The Pilotlighters, sponsored by their companies, report a phenomenal growth in professional skills: 93 per cent are better coaches as a result of their experience and 75 per cent say it increased their job satisfaction. Seventy per cent say that it helped with their career development. All recommend the experience because it increases their understanding of others and feelings of wellbeing. In 2016 there were 65 charities and 260 Pilotlighters in the programme.

Beyond Me has a similar mission. It started in the Big Four accountancy firms (as 'Young Philanthropy', 2011) and expanded into others. Over five years, 1,500 young professionals formed 143 BeyondMe teams serving over 80 charities and social enterprises. Teams of seven plus a senior leader collaborate to meet a charity's demand for volunteers to add capacity and skills in strategy, analytics and growth planning – and some fundraising. BeyondMe matches teams (there are 20 in PwC alone) with appropriate charity challenges, providing access to 'the talent, energy and resources of professionals eager to give' for a year. Ninety-three per cent of charities helped say that goals were met or exceeded whilst over 90 per cent of team members increased their giving habits and wanted to repeat the experience.

Case study: Ban the Box

Ban the Box is a BITC initiative supported by 78 companies (and Bristol City Council) to boost the employment of ex-offenders, an effective way of reducing reoffending – often making skills available in the workforce. 'The box' refers to that part of a job application form which asks 'Do you have any unspent criminal convictions?' An answer in the affirmative may guarantee no further consideration, even where many circumstances would have no relevance to the job in question. Such an approach, say BITC, is inefficient, unfair, short-sighted and potentially illegal (if used as a proxy for race). Pioneers of treating such jobseekers on their merits by 'Banning the Box' include Timpsons, Wates, Boots, Virgin Trains, the Southbank Centre and Interserve, who say that ex-offenders are often more committed, more reliable and more hard-working because they've been given a second chance.[40]

Health

Mental health problems cost British business 11.7 million working days in 2015–16, almost half of all time lost and significantly more than the next main cause, musculoskeletal problems, says the Health & Safety Executive.[41] The figures for stress, depression and anxiety have been static since 2010, before when they were falling. People trying to cope with stress often turn to harmful practices: over-eating, smoking or drinking too much alcohol. Stress, depression and anxiety account for one in five visits to GPs and the main causes of work stress are said to be inappropriate levels of pressure, lack of support from managers, violence and bullying. The Company Citizen tries to minimise or prevent these because that's what decent citizens do – and because the number of days lost per employee with a mental health condition is 24 per year compared with just 16 for those with a physical condition. Happy workers are also more productive, working harder and utilising their time better.[42] Mental health-related absences are often exacerbated by trying to return too early or by not receiving appropriate support from employers and workmates when return is attempted.

Exercise and relaxation help keep work-related stress at bay. Some employers have installed gyms and chill-out areas, encouraged lunchtime walking groups and promoted good habits like bike-riding, smoking cessation and healthy eating, which can all help stress management. Volunteering bestows upon an employee an element of control which they might otherwise lack in the workplace. The secret to coping with stress in the workplace, says Professor

Cary Cooper on the NHS web site, is that: 'Stress can be managed. It's about gaining control. The things that cause people the most stress in life are the things where people feel they have no control.'

Between 2005 and 2015 the proportion of British workers who said they had no control over how their work is organised grew by a third, from 42 per cent to 57.[43]

I keep coming back to dopamine; small amounts of dopamine produced by pleasurable experiences, including volunteering and 'doing good', help regulate the body's hormones to keep us happy and healthy. Constant over-production, caused perhaps by working to tight deadlines, stimulates over-production of adrenalin which in turn creates stress. Both dopamine (a neurotransmitter) and adrenalin (a hormone) work best in limited quantities. Stress ultimately drains the body's ability to produce dopamine, reducing the capacity to respond positively to those small but positive stimuli which normally generate feelings of reward and happiness. Chronic under-production of dopamine is linked by some studies to Alzheimer's, Parkinson's, heart disease, cancer and immune system disorders.[44]

Managers need to be able to spot signs of stress in others and employers have a legal duty to ensure the health, safety and welfare of employees. Half of all employees believe that being open with their employer about a mental health problem could damage their career prospects and four in ten have experienced stress, depression or anxiety at work without telling their employer.[45] This is unacceptable, though employers are more understanding today than they were even 20 years ago. Whilst huge progress has been made on physical health at work the workplace remains a major source of mental health problems, alongside financial concerns and relationship issues.[46]

Four hundred employers and almost 10,000 individuals have backed the Time to Change pledge. Led by charities Mind and Rethink Mental Illness, it's a commitment to change attitudes and risks around mental health. The charities help create a bespoke plan for the workplace backed up by a network and events to support mental health Champions. Longstanding supporters include Transport for London, Imperial College, E.ON, Anglian Water and Lloyds Bank. A manager in a big white-collar company noted that the main cause of death in adult males under 40 is suicide. He told me: 'Ours is a stressful business and our median employee is 29; we need to manage them carefully.'

Customers have mental health problems too: the Money and Mental Health Policy Institute argues that people suffering from depression or PTSD find remembering PINs difficult, those with bipolar disorder or ADHD sometimes behave impulsively, often with damaging financial consequences, and people with anxiety may fear to open letters, especially from the bank. These could constitute half of all customers, over time: do banks design services around such needs? No. As with disabled access ramps and improved signage, accommodations made for a minority could end up benefitting everybody.[47]

One cause of stress and under-performance is menstrual pain; the law allows women the option of (paid or unpaid) leave for a day or more each month in Japan, South Korea, Indonesia and China. Peer pressure is generally held to be sufficient to dissuade women from staying at home when they don't need to. Italy, renowned for its strong maternity rights, is considering becoming the first in Europe to grant such leave, though it's feared that their proposal – of up to three days per month – may discourage companies from employing women.[48] One in ten women suffer chronically from endometriosis, a condition of the uterus which can take years to diagnose, which produces crippling pains each month for one in three of those who have it. An employer that understands female biology and works around it is one that gets the best out of their workforce.

Physical health also concerns the Company Citizen: in 2013 sickness absence cost business £29bn, of which almost a third was caused by smoking-related conditions. That's 131 million days lost, over four days per employee, 400 times the 312,000 lost to industrial disputes in 2016.[49] 'Presenteeism', the tolerance of under-performance at work due to sickness, lethargy or long-term medical conditions, costs business £605/year per employee. Although academic studies of presenteeism are fairly novel there's evidence that when economic conditions are tight employees come to work and underperform rather than draw attention to themselves, as they see it, by taking time off.

Public Health England's Workplace Wellbeing Charter targets organisations of all sizes. They aim to create workplace environments which support health and wellbeing – and their associated business benefits. The Charter focuses on leadership, absence management, health and safety, mental health, smoking, physical activity, healthy eating and alcohol.[50] A self-assessment tool checks whether the organisation is legally compliant and reflects 'achievement' and 'excellence'. It's an effective but under-used tool: although over 1,000 employers have Charter status a quarter are in Liverpool, where the city's Business Improvement District is clearly very supportive.

PwC's 33 regional offices employ a comprehensive employee wellbeing strategy including paid 'People Managers' and volunteer 'Wellbeing Champions'. Their eclectic programme includes personal resilience training, on-site dentistry, active lifestyles, nutritious food and redesigning offices to maximise daylight.

'Health at Work' is a British Heart Foundation campaign.[51] Almost all companies who engage with it observe reduced sickness absence and higher morale, better team building and reduced early retirement on sickness grounds; the return on investment for a workplace health strategy can be £34 for every £1 spent, based on its impact on absenteeism, presenteeism, accidents and staff turnover. Better employee engagement and internal communications are also reported. The BHF also promotes the Workplace Wellbeing Charter, not least at Asda's distribution centre in Leicestershire. Here, on-site gym membership costs £3 per month and the company supports free fruit days, help for employees buying bicycles, smoking cessation clinics, health checks and even a 'coast-to-coast' static cycle event to raise money for the BHF. The Asda scheme initially reduced absenteeism by 1.5 per cent – this alone was worth £200,000 to the company.

Some law firms specialise in suing workplaces for health, safety and even wellbeing breaches. You don't want that to be you.

Measuring the difference

I've used 'value' ambiguously, reflecting the word's usage even in responsible business circles. We've talked of 'social value' and the 'value' of contracts. The latter is clearly monetary and we've seen that 'social value' can also be expressed in monetary terms but how meaningful is its measurement? Professor John Kay says:

> I'm . . . a very quantitative person, but there's an obsession with quantification, particularly of things that cannot easily be counted, and that leads people to make up bogus numbers. KPIs and so on are good for businesses to use but they are, by definition, company-specific.[52]

I sympathise. One purpose of monetisation is comparability, to understand whether three apples are worth more or less than four pears. Consider the following.

- 'My company measures everything by outcomes – except employee volunteering. That's measured in hours, inputs, which tells you nothing about what it achieves.'
- 'I listen to children read, it generates a great sense of purpose. But how do we measure its value? How much I'm paid in that hour? Is an hour of a lawyer listening worth more than a secretary? Or should we use minimum wage, as a teaching assistant might earn for the same work?'
- 'How can we compare what we do for the community in my company with what you do in yours if we don't measure the outputs in the same way?'

This debate isn't just academic. As any charity knows, funders are becoming more demanding, wanting to know what sustainable positive change their input has brought about. As Company Citizens grow more sophisticated, investors, shareholders, managers and CEOs will want convincing of the value for money of engagement programmes.

Consider an organisation which helps teenagers at risk of entering gang culture. It provides them with support at school and counselling for families. Some of what it does is under a council contract, the rest funded through charitable fundraising. The council wants to know whether repeat juvenile offending has been reduced and how much money public services have saved through keeping young people on the 'straight and narrow'. A foundation wants to know how many children have engaged with the organisation and how the community's perception of young people has changed. A potential donor wants an assurance that the organisation isn't spending excessively on administration, fundraising and running costs. A local business has offered to provide work experience for 15-year-olds – though not those at high risk of offending as they pose an unacceptable reputational risk (even though a positive outcome creates more public benefit value than for a lower risk one).

Here are four ways to arrive at a common approach to measuring impact:

1 make it simple, aiding comparability;
2 make it complex, maximising transparency, accounting for all outputs;
3 compromise, pleasing no one; and
4 measure impacts in different but appropriate ways for different purposes.

As Big Society Capital's Cliff Prior told the 2017 Unity Trust Bank AGM, there may be more ways of measuring social impact than there are organisations creating it. In the past, companies would simply count the hours: corporate CSR reports still contain phrases like 'colleagues volunteered for 5,000 hours in work time' which means nothing; it might be 20 minutes per year per employee, not very impressive, or describe activity with little impact.

Each year BITC organises 'Give and Gain Day', a celebration of employee volunteering. Its 850 member companies, mostly large corporates, focus on helping 'young people and vulnerable groups, budding entrepreneurs, charities and community organisations to problem solve, develop skills, build confidence, maintain and expand their services'.

This represents a qualitative improvement – fundraising and team building used to predominate. In 2016 the ninth such day saw at least 18,000 volunteers contribute in activity too diverse to make impact rationalisation easy. Twenty two people per corporate member sounds like only a few but is probably significantly under-reported; yet it's double the 2014 level and at least the event's positive impact on employees is now measured.[53]

When the London Benchmarking Group reported in 2016 that 168 of its member companies had contributed $3.3bn globally in the previous year to 'community and philanthropic investments, reaching 65 million beneficiaries' we know that all its members had used common metrics in obtaining these two numbers (which include time, talent, cash and kind). When they report that 41 per cent of employees volunteering had improved their skills as a result of participation then we're motoring. At last, a meaningful metric which demonstrates value creation, change, benefit for both the companies and individual participants.[54]

Three quarters of FTSE 100 companies have employee volunteer programmes, involving various degrees of sophistication. They overwhelmingly believe that volunteering can enhance workplace skills. By contrast, fewer than a quarter of Britain's five million SMEs have a strategy for engaging with the community.[55]

For reasons best known to itself, Britain's Government recently removed a requirement for companies to report on their corporate charitable donations. In recent years corporate philanthropy, the giving of company cash (or equivalent) to charity, has flatlined but it's nonetheless significant. In 2014 only a quarter of FTSE100 companies gave 1 per cent or more of pre-tax profits to charity, only a quarter of £1m+ charitable donations came from corporates and the total given by business was somewhat less than that from wealthy individuals.[56]

But who was actually doing the corporate giving? In many company reports it's impossible to distinguish between genuine corporate giving – the company donating some of its profit to a good cause – and fundraising by employees; sleight of hand does occasionally skew reporting. Some, like RBS, make a virtue – rightly – of match-funding employee fundraising but some company donations are definitely overstated by bundling them up with employee giving.

During the 2010 election David Cameron announced plans for all large firms to allow every employee up to three days of volunteering leave per year. In government, he repeated the pledge several times.

That pledge, like Mr Cameron, has since disappeared, without even the dignity of being withdrawn.

Notes

1 www.jnj.com/about-jnj/jnj-credo.
2 www.ippr.org/news-and-media/press-releases/businesspoll.
3 www.thersa.org/globalassets/pdfs/reports/rsaj3718-connected-communities-report_web.pdf.
4 http://researchbriefings.parliament.uk/ResearchBriefing/Summary/SN06113#fullreport.
5 www.bitc.org.uk/scotland/what-we-offer/business-engagement-early-years.
6 www.cbi.org.uk/news/getting-skills-right-more-vital-than-ever-post-referendum/.
7 www.samsung.com/us/solvefortomorrow/contest/.
8 www2.deloitte.com/content/dam/Deloitte/uk/Documents/about-deloitte/deloitte-uk-sustainable-procurement-policy.pdf.
9 www.retail-week.com/topics/supply-chain/the-benefits-of-local-sourcing/5010688.article.
10 http://assurance.redtractor.org.uk/who-we-are/annual-reviews.
11 www.theguardian.com/society/2017/feb/14/poverty-was-entrenched-in-preston-so-we-became-more-self-sufficient.
12 www.socialenterprise.org.uk/procuring-for-good.
13 http://socialvalueportal.com/about/.
14 www.croydon.gov.uk/sites/default/files/articles/downloads/socialvalue.pdf.
15 www.socialenterprise.org.uk/healthy-commissioning-how-the-social-value-act-being-used-by-clinical-commissioning-groups.
16 www.fujitsu.com/uk/Images/Fujitsu-SME-Charter.pdf.
17 www.gov.uk/government/uploads/system/uploads/attachment_data/file/576874/13DecFinal_publication_version_PPN_Steel_Procurement___2___4_.pdf.
18 Derby: www.thinklocalactpersonal.org.uk/_assets/BCC/Social_Value_of_Local_Area_Coordination_Executive_Summary_March_2016.pdf.
19 www.bitc.org.uk/programmes/business-connectors – see also *Welcome to GoodCo.*
20 www.westminster.gov.uk/ward-profiles.
21 www.gov.uk/government/uploads/system/uploads/attachment_data/file/465791/English_Indices_of_Deprivation_2015_-_Statistical_Release.pdf.
22 www.local.gov.uk/sites/default/files/documents/future-funding-outlook-co-18b.pdf.
23 https://voluntarynews.org.uk/news/2016/02/local-charity-services-lost-most-in-government-cuts/.

24 www.ippr.org/files/publications/pdf/third-sector-trends-in-the-north-of-England_Mar2017.pdf?noredirect=1.
25 http://wordpress.collaboratei.com/wp-content/uploads/Building-Collaborative-Places_Digital-Report-Pages.pdf.
26 www.theguardian.com/sustainable-business/2015/may/05/millennials-employment-employers-values-ethics-jobs.
27 http://smallbusiness.co.uk/workforce-dark-csr-initiatives-2536243/ and www.hrmagazine.co.uk/article-details/csr-could-be-the-key-to-boosting-engagement-and-productivity-research-suggests.
28 http://benefacto.org/employee-engagement-csr/.
29 www.businessnewsdaily.com/8830-corporate-giving.html?.
30 https://thirdbridge.co.uk and http://benefacto.org.
31 https://impact.msdf.org/report/.
32 http://gcgrapevine.com/pro-bono-action-by-herbert-smith-freehills-sparks-commercial-rejuvenation-in-sierra-leone/.
33 www.salesforce.org/pledge-1/.
34 Many of these examples were explored in *Welcome to GoodCo*.
35 www.iqbusiness.net/aboutusposts/iq-foundation/.
36 https://twitter.com/iqbusiness April 7–8, 2017.
37 http://fightforpeace.net.
38 www.youtube.com/watch?v=YbNgwzue8d0.
39 www.pilotlight.org.uk and https://static.beyondme.org/files/beyondme-impact-report.pdf.
40 A jobseeker's story: www.bitc.org.uk/our-resources/case-studies/ban-box-lucys-story.
41 www.hse.gov.uk/statistics/dayslost.htm.
42 www2.warwick.ac.uk/newsandevents/pressreleases/new_study_shows/.
43 www.bsa.natcen.ac.uk/latest-report/british-social-attitudes-33/introduction.aspx.
44 www.livestrong.com/article/366013-dopamine-and-stress-response/.
45 www.greatbusinessdebate.co.uk/opinion/is-mental-health-wellbeing-supported-at-work/.
46 www.nhs.uk/Conditions/stress-anxiety-depression/Pages/workplace-stress.aspx.
47 www.bbc.co.uk/news/business-38722210.
48 www.theworkfoundation.com/2017/06/06/more-than-womens-issues/ and www.independent.co.uk/news/world/europe/italy-menstrual-leave-reproductive-health-women-employment-a7649636.html.
49 www.ons.gov.uk/employmentandlabourmarket/peopleinwork/labourproductivity/articles/sicknessabsenceinthelabourmarket/2016. Note that ONS figures suggest different proportions of time lost for different reasons to those of HSE (Note 41), though on a comparable scale.
50 www.wellbeingcharter.org.uk/index.php.
51 www.bhf.org.uk/health-at-work.
52 'The Essence of Stakeholder Value', *ESG Magazine* 6, Winter 2016.
53 www.bitc.org.uk/sites/default/files/ggd2016_annual_review16.pdf.
54 www.lbg-online.net.
55 www.theguardian.com/voluntary-sector-network/community-action-blog/2012/apr/04/charities-voluntary-organisation-business.
56 www.thetimes.co.uk/edition/comment/businesses-are-the-skinflints-of-charity-giving-7mfg6259k.

8 The future is ready

Things could go either way.

If Britain is to cure the huge social deficit that we're allowing to accumulate, that growing difference between the support that people need and its available supply, exacerbated growing numbers of 'working poor' and the demographic time bomb of old age, then the Company Citizen has to step up to the mark. Without engaged business subsequent generations cannot experience the same quality of life that we've enjoyed for half a century.

The challenges that the planet faces will not be met if we continue to use resources and treat the biosphere as we have, ignoring the long-term consequences of our actions. Did we, as people or companies, systematically plunder those resources and dump on the environment – or was it all an accident? Forget blame, only business can deliver the solutions to put this right.

The country cannot be governed simply in the interests of business but nor can those interests be ignored. Business has a right to a voice and a hearing, a mutual recognition that good business is good for the people it serves and employs – and their neighbours.

Also our most vulnerable communities, those lacking skills, capacity and experience of self-sufficiency, can't retain whatever coherence they have or build upon it unless they're granted not simply the opportunities but the capacity, skills and ability to take more control. Not a conventional role for business, admittedly, but no-one else has the tools to do it on the scale needed, as close to the ground.

I'm hopeful about the future role of business in society: more will step up, become more inclusive and positive, lower their environmental impact, think more long term, better engage their employees and stakeholders. But the opposite will happen too: the temptation of the quick buck will never lose its allure. Short cuts will continue to be taken and 'tax efficiency' will still undermine the proper contributions that bigger company citizens, in particular, are asked to make to the society which is supposed to sustain us all. More will do good and more will undermine their efforts; fewer will sit on the fence – and there will be more companies in total.

The big corporate at the head of a supply chain of vertical, hierarchical relationships is a very 20th-century model: such simplicity is no more. Supply is managed these days through webs, not chains, so pressure will grow on companies to collaborate on common solutions to ethical and sustainability challenges in distant jurisdictions. Hitherto parallel businesses will find themselves dependent on each other.

Many shareholders and investors already realise that enlightened self-interest requires planning for the future, more will see 'returns' in colours as well as numbers, poetry as well as prose.

Whatever happens in the future, to the planet, nation or community, business will play an important part: it always has, always will. Business is the driver of innovation and we need that innovation desperately. We need it to achieve a circular economy that minimises waste, that sees end-of-life products as a resource in themselves, acknowledging that natural resources are not only finite but often severely time-limited in their availability. We need innovation to power inclusion, to create opportunities, not to compete against robots but to work with human qualities, concerns and empathies. We need innovation not simply to provide purpose for business but to address our social challenges with sustainable and affordable solutions. We need innovation to power productivity, the Holy Grail which has eluded the British economy for a decade, which we've never properly integrated into our commercial life.

Seven of the world's top 30 universities are in Britain and yet our record for creating innovative products and bringing them to market is poor. In America such businesses, frequently digital-led, are launched and grow and are then typically acquired by a larger company – a second-stage acquisition. Over here a stage is missed out with the result that inventors sell their ideas early, before they reach their potential, failing to maximise the benefit to themselves, often failing to retain intellectual property rights and failing to bring product diversity to the market place. The result is a less dynamic market with fewer players and less incentive to grow through productivity. Our market for acquisitions may be active and involved but it's usually focused on quantity, not quality.

This is unhealthy: acquisition is used to neutralise competitors and threats, to grow market share without effort, to asset strip and sell on or to capitalise on elements of the 'unreal' economy such as short-term changes in share prices. Real growth must come from responding to new opportunities in both new and existing markets, taking opportunities to innovate but also to democratise, by making goods and services available to those who would otherwise be excluded from those markets by virtue of their poverty.

In Chapter 4 we discussed the inclusive and the circular economies. These two essential concepts will determine the nature of our business world if, as I hope and believe it will, business becomes ever more of a power for good. The alternative is unthinkable: we've already had more than our share of that, thank you.

Before looking further at how business might respond to these challenges there are two complementary antagonistic trends within business which will grow in importance, making it easier to deliver positive outcomes. Those currents, of fragmentation and aggregation, will influence the world of government as well as business.

Agg and frag

If fragmentation is a rise in the granularity of the business world and aggregation a tendency towards accretion then both have historical precedents. Previously the words have described different phases of a cycle but today things are different. New technology allows both phenomena to rise simultaneously.

The fragmentation of big business is a good thing: it's the friend of innovative technology and it complements social policy liberalisation. 'Too big to fail' is arrogance personified, especially when poor corporate behaviour merits failure. The largest companies in some markets behave like monopolies, defying normal rules of competition. Markets demand that competition should flow and declare that cabals are anti-competitive, so on that basis the behaviour, perhaps existence, of some giants is difficult to defend.

Within some corporations the intrapreneur, the employee with an entrepreneurial innovative flair, is changing the way businesses are run.[1] Such people should be put to use rather than tied down, as used to happen. 'Disruption' has become a positive term both inside the workplace and outside in the market: there's even an annual business award for it. Outsourcing and spinning off will continue as departments, brands and functions enjoy opportunities provided by greater autonomy within companies, limited only by their mission.

Barriers to market entry are lower than ever because of the ubiquity of information technology yet the rise in genuine entrepreneurial self-employment has been obscured by the growth of the reluctant precariat in the gig economy, a less worthy example of fragmentation – that of the workforce.

The historical shortcomings of attempts to tame giants are clear and should generate significant changes in how business is organised. To state the obvious:

- Small companies are more agile than large, can adapt more quickly to changing markets and introduce innovation more quickly, even though they lack scale and its associated economies and therefore, individually, may lack impact. They operate closer to the 'grass roots' of communities and tend to treat their employees as 'family' by default. Pay ratios tend to be relatively moderate and it's not too difficult to create a sense of mission and purpose.
- The largest companies have greater impacts – both positive and negative. Many are conventional aggregators through acquisition. They can often produce products more cheaply than smaller rivals through economies of scale, good for financial inclusion, but such economies have their limits. Big companies are highly complex organisms where chains of command (and supply) can become stretched, rendering them vulnerable to poor communication and misunderstanding, inefficiency, even corruption. International companies can lack a focused geographical 'loyalty' making them more likely to prioritise internal, self-serving, often short-term interests over national or global ones, leading to low levels of accountability and transparency.

A hundred years ago farming, brewing and banking consisted of many small operations in local markets. As population and affluence grew so did demand, prompting aggregation though merger and acquisition, often aggressively. Agribusiness grew huge, especially in America, both by amalgamation and by tying smaller companies into supply chains so tightly they lost their independence. In Britain by the 1990s only half a dozen significant brewers dominated the whole country, not just making beer but controlling access to market through the tied-house system. Over 30 post-war years the idea of local independent banks – remember Captain Mainwaring? – disappeared as the Big Four pushed others out or took them over. The Big Four now account for three quarters of the UK retail banking market and there's little to choose between them in practice.

Suddenly, today, there are more brewers in Britain than even in the industry's heyday; the agri-business pendulum has swung as changing market demand has stimulated niche organic and other minority products, necessarily on a smaller scale. Meanwhile, a new breed of internet banking and finance entrepreneurs have even developed a vocabulary that's going rapidly mainstream: 'challenger banks' based on 'fintech' are poised to disrupt the Big Four's cosy retail hegemony. These industries are well and truly fragmenting.

The Dutch bank Triodos demonstrates that small can work; with only €13bn in assets and 50,000 UK deposit customers 'the world's most sustainable bank' is a major provider of social finance. In 2016 they financed 381 UK projects in renewable energy, 620 in community housing and 422 in elderly care. Triodos' goal is 'A society with dignity at its core'. Granularity promotes diversity, which is where banking as a whole should be heading.

Since the turn of the century government has been repositioning itself as an organiser, facilitator and coordinator/aggregator of semi-fragmented services rather than simply being a large-scale provider, and this trend will continue. However, there needs to be a wholesale review of outsourcing as the mega-contracts that sustained half a dozen corporate behemoths for 20 years are no longer fit for purpose, if ever they were. Government commitments to 'small' and 'local' solutions must, after years of talk, mean that commissioning services at that scale finally goes mainstream – at the expense of homogeneity. The developing sophistication of 'social value', in not some but all public-service commissioning, will help 'for purpose' businesses, social enterprises and new forms of volunteer-led active social networks. Ministers must tolerate greater diversity in the means by which 'their' services are delivered: we should welcome, not deride, the 'post-code lottery' of service provision, the antithesis of 'one size fits all', and celebrate the possibilities and opportunities of community-level devolution.

For the foreseeable future, fragmentation and aggregation will not alternate, as in the past, but coexist. The behemoths are still there but rather than build empires for the sake of it they themselves are outsourcing more: will any big company do its own catering, transport or cleaning in ten years' time? Would Tesla, pioneers of electric cars, have survived a generation ago? No, they would have been bought up by a giant and either exploited or, as in the apocryphal history of the everlasting light bulb, closed down. Having fought off the predatory intentions of Kraft-Heinz in 2017 what was Unilever's next reaction? To look to sell off the brands that were most peripheral to their core cause of sustainability and responsibility, to sharpen their message and accept downsizing as a consequence: fragmentation.

Business, pushed by investors, ministers and public opinion, must act to significantly control Britain's top pay free-for-all in the next five years (government will be too mired in Brexit to act). This isn't because companies will suddenly believe that people shouldn't get too rich; they will realise that having a few people take large amounts of money out of the system simply makes no sense – and that each company's licence to operate depends upon them demonstrably observing economic justice. Fragmentation will accelerate this response: instead of one company with a 100× pay differential there could be five companies each with a 20× differential. Though this will not significantly affect the distribution of money in society – those five will still be part of an economic elite – the move, if widespread, will contribute to a more meritocratic, less unequal society (in *Spirit Level* terms) as well as keep more money in circulation. Inequality isn't just a matter for the HR department but for those responsible for the reputation, purpose and mission of the company, its leaders, spokespeople and ambassadors and, not least, its investors and shareholders.

And paying the bottom of the pyramid more is a strong prompt to increasing productivity.

Smaller operations are utilising new ways of growing effectiveness, market share and capacity not through mergers but through the sharing of platforms: aggregation. This very 21st-century approach wasn't available before access to the internet was both universal and cheap. Amazon, for all its faults as Tax-Avoider General, is an aggregator par excellence. No one buys Amazon products: it's simply a platform which enables, facilitates, some might say 'liberates', smaller companies and individuals by providing low cost effective access to market. It makes its money through sheer scale; the platform has become its own message.[2] Think eBay, Uber, AirBnB. Peer-to-peer lending is another aggregator process: if your bank is reticent to invest in your small business then look to Funding Circle or Assetz Capital, where thousands who understand your predicament – they share it – each take on a small part of your fragmented risk (such lending platforms received full regulatory approval in May 2017).[3] Generating around 6 per cent annual interest for a typical investor this is a far more attractive prospect to savers, even after tax, than a traditional savings account or ISA, albeit with an element of risk.

There are low-tech aggregators too. Through the proliferation of common office space micro enterprises share everything – kitchen, wifi, cleaners, conference rooms, servers, sharpies – 24 hours each day, vastly reducing the cost of commerce. Another way to cut costs is to have your staff work from home, downgrading the physical office (fragmentation). Even coffee shops have rediscovered their 18th-century aggregator role at the centre of dynamic creativity, exponentially opening up more space – Samuel Johnson with wifi.

Ever-increasing collaboration between peers on supply-chain ethics is preferable to developing internal capacity solo; a collaborative aggregation culture will assist this process.

Aggregation isn't just a first-world phenomenon. Across the globe small producers coordinate what they grow, share opportunities and good practice, compensate for lack of scale by growing opportunity. The physical infrastructure required for aggregating a fragmented supply chain exists in the native Indian herb producers of the Amazon Basin, cultivated by Natura; the fair trade chocolate co-ops of Ghana, built up by Cadbury; the network of grain producers of Ethiopia aggregated by Diageo. In each case the net effect is not to enslave producers but to empower them collectively. This is also the idea behind M-Pesa in Africa where basic collaborative information technology is now mainstream.

Like globalisation, aggregation and fragmentation are neither good nor bad; they just are. Also, like globalisation, those that can ride these tides will benefit the most, Company Citizens please note.

Business must respond positively to global threats. It will remain the role of governments and intergovernmental bodies to identify them, outlining risks and priorities for planet and people, but much delivery of solutions will fall on the shoulders of Company Citizens. Business won't become a new arm of government, far from it: the driver of innovation will be what it's always been, business success, but broadly defined.

The three causes around which business needs to focus are:

- sustainability: today's global business can't survive the consequences of ever-depleting quantities of natural resources, hence the development of the Circular Economy;
- growing markets: at country and global levels new sales won't only arise from selling more into existing markets but through the economic emancipation of the poor, creating new markets in the Inclusive Economy; and
- responsibility: being a Company Citizen is not a charitable proposition but a business framework linked to the 'licence to operate', as the Social Economy is demonstrating through social enterprises, mission-led businesses and trading charities that are blossoming in Britain today.

Let's pull these strings together.

Going forward – sustainability

The crisis in resource conservation is discussed in Chapter 2 and the arguments for more responsible use of commodities and the environment need no rehearsal. Let's look at what can be achieved in the fields of energy and food.

We're half way to the tipping point, that two-degree rise in temperature since pre-industrial times that will be catastrophic for agriculture, water supplies, weather – for life, human and otherwise. Global warming shows little sign of stopping: whatever we do, Earth's temperature will continue to rise for a while because of impacts working through the system. More need to do more: if we rely only on countries and businesses that are already tackling climate change they'd need to make their actions six times more effective than currently planned to stay within that limit.[4] Governments agree that the world needs to reduce carbon emissions by 80 per cent by 2050, upgraded from 60 a decade ago, and that they need to act now: otherwise crossing that two-degree threshold will be inevitable.

There's good news; and the bad news could be worse. The good news is that, contrary to earlier expectations, the world's second biggest carbon emitter, China, has accepted the need to tackle climate change: as well as scrapping plans for new coal-fired power stations in favour of renewables it's developing urban forests on the sides of buildings, an effective means of capturing carbon. The bad news is that President Trump is serious about withdrawing from international climate programmes for reasons few claim to understand; fortunately American business is not only increasingly aware of the business case for reducing carbon emissions and their investor community even more so, but is doing something about it. There'll be no widespread rejuvenation of American coal, not least as poorer mid-West farmers have discovered a way out of recession-fuelled poverty – renting their depleted land to wind-farm companies for $10,000/year per turbine, complementing their fragile income.

The energy industry must embrace fragmentation.

Brits are familiar with those grey parabolic cooling towers on our horizons; these leviathans, monuments to wasted energy, symbols of big centralised production based on century-old technology, are doomed. Conventional nuclear energy will slip into the 'too difficult' box, not on environmental grounds but because the financial risks of slippage over 20 years of planning and construction are now beyond the pale, as Toshiba demonstrates.

June 2017 saw Britain's first ever day where half the energy we used came from renewable sources. Most communities and big companies will produce their own green energy locally by 2030. In London we already see combined heat and power schemes, the Sky wind turbine and the Bywater solar array, and micro-hydropower in the Peak District and Wales. Add increasingly sophisticated and cheap photovoltaic cells, the maximisation of energy efficiency in new buildings and greater urgency to conserving energy – the market will drive clean energy creation. We'll pass peak oil demand around 2024 as the real costs of generating renewable energy continue to fall. Peak energy demands may not match peak production from renewables but no matter, as battery capacity in 2030 will be many times greater (and cheaper) than now.

Sir Ian Cheshire, whose pedigree includes senior roles at Kingfisher, Whitbread and Barclays, told a business conference that the transition to low-carbon energy is not a threat:

> It's going to happen to you anyway, so you should frame it as an opportunity. If you don't figure out how to be one of the winners, I can predict, quite confidently, that you'll be one of the losers.

> This can't just be about future-proofing businesses because that is slightly defensive, the point is to be a future winner, and the opportunities for those who figure this out are huge. But it takes courage to look into what your business might be, compared to what it is now. Ultimately, this is about leadership.[5]

Quite so.

In 2015 Storm Desmond inflicted £5bn of damage to England in barely 24 hours. This was no longer 'a once in a 100-year event' as major climate incidents are now expected in Britain every year. Our flood defences have been addressed piecemeal over decades and it's clear that substantial, strategic, additional funding for this isn't going to come from government. However, there's every likelihood that 'green bonds', a new generation of collaborative financial instruments aimed at tackling and mitigating climate change and other evils, will prosper and help the economy deliver what's needed. The UK Green Investment Bank may be part of the answer; when controversially sold off by the Government some critics were reassured to discover that its new leading partners were to be Australia's Macquarie Bank and the Universities' Superannuation Scheme (USS). Combining Macquarie's existing green investment with GIB resources creates Britain's third biggest investor in renewable energy with particular interests in tidal lagoons, battery development and offshore wind. The presence of the USS golden share, with a generation of ethical investing behind it, might reassure those who point tremulously to Macquarie's past involvement in non-renewable shale gas exploitation.[6]

Our speed along the road to self-destruction will get significantly slower. Economically sustainable low carbon solutions involving the minimum of external (government) intervention will thrive. Designing climate damage out of industrial and social systems is in full flow, as are recruiting entrepreneurial vigour in biotech (designing drought- and heat-resistant agriculture, protecting against crop diseases emboldened by warmth); architecture (flood-resistant, minimum waste, energy-sufficient communities); and the re-generation of viable communities in areas where dominant industries have foundered. Preventing and mitigating climate change creates jobs: in 2017 in Britain 1,000 renewable energy businesses already employ 250,000 people.[7]

Food is our other sustainability focus; it's no less political.

There's an expectation that America will be UK's new best friend in post-Brexit trade. Presently American meat is allowed to contain growth-promoting hormones and prophylactic antibiotics, practices both banned in the European Union. Given growing concern that the unnecessary over-use of antibiotics cultivates microbial resistance and makes likely a resurgence of infectious diseases, we'd surely wish to maintain these particular European standards after Brexit renders Britain free to choose. Public revulsion against American meat, which can't presently be sold in UK, could scupper any bilateral trade agreement. However, I don't expect the UK to follow Denmark in considering a 'red meat tax' as part of its climate change controls. Yet.[8]

In the food industry fragmentation will again be the order of the day:

- urban farms (see Boston, Sacramento)[9] will become food producers rather than petting corners, smallholdings will be introduced into parks and suburban estates (perhaps associated with local energy production);
- mushroom farming will grow in scale, both to recycle organic waste and to produce material that can either be eaten or substituted for biodegradable plastic packaging;
- big food producers will invest in and partner small businesses producing healthier, less processed food, rather than acquiring them or mimicking them in-house;
- food collection vehicles (electric, of course) serving smallholders (an aggregator role) will become as ubiquitous as supermarket vans serving customers.

The number one food priority for the UK must be to avoid ingesting a whole day's worth of sugar at the breakfast table. The necessary response is already happening, not least to head off the threatened sugar tax. To the relief of many, a way of making chocolate taste as sweet with only half the sugar has been found, optimising the product's micro-geometry to enhance taste.[10] If only the giant newsagent WH Smith would cease haranguing customers to buy chocolate with every purchase; or is it their company mission to generate caries, obesity and diabetes?

Occasionally, accompanied by cosmetic flagellation, governments launch drives for healthy eating. 'Traffic lights' on food packaging are supposed to alert us to where harm might come from but seemingly incompatible scales of evil confuse consumers. In any case, such figures make sense only in the context of daily intake, which is hard to grasp. 'Low fat' is subliminally marketed as 'healthy' when it usually means 'high sugar'. The staple diets of the poorest and most vulnerable shouldn't be based on the least nutritious foods: deep fried gristle, fizzy sugar water, cereal boxes more nutritious than the product inside them. Busy families are told that they don't have time to cook, so adopt high octane 'ready meals'. Their children suffer from over-eating, lack of exercise, malnutrition, tooth loss and diabetes. Food companies need to address the qualitative needs of the inclusive economy, not just the quantitative.

Food should come back onto the education agenda, clusters of schools supplied by local kitchens run by community-based enterprises which put health first. In the medium term growing numbers of schoolchildren will need both free lunch and breakfast, prompted by increasing poverty not benevolence, and nutritional standards need to rise. Perhaps schools will grow their own vegetables, using plots donated by businesses both to supply their kitchens and to involve children in running them commercially as a learning resource. Vegetarian school meals would serve the cause of multiculturalism by reducing the risk of offending Jewish, Hindu and Muslim families.

Gene technology in agriculture will increase yields, develop pest tolerance and drought resistance. Such 'interference' with nature will be managed more sensitively than were the genetically modified 'Frankenstein foods' of the 1990s – and the population will be more amenable now, at least in relation to vegetables. Huxley's Brave New World included animal-free meat, grown from tissue culture. That's possible, thanks to gene technology, but it won't catch on (yet). The millennial generation, the parents of the future, will expect high ethical standards from food companies as from others.

Big Agriculture, like energy and other global industries, needs a flatter, more fragmented structure. Plants are not as innocent as they look, often farmed intensively in monocultures with a high chemical input. Vegetarianism may be less demanding on the environment than a meat-intensive diet, but not absolutely so.[11] Organic veg are often farmed in areas of water-stress, bear a large carbon footprint due to the countercyclical demands for out-of-season produce, and are sold at a premium, making them inaccessible to those on lower incomes.

In China, where food security for the world's biggest population is of concern, massive growth in investment in food production is being driven by welcome penalties on the use of environmentally damaging fertilisers and pesticides.[12]

The demands on our food industry are therefore:

- to provide enough low-cost food that's balanced and nutritional;
- to encourage sharing and family life;
- to minimise their carbon footprint and other negative impacts;
- to massively reduce the use of sugar, salt and other potential sources of harm; and
- to demonstrate the highest ethical standards.

These are challenges, not options.

Going forward – growing markets

A deprived community is easy to recognise in Britain: people tend to live in social rented housing, with higher levels of benefit dependency, disability, obesity, personal debt, smoking and malnutrition than the mainstream. They have lower levels of income, educational attainment, breast feeding, self-esteem and spontaneous social organisation; their social mobility is low, which means that they're trapped. They have a reputation for living beyond their means but actually they're well versed in managing debt. Trapped too are their families, often in poorly designed and substandard housing with few of the trappings of the community spirit that the middle classes take for granted.

Increasingly such people work, if at all, in short-term casual labour, with low levels of awareness of their legal rights as workers or of union organisation. They're more likely than others to be in the 'gig', 'informal' or 'black' economies, having little experience of paternalistic relationships at work or anywhere outside their often fragmented families. Deprivation is all too real in Britain today and one reason why it remains is because too many don't understand it, both in and outside that mysterious 'elite'. If you think that paying 50 per cent annual interest (APR) on a credit agreement is high then you don't know how such people live. For them 50 is cheap compared with 70, 250 or over 1,000 per cent (on a payday loan); if your experience is zero for your car loan, 3 or 4 on your mortgage and 19 per cent on your credit card (if you pay credit card interest at all), then you're not one of the quarter of adult Britons deemed to lack creditworthiness.

Liberating people on low incomes to take part in the economy that sustains your business is more than a matter of companies looking after their own. Customers deserve to be part of a relationship based on mutual success. Nowhere is this more clear than in the poverty premium, the sum of additional costs paid by people on low incomes to access goods and services. The poverty premium, a counter-intuitive consequence of being poor, is made worse by decisions deliberately made by companies.

- Franchised enhanced corner shops are major suppliers of food to deprived estates and often the only local retail outlets. Despite local incomes being low their prices are higher than in supermarkets, which are more likely to be situated elsewhere.
- Fee-charging ATMs are found in deprived areas, where people tend to take out smaller amounts of money more frequently – paying up to £2 each time they take cash from their own account. For people on low incomes banks provide 'basic' accounts, without full functionality, which charge for the use of services (such as direct debits) thereby subsidising what mainstream account holders enjoy for 'free'.
- Energy companies routinely don't allow people on low incomes access to their lowest tariffs. They may oblige them to buy electricity using pre-paid cards, the most expensive way of purchasing energy.
- Supermarket offers of '£5 off when you spend £50!' are also inaccessible to the poor, so too reduced fees for paying regular bills by direct debit.

Twelve million British people can't fully access mainstream banking because their creditworthiness is insufficient to allow them to sign a loan agreement for a washing machine or be granted a bank overdraft. If such people don't have access to ready cash they're prey to High Street rip-off merchants (who might sell a £250 washing machine for £10/week over three years, which is £1,500, then repossess it at the first opportunity) and pay-day lenders. There are rising numbers of loan sharks who enforce debt repayments through the liberal threat of a baseball bat. Such customers face the highest level of poverty premium. Against this tide an 'ethical' on-line lender has emerged, the social enterprise Fair for You (that same washing machine would cost £7/week for 1 year), but their impact on that huge sub-prime market is small.[13]

Cinemas that have some showings at a reduced price have got the idea – the business case is clear, selling a product to a customer who wouldn't otherwise have visited, at no extra cost to the business, makes sense. The pricing of (non-motorway) café menus invariably reflects the demographic of those who provide their footfall. Everytable is a Californian fast-food outlet which charges less for the same pre-prepared healthy dish in disadvantaged areas compared with wealthy ones; not only can they be proud of a business model that focuses on customer needs but they undoubtedly sell more product this way.[14] Within a country, companies grow markets by poaching, persuading customers to change from one brand to another; business as a whole can only grow its market by making the market bigger. The only way that can happen domestically is by inviting those financially excluded from the market to join it, by making them less poor (in the first instance).

The number of people in working poverty, perhaps half of those 12 million, is double the number of 2010.[15] These are the ones who mainstream business can most readily help – for mutual benefit – through their management of wages, prices and the availability of appropriate products.

The question of a universal income, below which no one in Britain should fall, continues to be discussed but I don't see it happening – partly because of a reluctance across politics to bring in another 'Big Brother' system to determine and administer taxpayers' money. It's partly also because if ever a Living Wage actually brings the minimum earned income up to 60 per cent of the median, the commonly accepted and statistically robust definition of relative poverty, it renders the need for a universal income guarantee less pressing. Three minority flies remain in that particular ointment: those not working or unable to work, the un-pensioned elderly and the disproportionate impact of housing costs, in some areas, on those on lower incomes.

Today the strongest determinant of personal 'success' is social class: only four of every 100 doctors are of working class origin, while the figure for barristers is six. Half a million children start school 'unready' and each year a quarter of a million complete their schooling without good exam results. Only one in ten adults on 'low pay' is ever going to get out of that trap due, not least, to that poverty premium. British social deprivation is the worst of comparable countries in Europe, said Alan Milburn's 2016 Social Mobility Commission – the task ahead is momentous.[16]

If unskilled work is no longer a good route out of poverty then skilled work must be a priority. That means a national debate on how our schools are organised – not in terms of who controls them (yesterday's argument) but on what they're for. There'll never again be enough money to fund our schools ideally – small classes, broad choice within the curriculum, equal esteem for academic and vocational subjects, quality careers guidance – so we need to agree instead on priorities. That debate mustn't be dominated, as it sometimes has, by a few universities but must include everyone – including business.

As a parent and former teacher, my priorities within 'education, education, education' are:

- skills – learning, literacy, mathematical, information technology, problem-solving;
- skills – vocational (facilitating social mobility), promoting cultural and creative fulfilment; and
- skills – for life, financial literacy, citizenship, health, fitness.

The word 'education' comes from a Latin root not of 'putting information and skills in' but of 'leading out': discovering what's inside the child and equipping him or her to express themselves with confidence and authority. It's too important a subject to leave to schools – the phrase 'lifetime learning' has never been more relevant and the workplace is part of that lifetime. Underemployed graduates have become a clichéd illustration of an economy which fails to make the most of its assets: this must change. Universities will become 52-week, 24/7 institutions with standard two-year intensive degrees, enjoying stronger links to business with no 'dumbing-down'. Businesses and students, empowered by their role of 'customer', will demand ever greater skills, knowledge and intellectual capacity. If schooling and employment are conducted with dignity then the citizens who emerge from them will practice that virtue too.

The campaign to create a new generation of aware, responsible and engaged consumers, carrying the minimum of deadweight in terms of purchasing power, must focus on the workplace. Employers should be aware of which of their employees (and those of suppliers) qualify for housing benefit or receive support from food banks – and aim to minimise both.

Globally the fight against absolute poverty must build on its modest successes since the millennium. The goal is to engage $3.75tn of new demand into the world economy by lifting 3.5 billion people out of penury and helping them become consumers, in the western sense of the word. Under the law of diminishing returns this is easier to do in Asia and Africa, where the middle classes are growing faster than expected, than in most of Europe, especially in a relatively affluent country like Britain.[17] The toolbox represented by those Sustainable Development Goals equips us to move forward in ways which are fair to all concerned: the beneficiaries, not least (but not confined to) those at the base of the pyramid, the governments of the world – and the businesses who will find themselves made more efficient and more sustainable in every sense of the word.

Eradicating poverty is therefore in the interests of business, but not because economics has a conscience. Poverty represents a dysfunctional demand market which the inclusive economy tackles by granting human beings both the right to participate in society and share in the outcomes of their labour, through profits and products. Poor people make poor consumers both in Britain and in the developing world. Where the taxpayer is actively subsidising people they can't be participating fully in a market that nourishes business. It may always be necessary to support the poor, those suffering exclusion by dint of fate; but it's not right for the State to subsidise companies who deliberately pay poverty wages. Why should such employers receive such favours when more generous employers do not?

Business must accept that the market isn't working for too many consumers, the poor, the squeezed middle, the just-about-managing, and that means it's not working for business either. Creating the strong and stable 'shared society' where 'we're all in it together' is partly their responsibility.

Inequality is more extreme than ever. Endowing so few with so much is economic madness: Adam Smith must be turning in his grave.

Going forward – responsibility

Traditionally poverty thresholds, below which people were not allowed to fall, are set and administered by government, which then provides a safety net to protect against what Beveridge identified as the 'five great evils'. That role cannot be left solely to governments any more – not least because they haven't proved very successful in discharging their responsibility long term. The market has to bend to the needs of those who are outside it and welcome them in. There is, as Legal & General's CEO Nigel Wilson reminded the Social Stock Exchange annual meeting in 2017, 'no Beveridge 2.0' and nor is there likely to be.

William Beveridge was a Liberal, commissioned by a Conservative/Labour coalition to produce a report in 1942 which even he described as 'revolutionary'. It created the welfare state to act against 'want, disease, ignorance, squalor and idleness' through a national health service and National Insurance reform. The 1944 Education Act is part of that movement but Labour's creation of the NHS in 1948, free at the point of use, was perhaps the jewel in its crown. The people had just fought a war together and were united in what needed to be done. The centralised economic control of Russia, a wartime ally, was a model for the nationalised industries – of coal, steel, shipbuilding, power generation and others – that Labour created after WWII. The NHS was also a centralised, all pervading giant.

When the NHS was born, British life expectancy had never been higher: it was 65 years, the figure chosen as male pensionable age. Such people were the generation of heroes, veterans of the First World War to whom a debt of honour was owed – but whose demand for long-term care in old age was much less than today's pensioners and, in any case, care was a family matter. A girl born in favourable circumstances today might expect to live to 100, spending almost half her adult life as a pensioner and much of that time receiving care – something for which today's regime, barely changed in 70 years, was simply not designed.

Our Health Service was thus constructed both by people of a different time and for people of a different age; today's ever-growing demands can't be met by established conventional means. Always a 'sickness service' rather than one that prioritised the promotion of good health, the NHS as we know it can't survive the current quantitative and qualitative growth in demand without change. We need business, Company Citizens, to do more to promote good health and wellbeing amongst the people they employ and the communities in which they live.

The Beveridge model still works below pension age: on average we each contribute to the state roughly what we take out, up to 65.[18] We contribute nothing before 16 years old, growing to an average of £24,000pa in our mid-40s, before falling steadily for the rest of our lives. Our peak annual cost to the state, pre-retirement, is £13,000 at age 11, mostly for education. This falls to a steady £6,000pa for the combined cost of welfare, care, education and health from our 20s to our 50s. Apart from education, every category rockets from the age of 65: at 70 we're costing the state £16,000pa rising to £28,000pa at 90 and beyond.

To cope with larger numbers of ever-older people – in this way – requires a massive increase in taxation. And that's not going to happen.

The reputation of public-service 'silos', relics of Beveridge's day, has deteriorated as both public and private sectors learn that 'big' is not necessarily 'beautiful'. Those megalithic nationalised industries of the 1950s and 1960s became the mixed economy of the 1990s and 2000s but since then a new beast, a more granular fragmented economy, is starting to reach more places, more quickly, than its predecessors.

Businesses, and Company Citizens in particular, have a duty to share society's need to respond positively to challenges. As we saw in Chapter 7 there are cost-efficient ways of promoting good health through the workplace, supported by a business case. Each may be small but together they represent a vital culture change.

Gaps in provision emerge not necessarily because the state will be providing less but because demand for care is growing through demographic change. Yet employment in the care industry itself, largely through private companies, has been falling, despite rising demand; one care company closed each day in the first quarter of 2017. Domiciliary and residential care remains a low-paid sector, desperate for reform. The boundaries between health and social care will inevitably become more fluid, generating or reflecting several trends over coming years.

- Reduced political faith in huge, bureaucratic, centralised services leading to a slow acceleration of fragmentation; the NHS developing its role as a macro-aggregator (though most services remaining free at the point of use).
- Care services being delivered by thousands of small suppliers from the public sector such as autonomous council-owned services plus social enterprises, charitable enterprises and values-led 'for profit and purpose' bodies, coordinated by aggregators.
- Opportunities for profit-generating 'for purpose' companies to work as both micro-aggregators (of small services and individual carers) and local bifunctional care providers. Bifunctionality is where a profitable enterprise, perhaps not even associated with care, is constitutionally bound to directly subsidise a caring service within the same company group.[19]
- Faced with the prospect of care supply falling further behind growing demand,[20] more capacity needs to be created and utilised in communities 'looking after their own' to reduce demand on the NHS.[21] Especially in deprived areas, companies might adopt local community 'neighbour hubs'

to promote vigilance, awareness, support and early warnings of health problems, and to combat loneliness; employee volunteers could enable the hubs to generate capacity, skills and long-term planning ability.

- 'Health and safety' alone is an insufficient minimum contribution to employee welfare; it's a Company Citizen's duty to promote healthy living and wellbeing. This approach helps employees work until an older age, reducing recruitment and staff turnover costs, retaining skills in the workplace and improving productivity by reducing sickness.
- Companies giving more support to employees who are carers – flexible hours, part-time working, workplace support groups, use of facilities, etc.
- A more professional care industry: better paid employees, not stuck on the minimum wage; more emphasis on training, career development and customer care.

This approach could rejuvenate the care industry through the 2020s. It's not just charities and social enterprises that will fill the gaps around state provision: 'for profit' and 'for purpose' motives will combine to motivate enterprise.

Business will also respond to demands for greater responsibility in health more specifically, in ways which are already evident though not yet at the required scale. Take the business pioneers of big pharma, using gene therapy to address Type 2 diabetes and cystic fibrosis. Big pharma needs to prepare for the next novel infection crisis: pooling resources cuts years off the time needed to tackle the next ebola- or zika-type outbreak. Companies need to act too to stop the over-prescribing of antibiotics, a campaign in which governments have been less than effective. This might sound like 'lose, lose', but it's backed by both a health and a business case: over-prescription leads to microbial resistance, rendering drugs ineffective, leading to falling sales and the need to spend millions, if not billions, on pharmacological solutions.

Within the investment community ethical and responsible impact investment codes will become the norm. Pension funds in particular, the sleeping giants of the investment world, are acknowledging that patient investment is more likely to generate sustainable long-term success than any number of knee-jerk reactions, whatever their 'independent' investment managers tell them. Indeed, a cohort of self-serving independent fund managers will be quietly replaced by conscientious millennials whose values are more of a natural fit to company missions – and who generate more long-term profit. They prioritise environmental, social and governance policies, including employee engagement at board level. Such policies, they will ably demonstrate, reduce corruption and inefficiency, boost engagement and productivity and could even, collectively, save the planet.

Responsible Company Citizens are committed to transparency in reporting. We must revisit the 2006 Companies Act, which introduced the notion of annual reporting by some on their social and environmental impacts as well as their financial returns; no company should be ignorant of its own negative impacts on people and planet and we, the people, need to know that concerted, consistent and effective action on sustainability is being effected. The Global Reporting Index is an existing convenient standard and many company AGMs have called for its adoption. Even small businesses won't find this an onerous imposition, since large companies have started to join local authorities in insisting on 'social value' criteria in their contract management. I expect voluntary British Standards to be adopted on both Social Value Measuring and the Circular Economy (BS8001).

There must be a review of global taxation. A 'Robin Hood Tax' on global currency and share exchange transactions was mooted by Keynes in the 1930s and the eponymous James Tobin in the 1970s. In 2016 China, perhaps unexpectedly, implemented such a tax to protect its currency against short trading (initially set at zero per cent, admittedly, so they can vary the rate as need arises). Hillary Clinton supported a version of the Tobin Tax in her presidential campaign and several EU countries are discussing it. Even a 0.1 per cent levy on currency trading to fund climate change mitigation in developing countries would be well worth having. Surely this door is opening?

Harmonisation of global tax laws would go a long way to address foul play. Taxes don't need to be identical across borders – the European Union hasn't done that, nor even the residually independent states of the USA – but they do need to respect each other's regimes and demonstrate common values. It's simply wrong that mega-corporations and the wealthiest individuals can avoid their citizenship responsibilities by playing one tax regime off against another. Allowing companies whose ownership is not known, and cannot be known, to hide in tax havens can never be in our common interest.

The demands that businesses need to make of governments are the demands of responsible Company Citizens: 'We need certain things to be delivered because our licence to operate depends on them.' Although governments still have the power to provide, their main purpose will be to manage a sensitive and facilitating framework. Palm oil is a good example: companies alone don't have the reach to guarantee its ethical production, without slave, bonded or child labour, free of corruption, grown at a fair price and in a sustainable manner. Inter-governmental frameworks and corporate commitments are required to make it reality. International partnerships, making common cause between businesses and governments, are essential.

Robert Philips, of the consultancy Jericho Chambers, describes business acting in the common good as moving from a 'licence to operate' to a 'licence to lead'; this is exactly what's required.[22]

Or a power for ill?

Businesses, acting together, have the power to destroy the world, even accidentally. They can't wage or prevent all-out war, nor even influence the machismo of all powerful dictators: those remain matters for the politicians.

But people will die in large numbers from the impact of global warming, both directly on food production and through skirmishes generated over access to water or fertile land, if we don't get things right in both preventing catastrophe and mitigating it. Conflict and climate change power migration, so globally destabilising in the 21st century. If business, government and people, acting in harmony, can't address these issues it would be a crime against humanity; though there may be no one left worth prosecuting.

Another global issue is resource depletion. Business – more than governments – has behaved for too long as though there's no tomorrow. Shortsightedness ignores the sirens that warn of supply-side failure: unreasonably rising costs, genuinely unreliable sourcing, ransom notes signed by OPEC. Business has wasted our natural resources in the past and failed to heed the warnings when calamitous shortages are imminent in oil, copper or water to name but three. Forget social responsibility: if business wants to survive as an economic entity it needs to better manage the planet's resources.

Obscene multi-million-pound salaries and astronomic bonuses do not, cannot, reflect the real value of people's relative contributions and there's no more dispiriting feeling than that which says 'this person is valued hundreds of times more than me; and that's not fair'. There's so much evidence that excessive inequality within a society is a stronger driver of unrest, disquiet, resentment, ill health and unproductive practices than is the absolute balance of wealth and poverty; those who perpetuate such inequities, who almost all reside in the private sector, must take responsibility for their actions.

We need investment in Britain but investment with a conscience. Forever seeking a better deal as land prices rise is never going to build those affordable homes that people need, in the places they need them, with the infrastructure to support them. Using land to acquire wealth through appreciation rather than development is unjustified and unfair, especially to those needing homes. Money for investment exists, but it's hived away where it can generate no public or social value. Working with planners, whose job it is to take a strategic view, business needs to deliver for the public, for they, including business' own employees, are the consumers without whom there is no business.

The most damaging of business' habits is short termism. If there are three priorities for Company Citizens and human communities alike, they must involve a holistic view of the consequences of our actions beyond the immediate:

- Think long term
- Plan long term
- Act long term

For business, long termism means going back to the way family-owned companies took a generational perspective of their planning, powered by a desire to leave a better company to their children than the one they inherited from their parents. Reinstating family ownership would be a bizarre application of the hereditary principle, which we've all but removed from government after 1,000 years; rather, long termism simply means not being seduced by the lure of short-term gain where that's not sustainable. In practice it means:

- ending quarterly reporting, which distorts our view of real impacts;
- taking a 25-year view of investment, such as on climate change mitigation (lengthening the accounting periods of expensive proposals makes much more business sense);
- ending that element of the bonus culture which relates to manipulable short-term results, replacing it with medium- to long-term stock-based team bonuses based on team achievements; and
- downgrading massively the importance of trading derivatives, the principal engine of the 2007 crash.

Our current approach to government mitigates against long-term thinking. Incoming governments front-load their plans to achieve as much as possible before risking it all in an election, whilst emasculated councils aren't even told what their budgets will be from one year to the next, making proper planning close to impossible. Business doesn't have these constraints yet often behaves as though it does, encouraged by banks, exhibiting the cautious risk aversion of the sloth. In a sensible world, where financial, social and environmental impacts are all afforded respect and recognition there'd be no call for short termism. Reporting would be more transparent and little that gets revealed at an AGM would be a surprise. Companies with ethical missions and responsible purposes create philosophical frameworks for their activities and priorities to reduce unpredictability still further. Also, whilst the direction of travel could be adjusted to avoid potholes, the destination would not change without consultation, engagement and appropriate levels of consensus.

It's not in business' own interest to cheat on competitors, suppliers, customers or others; the race to the bottom is one that no one can win, where everyone's a loser. Britain's a pioneer in effective anti-corruption legislation and halting the anonymous ownership of companies, but there's much more to do: British Overseas Territories, excluded from that progressive legislation, are mired in the proceeds of tax evasion and the laundering of the proceeds of crime, drug and people trafficking. The global amount of corrupt wealth hidden in secret bank accounts is greater than the combined declared assets of all the world's banks (Cockcroft and Wegener, 2017). That's both supremely unjust and economically very inefficient. Corruption has never been a more serious threat to the future of business – and democracy, for they're linked. Corruption is the abuse of business; it's not a victimless crime and business must do more to root it out.

There's one area of the economy which has become, and remains, so disconnected from real life that its values are literally inhuman, its activity so divorced from ethical protocols and its impact so disproportionately profound that it must be taken in hand. It operates on timescales which are unimaginably short, almost literally unreal, more properly the domain of quantum physics. We've let reckless parts of the finance industry get completely out of control, allowed investment banks to forget that their original purpose was to build relationships between loaner and loanee and allowed them to create a world of their own with little grounding in reality.

I'm talking about financial derivatives, artificial creations of gamblers which exist only in computer memories, the majority serving no honest purpose by any sensible measure; their rationale is simply to disguise risks which might otherwise be deemed wholly unacceptable to any sensible person. They caused the 'crash' – and could do so again.

It's no wonder that businessman/philanthropist Warren Buffett has called a type of derivative known as credit default swaps 'financial weapons of mass destruction'.[23] Their value today is ten times that of the Gross Domestic Product of the whole world. Read that again:

> Their value today is ten times that of the Gross Domestic Product of the whole world.

This is either value that doesn't really exist, in any meaningful way, or it's value that's been vampire-sucked out of the real economy. Either way the world of high finance has the power, at the touch of a switch, to wreak havoc equivalent to the other infamous red button, but without the same checks and balances.

Whilst we allow this market to so dominate our economies we are at great risk.

Take-away: a company citizenship code

Companies are neither saints nor sinners but each business has elements of both, in varying proportions. The following 20 thoughts, arising from this book, will help your company be a better Company Citizen.

- A Company Citizen thinks of others and works collaboratively.
- Wasting human and other resources, so 20th century, threatens the 21st.
- Long-term impacts matter more than short-term trends.
- Fragmentation is an opportunity not a threat.
- Customers reward good and punish poor behaviour; misrepresentation breeds distrust.
- Not all investors are motivated by 'profit at all costs'.
- The era of the Inclusive, Circular and Social economies is here.
- Responsible companies need their supply chains to be likewise.
- Employee engagement drives productivity.
- Mission is message: it's not what you say, it's what you do.

- Reporting what you do and the impact you create is not a sign of weakness.
- Impacts can be positive or negative; it's important to monitor both.
- More transparency means fewer surprises.
- If you don't play fair, others won't play fair with you.
- A race to the bottom has no winners.
- Addressing inequality creates consumer demand.
- Communities need Company Citizens to play their part.
- Every manager is a responsibility manager.
- Promoting Company Citizenship is the job of business.
- We only have one planet: we're all in this together.

Although proper leadership in Company Citizenship terms comes from the top it has to be inclusive, at all levels, to work; collaboration can drive this agenda. Within companies we expect every manager in every business to observe and discharge their responsibilities dutifully on issues like health and safety or non-discrimination – and so it should be with ethically and socially responsible business behaviour too.

Keeping things on a human scale doesn't rule out ambition nor any other positive virtue, nor the creation of value associated with business; we must just keep things real.

The job of the Company Citizen is both to help us do exactly that, keep things real – and to help us keep our planet, our nations and our multifarious communities alive.

The future awaits.

Ready?

Notes

1 www.bitc.org.uk/blog/post/david-grayson-top-ten-tips-social-intrapreneurs; see Grayson *et al.*, 2014.
2 https://dupress.deloitte.com/dup-us-en/topics/operations/heros-journey-landscape-future.html?id=us:2el:3dc:dup826:eng:tmt::dcpromo.
3 www.fundingcircle.com/uk/; www.assetzcapital.co.uk; and www.standard.co.uk/business/anthony-hilton-peertopeer-is-big-enough-to-be-regulated-a3548621.html.
4 'Living on the Edge', Elena Johansson, *ESG Magazine* 6, Winter 2016.
5 www.edie.net/news/12/Sir-Ian-Cheshire--Sustainability-leadership-will-be-defined-by--courage-/.
6 www.bloomberg.com/news/articles/2017-04-20/u-k-sells-green-investment-bank-to-macquarie-for-3-billion.
7 www.renewableuk.com.
8 http://food.ndtv.com/food-drinks/denmark-considers-taxing-red-meat-to-fight-climate-change-1402265.
9 www.theguardian.com/sustainable-business/2017/apr/16/boston-organic-food-farming-agriculture-startups?CMP=ema-1706&CMP=.
10 www.bbc.co.uk/news/business-38167241.

11 https://shift.newco.co/vegetarian-diets-are-not-going-to-save-the-planet-4f50d0c1f8cf#.cjjuu0vkb.
12 https://agfundernews.com/china-will-produce-4-of-top-10-global-food-companies-by-2027-says-leading-food-investor.html.
13 www.fairforyou.co.uk – I chair the charity that owns this social enterprise.
14 www.sustainablebrands.com/digital_learning/event_video/business_models/access_equality_drivers_fundamentally_new_business_mode?.
15 JRF 'Solve UK Poverty' www.jrf.org.uk/solve-uk-poverty.
16 www.gov.uk/government/news/state-of-the-nation-report-on-social-mobility-in-great-britain.
17 www.brookings.edu/wp-content/uploads/2017/02/global_20170228_global-middle-class.pdf.
18 From 'Re-equitising the UK', a presentation by Nigel Wilson of L&G, March 2017.
19 See Luta, in Chapter 7 and in *Welcome to GoodCo.*
20 www.parliament.uk/documents/commons/lib/research/key_issues/Key-Issues-The-ageing-population2007.pdf.
21 The Dutch Buurtzorg model is widely regarded as effective in health terms and motivating of nursing staff. It appears to reduce a lot of managerial roles: www.rcn.org.uk/about-us/policy-briefings/br-0215.
22 *Accounting and Business* magazine, May 2017.
23 http://fortune.com/2016/08/08/mass-destruction-buffett-derivatives/.

Further reading

Agrawal, S. *et al.*, *Beyond Integrity*, CAF, 2016.
Clark, T., *Hard Times*, Yale University Press, 2014.
Clarke, C., *The Too Difficult Box*, Biteback, 2014.
Cockcroft, L. and Wegener, A.-C., *Unmasked: Corruption in the West*, IB Tauris, 2017.
Cooper, Y. (Ed.), *Changing Work*, Fabian Society, 2016.
Dondé, G., *Corporate Ethics, Policies and Programmes*, IBE, 2017.
Grayson, D. *et al.*, *Social Intrapreneurism and all that Jazz*, Cranfield, 2014.
Greenhalgh, S. *et al.*, *Everyone's Business: Making Business Work for All*, CSJ, 2016.
Guthrie, L., *Managing the Sustainability Reporting Landscape*, ACCA, 2016.
Hierzig, S. and Philips, J., *Banking on a Low Carbon Future*, ShareAction, 2017.
Hoek, M., *New Economy Business: Seven Windows of Opportunity*, New Economy, 2016.
Hutton, W. and Chapman, C., *The Purposeful Company*, Big Innovation Centre, 2017.
Jacobs, M. and Mazzacuto, M., *Rethinking Capitalism*, Wiley, 2016.
Kay, J., *Other People's Money*, Profile, 2015.
Kibasi, T. and Jacobs, M., *Time for Change: A New Vision for the UK Economy*, IPPR, 2017.
Lacy, P. and Rutqvist, J., *Waste to Wealth: The Circular Economy Advantage*, Palgrave Macmillan, 2015.
Lalou, F., *Reinventing Organisations*, Nelson Parker, 2014.
Lansley, S. and Mack, J., *Breadline Britain*, Oneworld, 2015.
Last, A., *Business on a Mission*, Greenleaf, 2016.
Lawrence, F., *Eat Your Heart Out*, Penguin, 2008.
Lewis, P. and Yeomans, R., *Busting the Millennial Myth – the Power of Purpose*, Eaga Trust, 2017.
Love, C. *et al.*, *The Practitioner's Guide: Steps to Corporate Investment, Innovation and Collaboration*, Corporate Impact, 2016.
Mayo, E., *Values: How to Bring Values to Life in Business*, Greenleaf, 2016.
Milburn, A. *et al.*, *State of the Nation 2016: Social Mobility in Great Britain*, HMSO, 2016.
Peston, R., *How Do We Fix This Mess*, Hodder, 2013.
Pickavance, N., *The Reconnected Leader*, Kogan Page, 2015.
Sabeti, H., *The Emerging Fourth Sector*, Aspen Institute, 2009.
Saxton, J., *In Good Company: Taking Corporate Partnerships into New Dimensions*, nfpSynergy, 2015. Available online at: https://nfpsynergy.net/free-report/good-company-taking-corporate-partnerships-new-dimensions.

Scott, J. (Ed.), *In Our Interests: Building an Economy for All*, The Co-operative Party, 2017.

Studdert, J. *et al.*, *Get Well Soon: Reimagining Place-based Health*, NLGN/Collaborate, 2016.

Tantram, J., *Capitalism: What's the Point?*, Terrafiniti, 2016.

Tantram, J., *Developing Sustainable Strategy*, Terrafiniti, 2016.

Ton, Z., *The Good Jobs Strategy*, Lake Union, 2014.

Toynbee, P. and Walker, D., *Dismembered: How the Conservative Attack on the State Harms Us All*, Faber, 2017.

Wahhab, I., *Charity Sucks*, Biteback, 2016.

Walker, O., *Barbarians in the Boardroom*, Pearson, 2016.

Wilkinson, R. and Pickett, K., *The Spirit Level*, Penguin, 2010.

Index